Content Rights

DATE DUE			
7/14/09			
10/29/12			

Content Rights for Creative Professionals

Copyrights and Trademarks in a Digital Age

Second Edition

Arnold P. Lutzker

Focal Press

OXFORD AMSTERDAM BOSTON LONDON NEW YORK PARIS
SAN DIEGO SAN FRANCISCO SINGAPORE SYDNEY TOKYO

Focal Press is an imprint of Elsevier Science.

Library of Congress Cataloging-in-Publication Data
Lutzker, Arnold P.
   Content rights for creative professionals : copyrights and trademarks in a digital age / Arnold P. Lutzker.—2nd ed.
      p.   cm.
   Rev. ed. of: Copyrights and trademarks for media professionals . c1997.
   Includes bibliographical references and index.
   ISBN 0-240-80484-8 (pbk : acid-free paper)
   1. Copyright—United States.   2. Trademarks—Law and legislation—United States.   3. Mass media—Law and legislation—United States.   I. Lutzker, Arnold P. Copyrights and trademarks for media professionals.   II. Title.

KF2994 .L88 2002
346.7304'82—dc21   2002073879

British Library Cataloguing-in-Publication Data
A catalogue record for this book is available from the British Library.

The publisher offers special discounts on bulk orders of this book.
For information, please contact:

Manager of Special Sales
Elsevier Science
200 Wheeler Road
Burlington, MA 01803
Tel: 781-313-4700
Fax: 781-313-4882

For information on all Focal Press publications available, contact our World Wide Web home page at:
http://www.focalpress.com

10 9 8 7 6 5 4 3 2 1

Printed in the United States of America

For Mom

Contents

Preface to the Second Edition

In the five years since I began work on the first edition (entitled *Copyright and Trademark for Media Professionals*), much has happened to the world of copyrights and trademarks. I wanted to explore some of the tensions that led to reform as well as explain the changes that occurred and their impact on intellectual property rights in a second edition. Most notably, Congress passed the Digital Millennium Copyright Act (DMCA), the most comprehensive law reform in a generation, and extended the term of copyrights 20 years. On behalf of five national library associations, I was able to play a role in the passage of legislation that will shape the treatment of digital content by copyright law for years to come. The legislation not only established new rules to address the problems for online service providers like AOL and the telephone companies, but it also introduced several new legal concepts, including a prohibition on the circumvention of technological measures designed to control access to works.

Left hanging in the balance was the relationship of the Internet to distance education, the method by which the students log on and learn. The complex issues of distance education were the subject of intense debate during consideration of the DMCA, with no formal resolution occurring in 1998. It took a report from the Copyright Office and leadership by two committed senators to fashion a compromise that all interested parties have agreed to. This reform has the prospect of having an enormous impact on education in the coming years. However, the final bill is so complex in structure and language that educators, students, and content owners will need guidance in how to interpret its standards.

During the past five years, the Internet has burst fully onto the scene, creating a veritable revolution, not only in the way people communicate but also in the approach to ownership and use of content. A metaphor for the change is the story of Napster, the extraordinary music file-sharing technology that attracted upward of 40 million (mainly youthful) users by early 2000. These music hunters appeared oblivious to the concerns of copyright owners of recordings that were being shared without any recompense to those copyright owners. The fact that the price of CDs offended the sensibilities of many teenage buyers made Napster a natural ally of those who believed that traditional copyright law could not apply in cyberspace. However, after a legal assault based on very old-fashioned notions of ownership and exclusive rights, the upstart was brought to its knees.

The dot-coms also brought change to the world of trademark. The ease with which one could apply for and obtain a Web address made specious claims to words and phrases a simple method to attract online users to their sites. New systems for deciding conflicting claims to www.xxx.coms were instituted, including a mechanism for international arbitration to resolve cross-border disputes. All this happened amid the frantic boom and bust of Internet stocks on the NASDAQ.

Also, I wanted this book to appeal to a wider circle of readers. While the first edition focused throughout on media professionals, I believe that the topics and contents can have utility and interest for many others. Freelance authors, photographers, librarians, and educators (teachers, administrators, and students), in particular, need a better understanding of how the law of intellectual property affects their work and their thinking.

So, at the start of the new millennium, I decided to return to the topic of copyrights and trademarks. This edition has a new and more accessible title, *Content Rights for the Creative Professional*. My goal is to help professionals—those serious about the creation or use of works, words, phrases, and images, and the translation of ideas into form and substance—discover what they need to know about their ownership and use and give them the tools to apply in practice. Novels and short stories, biographies and news articles, photographs and drawings, films and multimedia works, sculptures and paintings, songs and dances, words, logos, and catchphrases are the subjects of our work.

The book is an update, not a total rewrite. It discusses many of the important changes of the past few years and offers new, practical features like a glossary, helpful hints, and some visuals. Also included is a CD-ROM with full text of relevant laws, cases, and original source materials to help those wishing to explore issues in greater detail. Let the games begin!

Preface to the First Edition

We are in the midst of a media revolution. There are more ways for people to communicate than ever before—television and radio, cable and satellite, telephone and cellular, newspapers and magazines, the Internet. Each means of reaching an audience has one ultimate goal: providing viewers, listeners, or readers with content—news and information, entertainment and opinions. More than at any time in our history, the value of content has skyrocketed. Whether it is box office favorites, news reports of special events, reruns of TV sitcoms, home videos, or scribblings on e-mail, people covet the content they own and seek new outlets for releasing it. Thus, while the channels of communication are expanding, it is what's on those channels that reflects their ultimate value.

This book explains, for those in the media and those who care about communications, what they need to know about content. It takes the laws of intellectual property (IP)—copyright and trademark—and translates them into plain English. It helps answer those puzzling questions about what can be used on the air or in print, and who really owns photographs, videos, storylines, and titles.

While these IP laws can be confusing, they are central to the media's effective operation. From program directors to advertisers, from scriptwriters to online access providers, from stringers to students, from home videocamophiles to Hollywood directors, the rules that we have set up to regulate the way we create and use content affect us all. Those on the front lines, whose jobs are to put programs and information together, are under the greatest stress. This book adds measures of understanding regarding the legal principles that shape our most precious commodity, the fruit of our intellect.

For creators and users of programming and content—which is just about everyone these days—the laws of copyrights and trademarks are the rules by which we organize the products of our intellectual efforts. These laws are challenged by an electronic system of communication that makes the ability to copy and disseminate, as well as to alter without a hint, simple and universal. At the same time, there are major realignments taking place among the owners of the media industries. Alliances between telephone and cable companies and acquisitions of television networks by movie studios are making current headlines. The passage of the 1996 telecommunications law reform has been lauded as one of the most significant legislative accomplishments of the Clinton administration. What are the economic forces driving these changes, and how will they affect what we see and hear on the media? The pivotal element is content. With the knowledge you gain from this book, you will be better equipped to face the coming challenges in communications.

About the Author

Arnold P. Lutzker practices copyright, trademark, Internet, entertainment, and art law. He counsels on issues of ownership and exploitation of intellectual property and assists clients in matters of selection and registration, licensing, infringement and effective management, and exploitation of copyright and trademark portfolios. He has special expertise in the copyright and trademark issues that surround the print and electronic media, television and film production, the Internet, multimedia, information infrastructure, and intellectual property policy.

In 30 years of private practice, Mr. Lutzker has advised many media companies, including Cox Enterprises, Multimedia Entertainment, Newhouse Broadcasting, USA Networks, Home Shopping Network, and Gannett Co., Inc. Since 1994, he has represented a consortium of five national library associations regarding copyright and Internet issues. He has also counseled numerous colleges and universities, including Ohio State, Arkansas, and Wisconsin, about intellectual property law and assisted institutions in establishing licensing programs. He has served as outside counsel to UDV (Diageo), handling trademark matters for the company's famous brands that include J&B, Ouzo #12, and Malibu.

A successful advocate, Mr. Lutzker has won U.S. Court of Appeals cases involving the cable copyright compulsory license, video monitoring, and trade dress. For the library associations, he filed amici briefs in the U.S. Supreme Court in *The New York Times* v. *Tasini* and *National Geographic Society* v. *Greenberg* (work-for-hire cases) and *Eldred v. Ashcroft* (the legal challenge to the Copyright Term Extension Act). He has also handled multimillion dollar copyright royalty claims for the producers of *Donahue* and *Sally Jesse Raphael* television shows and routinely counsels clients on music rights and clearances.

In the legislative and policy area, he advised the Directors Guild of America in connection with its effort to protect classic American movies and to secure residuals for directors. He has prepared prominent witnesses (notably Steven Spielberg, George Lucas, Woody Allen, Jimmy Stewart, Milos Forman, and Martin Scorsese) for hearings before House and Senate committees. In the Digital Millennium Copyright Act debate, he represented library and educational interests. He was chief negotiator for these associations on bills dealing with Online Service Provider limitation on liability, Copyright Term Extension, Fair Use, Distance Education and Database. Among legislation he has worked on are the following: The Satellite Home Viewers Act (1987), The Berne Treaty Implementation Amendments (1988), The National Film Preservation Act (1988), The Digital Millennium Copyright Act (1998), The Copyright Term Extension Act (1998), and The TEACH Act (2002).

In the arts, since 1988 he has served as General Counsel of the Cultural Alliance of Greater Washington, a nonprofit service organization comprised of more than 300 arts organizations and civic institutions. He is a member of the Board of Directors of the Washington, DC, International Film Festival and was special legal advisor to the American Russian Cultural Cooperation Foundation and its touring art exhibition, *Jewels of the Romanovs: Treasures of the Russian Imperial Court.* Mr. Lutzker is cofounder of Palace Arts Foundation and organized its critically acclaimed touring exhibition, *Palace of Gold & Light: Treasures from the Topkapi, Istanbul.*

He also is cofounder of three commercial ventures, InterStar Releasing (a theatrical motion picture production and distribution company that was sold to Westinghouse's Group W Division), Cineports International (a broadband startup that will provide on a streaming, subscription basis movies from more than a dozen countries), and Entera Entertainment (an entertainment company specializing in Spanish- and Hispanic-themed music, television programs, and film).

He is the author of two other books, *Copyrights and Trademarks for Media Professionals,* (Focal Press, 1997) and *Legal Problems in Broadcasting* (Great Plains University Press, 1974); a video, *Copyrights: The Internet, Multimedia, and the Law* (Taylor Communications, 1997); The Primer on the Digital Millennium Copyright Act; and numerous articles on copyright and trademark issues. Prior to establishing Lutzker & Lutzker LLP, he was a partner in the Washington firms of Fish & Richardson, P.C. and Dow, Lohnes & Albertson, and was legislative counsel to Congressman Jonathan B. Bingham. He graduated City College of New York (1968, magna cum laude) and Harvard Law School (1971, cum laude).

Part One

Copyright

Chapter 1

Overview of Copyright: The Big Picture

We begin with an overview of the texture of copyright. What is it and why everyone, particularly creative professionals and those who work with content in the media and education—those whose job is to *communicate*—should have a firm footing in copyright. Aside from an understanding of principles, our goal is to impart information to help with judgment calls. Each book or article, every photograph, video, or CD raises questions that touch on copyright. Because communication is instantaneous and ever more interactive, one cannot be paralyzed by uncertainty about what content can be used to teach, to share, to exploit. So we explain the traffic lights of the law—the green light that tells you when the road is clear to "go," the yellow light that urges "caution," and that red bugger that hollers "hold up, there's a problem here."

What makes copyright fascinating from a legal perspective is that it involves the tension between two bedrock constitutional principles. Article I, Section 8 instructs Congress to pass laws granting to *authors exclusive rights to their writings for limited times*, while the First Amendment prohibits Congress from passing laws that inhibit *free speech*. Copyright principles have been embodied in federal laws since the founding of our nation. Every generation or two, they have been updated to reflect technological developments, with the most recent major changes coming in the Copyright Act of 1976 (we refer to this throughout as the 1976 Act) and the Digital Millennium Copyright Act of 1998 (DMCA). The 1976 Act was amended several times in focused ways between January 1, 1978, the day it took effect, and October 28, 1998, when the DMCA took effect. Still, the core principles of the copyright law have remained the same. The statute

- Defines a copyrighted work and what is meant by *exclusive rights* in that work.
- Sets forth a term of years during which the *author* can commercially exploit the copyrighted work.
- Governs the ways in which copyrighted works are owned and can be transferred.
- Provides penalties for those who would take an author's copyrighted work without permission.
- Establishes limited exceptions so that important public policies can be advanced.

The tension with the First Amendment still persists, and in the age of cyberspace, it is more acute. How many times has it been said, "The Internet has no rules?" As this new medium evolves and electronic transmissions confront copyright barriers, the tension becomes palpable on the information superhighway. Rules of the road exist, but they are being resisted. We delve into that conflict and see how the challenges are being addressed.

Traditional media—radio, television, cable, even the venerable newsprint—have had to grapple with copyright principles from their start. Even with decades of experience, confusion reigns in many quarters. "How far can one go in using the works of another?" is an age-old question. Let's put this in perspective by some "fact patterns." They have been drawn from my practice and the pages of our daily newspapers.

Setting the Stage

1. A radio manager has had a long-running dispute with Arbitron (ARB), one of the leading firms that rate the popularity of programs. ARB measures audiences for radio programs and issues reports. Then, radio stations rely on the data to price the value of their air time for advertisers. But our radio manager felt his station consistently paid a king's ransom price for the diary numbers. Fed up, he decides not to renew the ARB contract. As luck would have it, when the very next ARB report is released, his station is credited with moving up five slots and is top rated in drive time (the prime time for radio, when most people drive to or from work). He obtains a copy of the diary report from his ad agency and highlights of the market numbers are printed in "the trades," specialized magazines that cater to radio and advertising executives. Determined to make a splash, his sales department prepares a chart based on the report, comparing the station's ARB ratings data with all competitors. The report is sent to 300 advertisers in the market. When ARB's representative calls to complain, the red-faced manager asks his staff, "Any problem?"

2. A drama is caught on videotape by a viewer—police beating a drunk-driving suspect. The viewer calls a television station's "hotline," and a reporter picks up the videotape. It is played on the noon news, and by nightfall, the network is clamoring for copy. The station sends it on, asking for on-air credit with its logo on-screen at all times. When the viewer who made the tape sees his video on national television, at first he is thrilled, then he gets angry: Who gave them permission, and where's *my* credit? He calls his brother, "the lawyer," who contacts the station demanding big compensation. Does the viewer have a claim?

3. A Tennessee television station's fall campaign has a VOLUNTEER theme. Every week for one year, the station produces five-minute pieces on the wonders of the state, from the statehouse to the mountain peaks. The series, which captures the native beauty of the countryside and the warmth of its residents, is scored with inspiring music from the Capitol Symphony Orchestra. The series is greeted with such acclaim that the station executives decided to market it commercially. They invest about $30,000 creating a two-hour video and release 5,000 copies to local chain stores. Their plans hit a snag when the Capitol Symphony Orchestra and agents of the composers contact the station. Is there exposure here?

4. Thanks to a provision of the Cable Television Consumer Protection and Competition Act of 1992 called *retransmission consent*, television broadcast stations can negotiate a deal with the local cable system for carriage. Instead of having their signals carried for free (as had been the case for 15 years), the stations can now say to the local cable system: carry my local channel only if you pay a fee or give me extra local access. Many stations receive local access in the form of a cable channel that they can program with a mix of local news and sports. With the popularity of regional sports networks, one station manager decides to capitalize on the wealth of local sports and blend it with a mix of highlights pulled from regional cable channels. While camera crews go to high school and college fields taping games, station engineers edit video feeds pulled from other cable channels down to two-minute summaries. The station also hires former local sports stars to simulate play by plays by reading box scores from daily newspapers. How does this plan sound?

5. A rival television station has the News Story of the Year breaking in its studio. A gunman, berserk but photogenic, storms into Channel 5's studio with a loaded rifle. He demands air time. The station executives have little choice but to oblige. What unfolds for the next hour is compelling, personal, and live TV. The gunman rants against his family, his city, his boss, his mindless life. Every television viewer in the market is riveted on the story. All the competitive stations can do is set their VCRs in motion, capture the drama, and wait

for it to end. The conclusion is sad and horrifying—the gunman shoots himself before startled onlookers. Instantly, the story is transformed into national news. When an arch competitor asks permission to air its off-air tape of the events, Channel 5's news director refuses. Spurned but insistent, the rival station leads its 6:00 P.M. newscast with the footage it taped off the air. Even after receiving a threatening call from Channel 5, the footage tops the 11:00 P.M. evening newscast. The next day, a lawyer's letter arrives. Concerned?

6. Breaking out of the crowded Internet pack requires creativity. One local phone company has a surefire campaign. It will build Web home pages for all its customers and pick the "Sweet 7" each week, creating hotkeys for quick access to them. The home pages are creative and informative. Some enterprising subscribers placed newly released CDs by top recording artists on their websites. Others pick photos from *Time* and *Newsweek* and give them new captions, while still others scan in chapters from best-sellers and rewrite the endings. The campaign proves instantly popular and subscriptions soar. The telco's Internet Access Group is sky high until it receives a letter from a publisher threatening a multimillion-dollar copyright claim. What gives?

7. George Lucas announced he would do it again! *Star Wars: The Phantom Menace*, the first episode in his Star Wars saga to be released in almost 20 years, hit the theaters with more ballyhoo than any film in a generation. However, between the release of *Return of the Jedi* in 1983 and this episode, the Internet craze and digital communications hit high gear. With computers more sophisticated than the ones that helped land a man on the moon sitting in every teenager's home, Lucas and his film company are concerned that the new Star Wars movie would be pirated and shared around the world. To beat the pirates to the punch, Lucasfilms launches an attack, not directly against known infringers but against the unidentified thieves. They do so by advising online service providers (OSPs), the Internet middlemen (including many colleges whose students log onto the Internet via school servers), that a copyright menace—pirated versions of the film—is about to be unleashed. Every OSP, they warn, has an obligation under the new DMCA to search websites for infringing copies of the movie. Does the Lucasfilm effort make the grade?

8. The Recording Industry Association of America (RIAA) is intent on cutting down what it views as the 20th century version of the black plague, the seemingly uncontrolled copying of digital sounds. Despite creation of a technical system nicknamed CSS, a program that scrambles digital codes to hinder copying, a teenager from Norway devised a computer program to defeat the scrambling system. Dubbed DeCSS, the program becomes a popular rallying point for hackers and others outraged by the high price of CDs and feeling

challenged by RIAA's aggressive campaign to shut down unauthorized copying of musical CDs. When a Princeton professor wants to give a talk about the DeCSS program, RIAA threatens reprisals. To RIAA's surprise, the professor sues, defending his First Amendment right to speak his mind. RIAA counters that it is just kidding—although it is intent on shutting down DeCSS, it has no gripe with the learned professor. Is this a real dispute?

9. The death of George Harrison of the Beatles is a sad reminder that the free-wheeling days of the 1960s are long since gone. Stories about the events in his life made the headlines fall and winter of 2001. One of the more curious events was the retelling of a copyright infringement tale that Harrison inadvertently experienced. It seems that the melody of one of his most popular songs, "My Sweet Lord," too closely parallels the tune of "He's So Fine," a 1963 hit by the Chiffons. But Harrison neither intended to copy the prior work nor was aware that he was doing it. Should that have been the basis for a legal complaint?

What is the common ingredient in all these stories? In each case, someone uses content without regard to the consequences of copyright law (Figure 1-1). These are textbook examples of how to get into trouble with copyright, real fast. They also reveal the double edge of copyright. The content is tantalizing and useful. In each instance, a clear, discernible benefit flows from the use of the material. The harm to someone else's interest may not be at the forefront of the users' minds. But it should be. A calculation needs to be made, one that balances the attractiveness of using the content with the right to do so. That assessment is not measured simply by the urgency of delivering news or information or by a subscriber's desire for access. What must be assessed is whether the publisher has the *right to use* the content as planned. Could someone claim a superior right and stop the use? Must the content be cleared? Or can it be used, no matter what anyone says?

These are the copyright questions. Now, let's discover the answers.

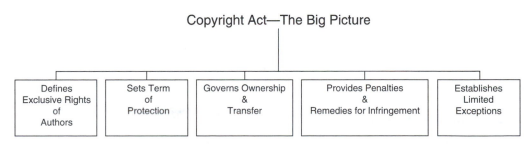

Figure 1-1 Copyright Act—The Big Picture

Chapter 2

What Is Copyright?

The Constitution of the United States gives Congress power to pass laws in order to encourage authors to create works. The encouragement comes in the form of exclusive rights to their writings for a limited time. Those rights are defined in the Copyright Act. There are only two key requirements to qualify as writings covered by copyright law: fixation and original and creative expression.

Fixation

The work must be *fixed in a tangible medium of expression*. Expressions come in different forms. They can be words contained in an article or a book; images preserved in photographs or film; sounds secured on sheet music, audiotapes, or CDs; or code stored on computer disks or hard drives. Rules defining how a work is fixed are flexible; over the years, new media have been incorporated. From piano rolls to computer disk drives, the law covers a broad swatch. Thus, the authors of books, articles, movies, tape recordings, snapshots, software, sheet music, newspapers, charts, graphs, choreography, and costumes can all lay claim to copyright protection in their works.

A glaring exception is unrecorded conversations: If words are not fixed, there is no copyright protection. However, flip on the tape recorder and, voilà, fixation and hence a copyrightable work. During one of the big trials of the 20th century, the O. J. Simpson murder case, one of the most infamous conversations of recent years, Mark Fuhrman's private conversations about cops and blacks, was recorded without his awareness. The tapes debuted during cross-examination in the trial. They were used to prove something about the state of mind of the witness. But, curiously, by making a tape recording, the aural remarks became copyrighted works. Using them as evidence in a trial is one thing; exploiting them in the marketplace requires a copyright analysis. Had they never been recorded, the world would have lost an insight into the mind of a key witness. In addition, at some time in the future those tapes may have a publishing value. If the tapes are ever exploited, as they are *his* words, Mark Fuhrman will certainly have something to say about it.

When television was in its infancy, live performances were the norm. Some of these performances were preserved by kinescopes, recordings made off a monitor. The kinescopes qualify for copyright protection. Indeed, what we know about the early days of television, from *I Love Lucy* to *The Honeymooners* to *Today* and *Playhouse 90*, is owed to those kinescopes. Some of those programs make up formidable parts of valuable cable networks such as Nickelodeon. Even without the kinescopes, many of the old TV performances have a copyrightable form, written scripts. Those scripts are fixed works.

Television's predecessor entertainment medium, vaudeville, with its stand-up comics, was notorious for "gag theft." The stars of the "Borscht Belt" regularly stole punch lines from each other, but they always did so with a copyright risk. If the gags were scripted, a copyright claim could have been made. However, when the live performances were ad-libbed and no script or underlying text was used and no recording was made, they fell outside the scope of copyright protection. In sum, if a work is fixed in a tangible way, copyright law claims dominion over it.

Original and Creative Expression

The other key for copyright law is that the fixed expression be *original* and *creative*. *Originality* means the work is not copied; *creativity* means that it evidences at least a modicum of thought. If the expression is extremely short, a word or a phrase, then trademark law takes over. However, string together 15–20 words (much like a poem) and you have sufficient creativity for copyright. But—and this is important—you cannot reproduce another's work and claim protection for it. How much of another's work you can use, with or without permission, is a topic addressed soon. For the moment, it is important to understand that copyright law protects a work's original creator.

The question of how much originality is sufficient for copyright protection is particularly troublesome in the context of photographs. In a controversial decision in 1999 (*The Bridgeman Art Library, Ltd.* v. *Corel Corp.*), a New York court held that transparencies and digital images of works of art were mere "slavish copies" (similar to photocopies) and therefore not entitled to copyright protection, although the court believed that the "overwhelming majority" of photographs would have sufficient originality to qualify. Not surprisingly, the case attracted a great deal of comment and criticism.

A copyright maxim that underlies the willingness of the law to protect original and creative expressions is this: *Expressions are protectable; ideas are not.* For copyright law to coexist with principles of the freedom of speech and the free flow of information, it is vital that ideas and facts not be owned exclusively by anyone. They are the building blocks of speech and knowledge. Therefore, the fact that something happened—a crazed gunman took over a station, ranted for an hour, and then killed himself—is available for anyone to explain, discuss, and put into *his or her own words*. Copyright law defines ownership of those words. At the same time, the Constitution and the copyright law ensure that anyone can report on those same facts.

The *idea/expression dichotomy*, as it is known, becomes more complex when a photographic image captures an actual image in place, the narrative of a reporter on the scene embraces the essence of the event, or an author of a historical biography relates events from his subject's life. Trying to put the expression into any other form may be difficult, if not impossible. The quintessential example of this statement is the Zapruder video of the assassination of JFK. That tape, shot by a bystander and later purchased by *Time* magazine, is a copyrighted work. But it is also the essence of a historic event. Can the visual retelling of that shooting be done *without* visual quotations from the Zapruder video? An even more profound question from a First Amendment perspective is, *Should an author be prohibited from using this work without the consent (and likely payment) to the copyright owner?* This question points to the core philosophy of copyright law—the economic incentives of encouraging copyrightable creativity—to which we often return.

A few years ago the U.S. Supreme Court had some things to say about the idea/expression dichotomy in a case involving the telephone directory. The ruling, *Feist Publications, Inc. v. Rural Telephone Service Co.*, or *Feist* for short, held that the names and phone numbers in the telephone books are *facts*. Facts, as we know, are *not* copyrightable; therefore, one could copy information from the directories, without asking permission of the copyright owner of the telephone directory. The significance of the ruling was certainly substantial for the telephone industry. Yellow and white pages have proliferated; today, CD-ROMs are sold with 100 million names and numbers; all that information is free for anyone to use. The fact that the original directory was compiled by "the sweat of the brow," a previously respected basis for developing a copyright, became irrelevant overnight.

For those creative professionals who mold and use content, this ruling has profound implications. Yet, the precise impact on one's works may be uncertain until all the relevant pieces are known. Take the news media, for example. When one's business spends large sums to find facts and be the first to report them, "ownership" of those facts becomes vital. As employees of media outlets in a highly competitive business, managers want the public to "see it first" on their station, in their newspaper, on their website. The race to uncover facts, assemble them, and attract a regular audience is what the business is about. However, if facts are not protectable, then guarding information and exploiting it prudently requires great care. Incorporating sufficient expression in the story overcomes the dilemma, at least from the copyright perspective. If facts are presented in a way that is replete with individual expression, then copyright law protects that expression. So Woodward and Bernstein's insider reports on the doings of Watergate were protected, as are Woodward and Balz's detailed reports of the handling of the September 11 crisis by President Bush and his cabinet, while the headline summaries of these articles are not. Similarly, the photo of the soldier and the girl kissing in Times Square to mark the end of World War II was reality, but one captured with a creative photographic artistry respected by copyright. Even the videographer who happened to train his camera on some cops beating up Rodney King achieved something more by framing his story and zeroing in on the event. He made a video that copyright law protects.

Sometimes, what appears to be a fact—say, the overnight rating of a popular television program—is often more complex from a copyright law point of view. The market report, which estimates viewing of television or radio programs based on application of complex research data and statistical analyses, constitutes not a fact but rather the rating service's *opinion* about the number of people projected to have seen a particular television program at a given time. Thus, that *West Wing* scored a 16 rating (meaning that about 16 million people watched the show last Wednesday) is not a statement of a fact but one rating service's best guess on the viewing total. What is more, another research firm might reach a different result, even with identical raw data. Therefore, those rating reports are copyrightable, even though they represent one entity's attempt to define the "facts" of the viewing marketplace.

Contrast the statement that 16 million viewers watched a television program with the statement that 16 million Hispanics voted in the 2000 election. If the statement about voters is the result of an electoral tabulation, that number is a fact that others can exploit without fear of copyright reprisal.

That *Feist* is having an important impact on the collection and exploitation of information is unquestionable. In the 1990s, when Congress modernized copyright law for the digital millennium, a burning issue was *database protection*. Creators of databases, or collections of information, vigorously complained that their investment in constructing and maintaining databases was being seriously eroded by unrestrained application of the *Feist* principles. Proponents asked Congress to amend the Copyright Act by creating a body of laws designed specifically to protect data. They argued not that their data is copyrighted—that path was foreclosed by the Supreme Court—but that they made an investment in finding the

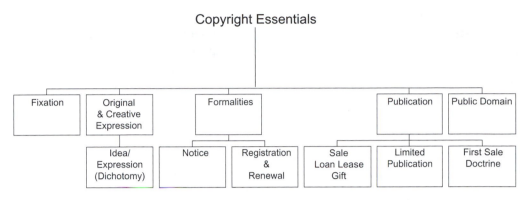

Figure 2-1 Copyright Essentials

data and maintaining the database. The "datamining" investment should be protected from third party uses that are unauthorized and uncompensated. The effort stalled, and a DMCA compromise required that the database title be removed from final legislation. But this issue persists. Congressional committees have asked interested parties to participate in a series of negotiations to see if a compromise on the matter can be worked out. We devote more attention to database protection later in the book.

Four other introductory concepts should be explained (Figure 2-1): the public domain, copyright formalities, publication, and first sale.

The Public Domain

Here is a concept full of confusion. Works in the public domain are, by definition, not covered by copyright. They are free to be used and reused, with no worry about clearance or compensation. In some cases, public domain works are easy to identify. Remember what was said at the start: the Founding Fathers empowered Congress to grant exclusive rights to works for *limited times*. In copyright terms, this generally has meant decades, not centuries. Once the term of copyright ends, no restrictions remain on making, distributing, or performing works.

As to the evolution of the statutory term, here is a capsule review. In 1790, the first copyright law set the term of protection at 14 years, with an extra 14 years if the author was still alive at the end of that term. The initial period of protection was extended to 28 years in 1831, with a renewal term of 14 years. Starting in 1909 and continuing until 1977, the copyright term for published works remained 28 years, but if some formalities were followed, it could be renewed for an extra 28 years. From 1978 (when the 1976 Act took effect) to 1998, the copyright law generally granted protection for a period of life of the author plus 50 years, or 75 years from creation in the case of works for hire. With passage of the Sonny Bono Copyright Term Extension Act of 1998 (CTEA), 20 years were added to the copyright term. Also, special rules apply for unpublished, anonymous, and pseudonymous works, so calculating the precise duration of particular copyrights can be complicated in any individual case. We provide a short primer on the subject in Chapter 7.

CTEA was passed after many years of debate. The law is named for the popular singer-turned-congressman, Sonny Bono. Bono, who personally composed many of the hits he sang with his musical partner Cher, became a well-liked politician after decades of performing. He was a particularly strong advocate for authors' rights. After being elected to Congress, he sponsored the legislation that became CTEA. When he met an untimely death after a skiing accident, Congress chose to honor him by making term extension his legacy. Sonny's legacy, however, may have a dark side. A group of educators and advocates for an expanded definition of the public domain filed a legal challenge to CTEA. In February 2002, the U.S. Supreme Court said it would hear the case of *Eldred* v. *Ashcroft*. A key issue before the Court will be whether extending the term of copyright of works already published and new works violated the Constitution's *limited times* requirement. A decision is due by June 2003.

Here is a *big yellow caution light* in the public domain: Unpublished works have a totally different time rule. For family heirlooms (private letters and photographs from the 1800s that may be gathering dust in an attic) or the great American novel that someone's great-great-great uncle wrote but never showed anyone, copyright may still apply (more about this later).

The limited term is why many of the great published works of 19th-century literature (Mark Twain, Herman Melville, or Jane Austen, for example) are exempt from copyright protection. The authors were entitled to exploit their works during the copyright term, but now the works are freely available to be copied by others in original form or adapted to new media. Bear in mind, however, *new matter is entitled to a new copyright term.* Indeed, changes can effectively transform a public domain work into a protectable copyrighted work. For example, a movie based on a book has its own term of protection; the storyline may be as old as the ages, but the photography, dialogue, music, costumes, scenery, and direction all raise new copyright claims. Recently, an enterprising scholar translated the 1,000-year-old Japanese text, *Genji the Shining One*. While the work of a millennium ago was written before the English language word *copyright* was created, the modern translation enjoys the benefits of our legal protections. Anyone can return to the original Japanese and translate the text, but no one can copy the translation without permission.

Many television stations received notices from film distributors who claim to be selling "public domain" movies. If a classic film was registered but the registration was not renewed, then the movie fell out of copyright protection and into the public domain. Rather than pay nasty license fees, these folks provide lists of films that they claim are free of any copyright restraint. With the rising cost of licensing films, these circulars can be pretty tempting. In some cases, they may even be correct. Many films, for reasons that defy commercial logic, were not protected as they should have been. While copyright law permitted the owners to keep the works under the full scope of legal protection, administrative lapses or plain old carelessness permitted the work to drift into the public domain.

When station managers or personnel with any media outlet receive notices about these works, they should do some homework to determine if, indeed, the work is in the public domain. The titles can be identified from the records of the Copyright Office in Washington, D.C. The benefits of this research can be substantial. With the exorbitant costs of securing broadcast rights for programming, obtaining public domain works that retain their broadcast appeal can fit the bill when stations are looking to reduce expenses.

But beware, many of the works touted as in the public domain are not. And some that used to be public domain may have been resurrected by clever entrepreneurs.

A favorite illustration of this point can be found at the National Association of Television Program Executives (NATPE) shows of some years ago. NATPE is *the* broadcast syndication trade show. Vendors of new and old programs sport their stuff there for television affiliates seeking programming products. One enterprising executive discovered that the old Basil Rathbone *Robin Hood* films were in the public domain. The copyright owner of the movies failed to meet the renewal requirement, and the movies' copyrights lapsed. This creative professional had a plan: By adding some new musical score to the old films, he was able to obtain a new copyright for the derivative work, the public domain film with the copyrighted music. Thus, while the principle of public domain meant that the films could be copied or broadcast by any media company without paying a license fee, the new music could not be copied or performed without the executive's consent. While a few original prints of the public domain films were floating around, the newly scored copies contained an updated copyright notice. Unless a broadcaster could secure a copy of the original, it was difficult, if not impossible, to know what was new material and what was old. The executive, who trouped around NATPE dressed à la Robin Hood and his merry men, made a modern morality tale with a twist; he took from the rich (the original movie producer) and gave to the poor (himself).

With digital technology today, the ability of a creative computer graphic designer to review a public domain work and claim new protection is as easy as logging on to a computer and utilizing specialized software that changes color and content at the creator's fancy. In photography and graphics, for example, the ability to make subtle but copyrightably meaningful changes in form and color permits the blending of an old work into a new copyrighted creation.

In addition to works for which copyrights have lapsed, works of the federal government are exempt from copyright protection. The works of the federal government, whose creation is funded by tax dollars from all citizens, are not entitled to copyright protection by statutory decree. This means that many works, such as government films produced by military filmmakers, reports released by federal agencies, and photographs taken from U.S. satellites, may be copied.

Even with a clear statutory dictate, however, there is a cautionary note to interject: If the government works were made under contract with a nongovernment entity or individual, then the contract covering the creation of the work may transfer the copyright interest to the independent contractor. This crucial limitation, which can wreak havoc with plans to use government works, is often misunderstood. Therefore, if the actual creator of a work published by the U.S. government is not an employee of the government, that creator may have a legal claim to copyright in the final work. For example, film footage of U.S. troops landing during the war in Afghanistan shot by a cameraman accompanying the forces *looks* like a government work. But, if the photographer was not a U.S. military employee but rather a private photographer hired to accompany the soldiers, that video may be used by the government, but it is *owned* by the photographer. One would have to review the contract between the military and the individual to know for sure.

With contracts like these generally inaccessible, what is a copyright maven to do? First of all, look at any notices published with the footage. Is there a copyright notice? Is any other legend associated with the tape? If so, in whose name is it? Assuming that information is not available, recall how the tape was obtained. Was it released to the media during a press briefing and, if so, by whom? Was it downloaded from a channel, and, if so, whose? Was there any accompanying printed text? Doing your copyright homework is a necessary chore.

Copyright Formalities

Copyright law used to be laden with formalities. This was a relic of the English legal tradition from which U.S. copyright standards developed. For almost two centuries, American copyright proprietors had to follow the rigors of the system or risk losing all of a work to the public domain. Therefore, formalities such as *notice* and *registration after publication* had strict requirements. Disobey these rules and you almost always lost your right to copyright protection.

Today, all those requirements have been eliminated as a by-product of the U.S. government's decision to join the Berne Convention for the Protection of Literary and Artistic Property in 1988. Berne, the leading international copyright treaty, defines the terms by which its members must live and provide copyright rules in their countries (see Chapter 19). While the convention allows each member nation certain flexibility in conforming its laws to the terms of the treaty (so-called national treatment), the Berne Convention resolves that the copyright owner should not be subject to formalities to enjoy copyright rights. Hence, in 1988 U.S. copyright law finalized a process begun in 1976, which stripped the law of formal requirements to smooth the way for entrance into a key part of the international copyright community. This is not to say that, prior to 1988, the United States was not already a world copyright leader; indeed, it was *the* leader. Moreover, by other multicountry and bilateral treaties, the United States had copyright relationships with most of the industrialized world. But the Berne Convention offered special legal access for U.S. copyright proprietors, especially owners of films and software, enabling them to attack directly the growing problem of international copyright piracy, the commercial theft of their copyrighted works.

Prior to the 1976 Act, the formalities of U.S. copyright law were one of its enduring and distinguishing features. Indeed, for users and owners of copyrighted works, formalities offered vital information: Since publication required notice of ownership, one could tell who claimed ownership of works simply by looking for notice. Works published without notice risked being thrown into the public domain, and registration was required promptly after publication. However, in one of the more noticeable efforts of judges to modernize the copyright law without waiting for congressional action, courts ultimately interpreted the obligation to register "promptly" after publication to mean registering any time within the initial term of copyright, that is, within 28 years of publication.

Nevertheless, until 1978 (when the 1976 Act went into effect), the formal requirements of copyright law were essential guidelines affecting the legal status of works. As explained in the discussion on public domain, careful research regarding an author's compliance with these rules can yield proof that the works that look like they should be under copyright are actually free for anyone to use.

For those in the know, copyright law provides the possibility to salvage even works thought to be public domain for many years. For example, the Frank Capra classic, *It's a Wonderful Life*, became a Christmas season staple when its copyright lapsed—the owner forgot to follow the formality of renewal and the movie fell into the public domain. However, an enterprising film distribution company, Republic Pictures, recently claimed that it held the copyright to the *underlying script* for the film and therefore telecast of the film without its consent is copyright infringement. Strange as the result may seem, this is sound copyright theory. Legal precedent has held that the copyright in the underlying script from which the film is derived is a separately copyrighted work. Even if the copyright in the film has lapsed, the owner of the underlying story may claim rights to the film as a derivative work (more on this later). For broadcasters, caution may be necessary next time they decide to air this Christmas classic. A check with a copyright lawyer will tell you whether Republic Pictures has succeeded in enforcing its claim.

Publication

When copyright law was updated in 1976, Congress merged all copyright principles into a unitary federal system. In the process, it eliminated the notion of *common law copyright*. Prior to this reform, if a work was unpublished it could remain the exclusive property of its owner and his or her heirs *forever*. The critical dividing point was publication. When a work was sold, loaned, licensed, or given away, the law deemed the work published and subject to all the formalities of federal law. Because the dividing point between published and unpublished works had dramatic legal consequences, an entire body of copyright law interpreting the concept of *publication* evolved.

One important rule in this area is that performance is not considered publication because no copy changes hands. Hence, live concerts are not publication of a musical score. By analogy, when broadcasting began to have an impact on copyright law, it was ruled that a telecast was not a publication of a work. If copies were sold or given away, that constituted a copyright publication, but the mere airing of a program on radio or television did not constitute publication. Thus, all the old network radio shows, which were broadcast live in many cases, with recordings made simultaneously, did not constitute published copyrighted works.

This means that a body of works for which copyright registration was not secured remained under common law copyright protection. Only if tapes of the shows were distributed would the program cross the copyright divide. At that point (prior to 1978), failure to follow the formalities created the potential that the work could fall into the public domain. Complying with the formalities meant that the owner was entitled to claim the benefits of federal copyright for the work during the years it was protectable. Because the consequences of publication without compliance with the formalities were so severe, courts created a *limited publication* exception. This halfway measure means that a loan of a very limited number of copies—to friends and family, for example—does not equal a divesting publication if formalities are ignored.

While the elimination of formalities has diminished the legal significance of publication, the concept still has important consequences. First of all, when the law was reformed in 1976, common law copyrights were given a federal term of protection. Even though they may have been created a century or more before, the term of copyright protection for unpublished works was extended at least to the year 2002. For works first published between 1978 and 2002, the term will last at least until 2047. Thus, for a vast body of unpublished works, including private manuscripts, photographs, letters, and the like, a cautionary word applies: Even though the works are very old, some even dating back to the early 1800s, they can still be owned and subject to full federal copyright protection. Then, too, several treaties in the 1990s—General Agreement on Tariffs and Trade (GATT) and North

American Free Trade Agreement (NAFTA)—establish procedures that restore the copyrights of foreigners (see Chapter 19).

First Sale

A copyright doctrine related to publication is called *first sale*. The core idea of the first sale doctrine is that the law gives the creator of works the right to choose the forum of first publication. In general, the courts have been very solicitous of the copyright owner's right to choose the first release of a work. If a work has not been published and someone wants to exploit it before the owner, the copyright law plants a red flag: "Wait a second." Almost always, the owner can stop the use.

This principle can even catch the experienced. A few years ago, Random House, one of the nation's leading book publishers, prepared a biography of reclusive author J. D. Salinger. In the book, many private letters written by Salinger were to be published for the first time. Even though Random House and the biographer came by the letters lawfully, the legal issue they faced was whether the book could be published against Salinger's expressed opposition. Anticipating substantial sales based on advance publicity, Random House had a huge first-edition run. To the publisher's dismay, Salinger sued for injunctive relief, demanding on copyright grounds that the publication be halted. The court agreed with Salinger. Salinger, the author of the letters, wanted to control first sale. Through appeals, Random House learned that its case was a loser, a victim of common law copyright and the first sale doctrine. Because Salinger's letters were unpublished, the court reasoned that they were entitled to a higher degree of protection. The First Amendment rights of Random House's author, who sought to bring new insight into the life of this literary hermit, suffered in comparison with Salinger's first sale rights to his private letters. Even though the letters passed from the recipient to another (a limited publication) and someone else owned the physical paper on which his words were written, the copyright to those words remained with Salinger. Random House had to destroy the books in its inventory. Many years still remain before Salinger's rights will be extinguished.

The first sale doctrine as codified by the copyright law also explains why copyright law does not prevent someone from reaping a profit from the sale of an antique book. When an author has benefited from the sale of a copy of his or her work, the law allows the owner of that copy to dispose of it as he or she pleases. It can be given away, sold, loaned, whatever. The *copy* in which a work is embodied is legally distinguishable from the *work* itself.

Following the passage of the DMCA, the application of the first sale doctrine to digital works became the subject of special debate. One of the open issues in the DMCA was the relationship of the first sale doctrine to digital works in the form of software, CD-ROMs, DVDs, and so forth. The Copyright Office was instructed to research the matter thoroughly and report to Congress on whether the law needs to be upgraded to deal with the first sale of digital works. The Copyright Office concluded that no changes were needed, rejecting the notion of a digital first sale doctrine. We spend some time reviewing this report and its conclusions in the chapter on digital rights.

This discussion of the first sale offers a useful transition. We now move from a general discussion of the principles underlying copyright law to the rights themselves.

Chapter 3

The Copyright Rights: The Coin of Copyright

What *precisely* do we mean by copyright? The copyright law sets down six exclusive rights of owners:

1. The right to reproduce the work.
2. The right to prepare derivative works based on the original.
3. The right to distribute copies to the public.
4. The right to perform the work publicly.
5. The right to display the work publicly.
6. The right to copy, publicly distribute, and prepare derivative works that are digital audio sound recordings.

To copyright purists, these rights are expansive and embrace every conceivable way in which a work can be copied. Therefore, as technology revolutionized modern communications, copyright kept pace. Whether on radio and television, photocopy or fax machines, the Internet or transnational digital satellite signals, copyright law applies.

These six rights, and all exploitation associated with them, are within the exclusive province of the copyright owner. They represent economic gold, the coin of copyright, because they can be sold, licensed, or loaned for a fee. They can also be given away for nothing. These rights define copyright interests. But read the listing carefully. They also set parameters: If a third party wants to use another's copyrighted work in a way not embraced within these rights broadly defined, then copyright law may not apply.

The most significant area open for discussion is the *public vs. private* distribution, performance, and display of works. This area is at the focal point of a current digital debate to which we often return, namely, whether transmitting copyrighted works via e-mail or the Internet is an exempt private distribution or a public transmission (and thus a copyright infringement). Some courts have already ruled that unauthorized electronic transmissions via bulletin boards are copyright infringements. The debate over the right of Napster.com to facilitate file sharing of music is covered by this issue, as is the matter of downloading movies from renegade websites somewhere in cyberspace. However, during the DMCA debate, there was sufficient uncertainty in the interpretation of "public distribution" that copyright owners supported amending the copyright law to make it clear that electronic transmissions are public distributions.

We now take a closer look at these crucial copyright rights (Figure 3-1).

Reproduction Right

The reproduction or copying right is what most people think about when copyright comes to mind. The ability to control copying is the signature of the act. Copying can be done in different formats, and copyright law has something to say about each type. Traditionally, copying meant grabbing a pencil and paper and writing down what someone else wrote. As technology has advanced, it has come to mean the ability to record by film, tape, and photocopy machine. In today's digital environment, the copying issue has become rarefied. It is easy to understand that duplicating a floppy disk is copying, so too is storing a work on a hard drive. However, when a computer is turned on and a working copy is entered into a computer's random access memory (RAM), that, too, is a reproduction (albeit a temporary one that disappears when the computer is turned off). Indeed, the copyright law was modified in 1980 to ensure that a licensee or owner of a software program has the right to put that computer program into his or her working files without violating copyright law. It is a simple concept, and one that is essential to the smooth operation of technology, but it still required an act of Congress to accomplish the result.

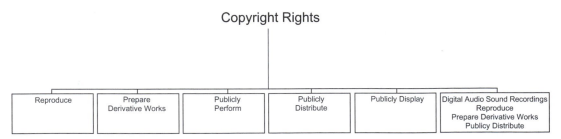

Figure 3-1 Copyright Rights

In broadcasting, the analogous issue is called the *ephemeral copy*. When radio stations play music, it is often necessary to make a copy of the tape or disk to permit smooth access for on-air play. Stations that promise "10 hits in a row, with no commercial interruption" prepare the tapes in advance so they can mix and match songs and themes. These stations, which are licensed to perform works by performing rights societies—the largest of which are American Society of Composers, Authors and Publishers (ASCAP), Broadcast Music Inc. (BMI), and the Society of European Songwriters, Authors and Composers (SESAC)—are not separately licensed by those societies to reproduce them. However, the Copyright Act offers an option. It allows broadcast stations licensed to perform music to make ephemeral, or short-term use, copies to facilitate their transmitting activities. We have more to say about music rights issues in broadcast and cable in a later chapter. For now, it is sufficient to understand that the copyright law allows responsible but limited use of those copies.

Derivative Works Right

Under copyright law, once you create a work for one medium, your rights extend to all media. Adaptations, translations, updating, and sequels—all are embraced within the derivative copyright. The paradigm example is a successful book that has many incarnations. The author of the book holds rights to all its progeny—a movie, a play, a television series, a video game, a theme park ride, a book on tape, a sequel, posters, note cards. Often, the book itself is derived from a shorter piece, such as an article, treatment, or poem. Like a precious jewel, a successfully copyrighted work has many cultural surfaces. Copyright law allows the author to claim all facets of creativity.

But, even as the derivative right offers the copyright owner multifaceted entitlements, residing in the jewel is a copyright flaw: the idea/expression dichotomy. While the preparation of a derivative work belongs exclusively to the owner, copyright law does not find fault with a third party who only takes the mere *idea* and then creates a distinct work. In the media, this translates into the honored art of catching up with the leader. When CBS had the hit series *Survivor* capturing viewers every week, Fox came along with *Temptation Island*. When ABC drew huge audiences with *Who Wants to Be a Millionaire?* NBC responded with a quiz series of its own, *The Weakest Link*. In the 1980s, prime time soap opera *Dallas* spawned *Dynasty*. Different personalities, characters, and plot, but a similar idea—prime time, soaps, game shows, artificial reality shows, with money at the core.

When the movie *Twister* opened to long lines and public fascination in summer of 1996, local television newscasts began running reports on violent weather, while some movie studios were racing to develop themes about natural catastrophes.

To take the Michael Crichton book and replicate it would violate the derivative right; however, taking the theme of scientists chasing weather phenomena and creating stories about hurricane hunters or volcano trackers is borrowing only the idea. If the new work is invested with such novel expression, it is copyrightable.

Public Distribution Right

As we have seen, for most of American copyright history—that is, until 1978—copyright law was a twofold system: common law copyright and federal copyright. The dividing point was publication. If a work was published, it was subject to federal controls and granted a copyright term embracing a limited number of years; if it was unpublished, it could be owned by its author forever. Public distribution was a legal synonym for copyright publication.

The statute defines *publication* as a distribution of copies to the public or other transfer of ownership by means of sale, lease, loan, or otherwise giving away copies of a work. Offering copies to a group of people for further distribution, public performance, or public display also qualifies. Thus, the ability to provide a single work to a multiplicity of people, even if no money changes hands, constitutes public distribution. Good Samaritans, who believe the world would be better off if people could receive free copies of video, software programs, or CDs of popular music from leading bands, actually violate copyright law, even though they do not profit, because they are wrecking the legitimate, public distribution market of the copyright owner.

This issue reached a boiling point in the world of electronic communications. Copyright owners are so nervous about the capacity of new technology to create perfect digital copies of original works and the mindset of ardent advocates of freeware on the Internet that they convinced Congress to adopt a new set of rules governing communications in the digital, electronic world. The advocates of reform fell short of their goal of enshrining the principle that any transmission or electronic communication is a public distribution, which would have broad implications for all kinds of communications, not just digital ones. Nevertheless, the reforms achieved in the DMCA will play a vital role in the exploitation of all content in the next decade. We discuss these implications throughout the book.

Public Performance Right

There is no copyright right more central to stage and screen, radio and television, even educational lecture halls, than the public performance right. Everything people associate with these institutions involves performing works for the public. In the case of stage and screen, while copies may or may not be made of works (as a practical matter, virtually all content, even news reports on live telecasts, is recorded in some fashion), programs sent out over the airways or by wires to a public audience, as well as live performances to adoring audiences, constitute public performances.

For the television, film, and theatrical industries in particular, copyright clearances are the protein of its life system. Knowing that the broadcasting station has the right to transmit programs to the public is essential to operation. Acquiring interests that fall short of public performance means that the ability to telecast is in question. Due to the breadth of material used on the air, in film, and in theaters and the fact that public performance rights to the various elements of a program may be held by many parties, it is necessary to ensure that all pertinent copyrights have been cleared. This may be a tedious task but one vital to the smooth operation of all media.

The public performance of a work occurs in most face-to-face performing environments, such as in a nightclub, concert hall, convention hall, or at a street fair. The copyright law fully embraces the delivery of works by individual speakers, as well as musicians and performers, in all public settings. In fact, any rendition before an audience in a public place or beyond a normal circle of family and friends is covered.

Describing the public performance right is useful in mentioning three related concepts. First, copyright law makes it clear that performance is not distribution. The cases that developed this maxim predated video recording devices; nevertheless, the concept is sound. Merely performing a work for the public in no way means that the public is entitled to retain a copy of the work. Conversely, being allowed to perform a work publicly does not mean that one holds the right to give copies of that work to others. As a result, the ubiquitous warnings that accompany many telecasts, such as "No reproduction, distribution, or use of the telecast may be made without the express written consent of Major League Baseball" or the warnings in theaters or other venues against using tape recording devices or even taking still photographs mean that the publicly performing entities may not hold the additional rights to distribute copies or to prepare derivative works. In simple terms, the right to perform does not ensure the right to distribute copies. Anyone publicly performing a work must approach a request from the public to make copies of the performance with great care.

Second, we must distinguish "performers' rights" from "public performance right." Under copyright law, the people who deliver the work to the public in a performance—in particular, the actors and actresses or the musicians and the singers—hold no copyright to their performance. This means that, even though the people who wrote the words and the music for all compositions aired on the radio are entitled to copyright royalties whenever their songs are performed (see Chapter 21 for a discussion of the funds collected by the music performing rights societies), there is no comparable statutory right for the singers and musicians. While their contracts may allow them a spot of revenue whenever their rendition of the work is performed on the air, they are not copyright owners of their own performances.

Periodically, there is talk in Congress about amending the copyright law to extend rights to performers. Throughout the 1990s this movement received renewed attention because some other countries have granted more expansive rights in this area. As a result, internationalists pressed for increased protection in the United States for the actual performances of actors and actresses. Among the first concessions were provisions in special compulsory licenses adopted for use of digital sound recordings. A fraction of funds go to performers, lead and backup (see Chapter 4). At some point in time, the performer's right and the rights of all who participate in making films and videos may be even better defined under copyright law.

Nevertheless, protection purists have a different body of law that offers collateral rights for individuals. We discuss these rights in more detail in Chapter 16, dealing with the rights of publicity and privacy. For now, it should be noted that rules covering publicity, a body of law designed to permit celebrities to control their names, images, and voices, give protection where copyright law does not.

Right to Publicly Display

Placing works in public places for people to view is a time-honored raison d'être of museums. For many in the traditional media, the display right was ignored. The computer revolution changed all that: Public display takes on new meaning in the digital world. When electronic transmissions are received on many computer screens, the operative principle is that *they are displayed*. We already mentioned the flexibility of copyright law to adjust to new technology and define certain uses and practices as coming within the scope of recognized rights. However, the question posed by digital transmission, which are directed to individuals on their private computers, is whether the transmission, once received, constitutes a *public display*. Certainly, it is a far cry from an Andy Warhol painting hanging in the local museum.

Rights in Sound Recordings

Finally, there is the notion of a performance right in sound recordings. We have more to say about this issue in the discussion of musical content in broadcasting and webcasting, but, briefly, record label companies have long claimed they deserve royalties when their recordings are played publicly. Copyright protection for these companies is only relatively recent. Copyright law first recognized certain rights of sound recording companies in 1972, when an amendment was passed in response to a wave of piracy of audiocassettes. To stem the tide of bootlegged tapes, Congress granted makers of sound recordings (in those days, LPs, 45s, and cassettes, later CDs and digital audiotape [DAT] machines) the right to control copying, public distribution, and preparation of derivative works. Importantly, no public performance right was granted by the 1972 amendment. In other words, when radio stations played tapes, they still did not have to clear the performance with the sound recording company like they had to with ASCAP, BMI, and SESAC.

Despite the new rights, the sound recording companies did not rest. They sparked a debate that raged for almost two decades. When digital came of age, the battle was won. Arguing that digital technology permits the making of perfect copies that duplicate the best sound quality, RIAA persuaded Congress to act. In 1995, Congress established a public performance right in digital audio transmissions. This amendment, coming just as the Internet and e-commerce were coming into public consciousness, gives the big record companies a crucial basis for exercising more control over digital exploitation of their works. Coupled with changes enacted in the DMCA, including the prohibition on circumvention of technological measures designed to limit access to content and a new compulsory license covering the use of sound recordings in webcasting, the RIAA membership gained gigantic legal clout, which it has used against many digital foes like Napster. We have much more to say about these changes in the chapters dealing with music and performing rights.

In sum, these are the copyright rights. They are statutorily defined grants, which means that they are creatures of our legal system. In a world where the intellectual property of the United States is one of the hottest commodities of commerce, these rights are the building blocks for exploitation. Other nations define them differently, but thanks to international treaties, most of the elements of U.S. law are replicated all over.

The copyright rights, however, come with strings attached. Attached to each right, and therefore attached to each work, are a series of exceptions or limitations. These qualifications are the way the law reconciles copyright principles of exclusivity and economic exploitation with competing public interests such as free speech, library and educational entitlements, and the complex needs of cable television and broadcasting. We turn our attention to these limitations.

Chapter 4

Limitations on Copyrights: The Chili Pepper of Copyright

If all the copyright law did was grant rights to authors, our task would be simple, because any copying would require advance permission and a user would always have to seek approval to use even small portions of a work. However, while the granting of rights is broad and quite inclusive, there exists a series of statutory limitations to those grants. Within the parameters of these limitations lies much play and much confusion. In all, the limitations represent the chili pepper of copyright law, which creates the spicy intellectual mix.

Fair Use

The most important limitation in copyright law is *fair use*. Fair use is a defensive claim that can negate a charge of infringement. It provides that, in the course of activities such as "criticism, comment, news reporting, teaching, scholarship or research," one can use a copyrighted work without the consent of the owner. To determine whether the use is indeed fair, four factors are considered:

1. The purpose and character of the use, including whether the use is for commercial or noncommercial purposes.
2. The nature of the copyrighted work.
3. The amount and substantiality of the portion used in relation to the work as a whole.
4. The effect of the use on the potential market for or value of the original.

While these criteria are deceptively simple, they have been the subject of more litigation than any other limitation in the copyright law.

Fair use has no bright-line test. Because analysis of the legal criteria varies with the facts of each case, one cannot know with certainty in advance whether the fair use assertion will be sustained. This poses a real dilemma for a potential user who does not want to be labeled an infringer and subject to the penalties the statute imposes for violation of someone's copyright. However, since fair use is a defense to a claim of infringement, the user must exploit another's copyright, then justify the activity after the fact, as allowed under law. This uncertainty can be both an advantage and a curse.

Due to a special provision of copyright law that allows the prevailing party in an infringement lawsuit to seek payment of legal fees, if a copyright owner challenges a user and loses the claim of infringement to the defense of fair use, the owner could be forced to pay the fair user's legal fees. However, the user who fails to defend his or her exploitation could likewise be burdened with the legal costs of both sides to the litigation in addition to financial penalties. Therefore, all parties must exercise reasonable caution when a fair use claim is involved.

As a handy reference for understanding the limitation, think of a baseball park, which we call "The Field of Fair Use Dreams" (Figure 4-1).

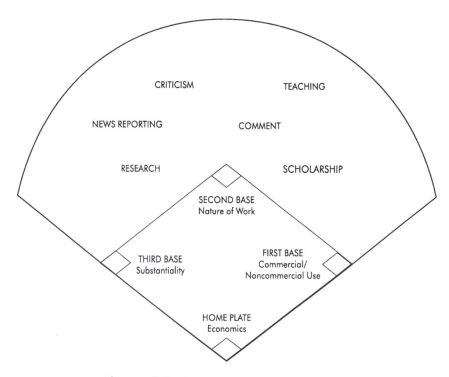

Figure 4-1   The Field of Fair Use Dreams

The Field of Fair Use Dreams

The statutory exemption defines the parameters, or the ballpark, in which fair use is played. News reporting, comment, criticism, research, scholarship, and teaching are in the field of play. For those in the news media and education, for example, most of the core activities come within these terms; therefore, these activities are favorable for a fair use analysis.

But being in the ballpark does not mean that using another's work is fair. To make that judgment, one must consider four criteria, which are like the bases of the infield diamond. You cannot claim fair use unless you successfully touch all the bases. So let's zone in on these four criteria.

First Base: Commercial or Noncommercial Use

This factor assesses the economic motivation involved in the exploitation. For some time, it was thought that any commercial use would doom the likelihood of winning a fair use argument. However, under more modern interpretations, while a noncommercial use is favored, a commercial use is not fatal to a fair use claim. Nevertheless, to the extent that the use is not directly tied to a commercial activity, the user has a better chance of prevailing. By definition, public (noncommercial) television stations and nonprofit educational institutions have an easier time establishing fair use than their commercial counterparts. Similarly, if the use is part of a product sold to the public directly for a fee, the use is less likely to prevail. It does not matter that the user is a single individual as compared with a multinational corporation. What matters for this factor is whether the user can claim to be noncommercial. In baseball terms, this factor also affects the speed with which one circles the bases, so that the swifter noncommercial runner may make it home while the slower commercial runners may be cut down.

Second Base: The Nature of the Work

This factor looks at the copyrighted work being used. The more factual the original work, the thinner is the line of protection. Biographies, historical writings, and photographs can be distinguished from works of fiction and abstract art. Further, expensive works like movies, which have great potential for commercial exploitation and may be available if the user pays a fee, are less likely to be subject to a fair use defense. For these reasons, one needs to understand the economic marketplace for copyrighted works. For example, movies and complicated software programs are among the most expensive copyrighted works to produce. The average box office feature costs close to $50 million to produce and distribute. Many software programs and video games are years in the making, involve teams of engineers, and contain thousands of lines of coded information. Understandably, copyright owners try to recoup every dollar, and the law discourages taking from those works. Conversely, works that are cheap to produce, have exhausted their market, and have limited value are fairer game. In between lies the vast bulk of current copyrighted works for which claims of fair use hinge on an analysis of the final two factors.

Third Base: Substantiality of the Taking

How much can you safely take from another's copyrighted work? The best advice is this: Borrow only what you must to create your own new work. In some instances, however, taking the whole work is hard to avoid. A photograph, a short poem, a one-page news article—these are all tempting targets. In the copyright analysis, substantiality is measured in relation to the entirety of the original work. The mathematics can be crucial: Judges will count words, minutes, inches, and then form their own opinions about the fairness of the taking.

A rule of thumb is to take no more than 5% of the original work. The chances of winning against an irate copyright owner are greatly improved when the borrowed piece constitutes less than 5%. While, in a few cases courts have ruled that 25–50% may be fair use (and even 100%, in the case of a photo), the danger zone is clearly marked in red when you take more than 25%. Taking 5–25% of the original leaves you in a yellow zone, where other factors come into play.

Still, even the 5% test has its limitations. In the case of film, taking a short clip (less than 1 minute of a 2-hour movie) might be questionable, but in the case of music, using several bars could constitute fair use. When the 1976 Act was adopted, Congress helped educators by setting forth some guidelines for in-class use. Included in the recommendations was taking no more than 250 words of a poem or 1,000 words of prose. But be advised: Guidelines are not a guarantor of the fair use conclusion.

In one of the most significant fair use rulings, *Harper & Row, Publishers, Inc.* v. *Nation Enterprises (Nation)*, the U.S. Supreme Court held that the use of just 300 words out of a 200,000-word book constituted unfair use. The book (the memoirs of former President Gerald Ford) featured a first-person narrative by the man who pardoned President Richard Nixon. Indeed, President Ford and his publisher had a magazine serialization deal with *Time*, which promised a preview of the work a few days before formal release. Relying upon a purloined copy, *Nation* magazine published the part of the book that contained Gerald Ford's own description of that pardon. So, even though the percentage (0.0015%) was about as low as you can go, the use was considered to be the heart of the book.

Moreover, not only did *Nation* take a crucial part of the book, it beat *Time* magazine to publication. Since one of the bedrock copyright principles is that an author has the right to determine the time and manner for *first sale* of a work, *Nation's* audacity in scooping the author left the court very reluctant to find fair use.

As a result of the *Nation* decision and the case previously discussed involving J. D. Salinger's letters, it had been thought that a winning fair use claim could never be made if the work in question was unpublished. After all, if the owner is entitled to choose the forum for first sale and if an unpublished work means that the creator has not yet decided how or what should be done with the creation, why should anyone—even a distinguished researcher—be allowed to trump the author's plans? However, in 1992, Congress amended the fair use provision to explain that fair use could apply even to unpublished works. Nevertheless, it remains very difficult to prevail in a fair use claim if the original is unpublished, even where only tidbits of the original work are taken. Now, assuming that you have made it as far as third base, the hardest part is still to come.

Home Plate: The Economics of the Taking

Copyright interests are economic rights in works. Perhaps the most important question in assessing fair use is this: What is the impact of the use on the market for and value of the original? If the answer is that the economic interests of the copyright owner are not damaged, you may round the bases and get home safely.

There are two ways to test economic impact:

1. Has the value of the original work been diminished?
2. Has the owner been deprived of just economic rewards?

We must bear in mind that most uses have some economic impact. Surprisingly, it is often argued in copyright infringement cases that the user has actually benefited the copyright owner by making the work more popular, giving it broader exposure, or opening new markets that the owner did not tap but are now ready for exploitation. That argument, although it sounds convincing, has been stated by those who never made it to home plate. The reason is that it is not for the infringer to control the way the copyright owner exploits his or her work. The law gives that right exclusively to the copyright owner. Moreover, how can anyone know for sure that the benefit derived from the infringement was greater than the benefit the author could have achieved if left to his or her own devices? A judge reviewing such an assertion will always side with the copyright owner.

There is an obvious relationship between the first-base test (whether the use is commercial or noncommercial) and the economic factor. It is easier for those claiming noncommercial status to argue that they have not profited by the taking. However, to the extent the user generates any funds from the use (for example, even a public broadcasting station may raise donations) or the owner can argue it has lost revenue (for example, a nonprofit foundation uses software without paying the license fee), the taking can have economic impact. Even the failure of the copyright owner to exploit a market is not sufficient support for a fair use defense. Just as the law allows the copyright owner to market the work, it allows the owner to withhold the work from a market until he or she is ready. The copyright owner is free to decide that such a time never comes. Remember, unpublished works are still protected by copyright law; J. D. Salinger can insist that his private letters never be placed into someone else's book.

The economics of the taking are also closely tied to the issue of substantiality. The less taken, the stronger is the claim that the user's work as a whole is what is attracting the market, not the portion of it borrowed from the original author. If only a snippet of a film or book is copied and the snippet constitutes only a tiny part of a new work, then it is hard for the original owner to assert either that the infringing work relies for content on the original or that its own marketplace has been severely damaged.

Well, there you have it. A round-tripper. Touch every base successfully and you can score, using someone else's work without permission or fee. However, if you fail to touch each base or overrun any one of them, the claim of fair use will fail. When we discuss damages and remedies in the next chapter, you will appreciate how costly a mistake that can be.

Educational Exemptions

Libraries, archives, educators, and public broadcasters are given modest leeway to conduct their public purposes while making use of copyrighted works of others. Some of these limitations (Figure 4-2) were the product of intense negotiations between copyright interests and these public-spirited institutions. Nevertheless, the narrowness of their scope suggests an important caution: Given that copyright proprietors fight hard to limit the exceptions for educational institutions, the private exploitation of copyrighted works are targeted even more.

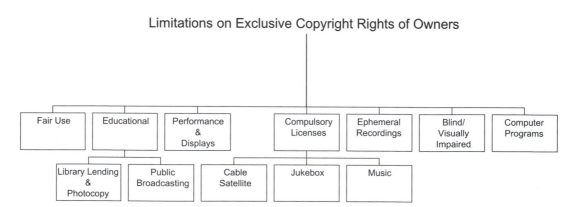

Figure 4-2 Limitations on Exclusive Copyright Rights of Owners

Library Photocopying and Lending

Borne out of the advent of 20th century photocopy technology and in the wake of a unique split in the Supreme Court in *Williams & Wilkins Co.* v. *United States* (a decision that ended in a four–four tie with one justice having withdrawn from the case), Section 108 of the Copyright Act attempts to explain how one can use the copier in a library without paying dearly for the privilege. The provision is divided into three parts: copying for preservation; copying for scholarship, research, and private use; and loaning copies of works.

The first principle is that libraries can duplicate works in danger of being lost due to age or condition, but only if the copies made are for preservation, not for resale. The second precept is that the copies can be made available to the public, provided that they are done on a single-copy basis and the library has no knowledge that the duplicated works will be resold. The libraries are instructed to post copyright notices near photocopy machines, advising the public about the limits of the law. Finally, libraries are free to publicly lend (distribute) to others copies of works they own. This is a corollary of the *first sale* doctrine, the same doctrine that got *Nation* into trouble when it scooped the story of Gerald Ford's memoirs.

The point here is that copyright law recognizes a distinction between copies and copyrights. One can buy and own a copy of a book, a video, or a record. Again, remember the lesson of Salinger and Random House. That physical copy can be resold or given to anyone else. If it becomes rare or if it increases in value, the possessor of the copy can keep the appreciation. Owning a copy, however, does not translate into owning copyrights. The six statutory copyrights belong only to the author. In short, the library limitation makes it clear that, while individually owned copies of works can be circulated without violating the exclusive distribution rights of the copyright owner, no such right entitles the holder of the copy to make widespread use of that copy.

With the digital debate of the DMCA, the library community pressed the point that it was time to update the exemption so that digital works could be covered. The 1976 Act allowed libraries to make copies, but only facsimiles. However, within the compromises of 1998 were some gifts to libraries, including the right to make digital as well as facsimile and analog copies, the right to make three copies of endangered or damaged works (one for use, one for copying purposes, and one to store away protectively), and the right to make digital versions available within the confines of the library.

Public Broadcasting

Under copyright law prior to 1978, certain nonprofit uses of copyrighted works were exempt from liability. As nonprofit activities expanded dramatically in scope in the 1950s and 1960s, pressure mounted to modify the free ride for nonprofits.

However, the copyright compromise of 1976 left intact certain limitations on owners' rights.

One of the industries that benefited from special treatment is public broadcasting. In a provision that tries to strike a balance, Section 118 of the Copyright Act allows public broadcasters (as defined by the Communications Act) and copyright owners of published nondramatic musical and published pictorial, graphic, and sculptural works to negotiate a *voluntary license* allowing the radio and television outlets to perform, display, and produce works incorporating the copyrighted material. However, if voluntary licenses are not agreed on, then the copyright law provides that a government entity (originally the Copyright Royalty Tribunal and now the Librarian of Congress) can set royalty rates.

Thanks to the successful lobbying efforts of movie interests, the public broadcasting exception does not cover the use of movies or nondramatic musical works. It also does not authorize the production of a program drawn to any substantial extent from a published compilation of pictorial, graphic, or sculptural works. If they are unlicensed by the copyright owner, they fall in the province of fair use because, without a license or permission, the use must be defended, and there are no other explicit exceptions that would apply. In practice, voluntary licenses rarely materialized, so every year the Library of Congress reviews the government-mandated rates and makes adjustments. Payments from the stations go to the owners.

Performance and Display Exemptions

One of the most hotly debated issues in copyright law is the appropriate limitation on the performance right. The heat generated by this issue is due in part to the strength and cohesion of performing rights licensing societies. ASCAP, BMI, and SESAC represent the vast majority of people who write popular songs and lyrics. They are tenacious in their efforts to sign up licensees, and under special legal rules, they are allowed to offer licenses not only for individual works but also for all the works in their repertoire, the so-called *blanket license*.

Although, prior to 1978, nonprofit entities, including educational institutions and public broadcasters, were free to perform copyrighted works, the 1976 Act struck a new balance in Section 110. The limitations set forth in this provision allow the performance of all kinds of works in classroom settings. Face-to-face teaching by nonprofit educational institutions and government bodies has a broad exemption that permits the performance and display of works without requiring permission. The primary qualification relates to the performance of motion pictures in classrooms. The law requires that the movie be "lawfully acquired"; that is, no bootlegged tapes or DVDs can be used. This requirement is one of many markers throughout the copyright law that evidence the quiet and effective work of the

Motion Picture Association of America (MPAA). MPAA has been engaged in copyright debate for decades, and the respect the act repeatedly shows to the economics and value of movies is testament to MPAA's effective lobbying activities.

When works are transmitted from a classroom setting to another locale, however, more constraints emerge; most significantly, audiovisual works (movies and videos) fall out of the exemption that allows their performance in classrooms. This means that distance education, particularly digital distance education, must rely on fair use to justify exploitation of third-party material not individually cleared. Further, the transmission must be made primarily for reception not just anywhere but in keeping with an educational motive in places devoted to instruction.

The transmission of teaching outside of a classroom, an updated version of the *Sunrise Semester* television show of the 1950s, is at the heart of a larger legal issue of *distance learning*. The more that classroom transmissions have the look and feel of television programming, the more copyright owners require that any use of their works be cleared at the source and resist the claim that they are subject to unlicensed exemptions. The debate is coming into clearer focus and will be hotly contested in the next few years. See Chapter 31 for the discussion of the digital distance education debate.

Another performance exemption that has been the subject of U.S. Supreme Court opinion and legislative reform is the playing radio and television signals in commercial establishments. Since anyone can play a radio station in his or her own home, we might wonder whether there should be any limit if someone wants to keep the radio on for background music on the job. Since the performing rights societies have licenses to cover background music, their answer has always been, "Get a license." However, Section 110(5) of the Copyright Act allows small store, restaurant, and bar owners to keep the radio or television on, as long as the equipment used is similar to that found in a home, no charge is made to hear the transmission, and the broadcast is not tampered with.

To explain the exemption, the statute clarifies what is meant by "equipment similar to that used in one's home." At base, for radio programs, no more than six speakers total (four hooked together in one room or space); for television, no more than four sets and one per room. The physical area of the store must be less than 2,000 square feet (3,750 feet in the case of bars and restaurants). So, the owner of a downtown department store cannot play a radio station's music throughout the building and claim an exemption. If the department store wants to play that station, it must get a license from ASCAP, BMI, and SESAC.

Beyond these performance exemptions, the Copyright Act details a host of other instances where publicly performed music is exempt from copyright liability, principally in the context of religious services, government meetings, state agricultural fairs, nonprofit veteran and fraternal organization functions, music stores, and transmissions to the blind. These limitations are detailed, and when issues arise, the precise language of the statute should be consulted to confirm that the exemption applies.

A word of caution should be added here: Radio stations have been known to get drawn into the middle of performance exemption disputes. A local merchant who advertises on a station may ask for permission to carry the station's programming free of charge. It is always tempting to keep the advertiser happy; however, the radio station's license with ASCAP, BMI, and SESAC does not allow the station to grant the rebroadcast right without regard to the copyright interests of the folks who wrote the music. A station may authorize anyone to perform works the station owns, but it cannot encourage retransmission of licensed material without clear authorization. When these questions arise, the station should exercise care in making sure that it has the right to do what is asked of it or else just say no.

A similar problem arises when a station's programming is used by businesses for telephones put on hold. Even though it seems innocuous, a radio station has no authority to grant a local business the right to play the station when the business phone is on hold. The performing rights societies have licenses specially drafted to cover this situation. If a station is asked for permission and grants it despite the absence of a clear right to do so, it may be liable to the copyright societies for contributing to the infringement of the performance right. Therefore, any such request should be carefully considered, and consents should be clearly limited to programming owned by the station. At the same time, the station should refer the enterprise to the performing rights societies for music clearances.

Cable and Satellite Compulsory Licenses

Compulsory licensing is a creature of the copyright laws. It is a government-mandated loan of copyrighted material in exchange for a fee set by the government—not an arrangement governed by supply and demand, but an economic bargain nevertheless. The theory of compulsory licensing is that the true marketplace is so unwieldy and technology so pervasive that public policy must reconcile these competing interests to allow consumers access to the copyrighted works.

When copyright law came face to face with content-eating technology such as cable television and satellite-delivered programs to home dish receivers, complicated compromises were devised. The compulsory licenses for the cable and satellite industries qualify as winners of the Blue Ribbon of complex federal law. We discuss these rules in depth in the next chapter. For now, it should be understood that, at the core of these rules lies the principle that copyright law should not stop the technology. Indeed, Congress found a way to require the cable and satellite resale carrier industries to pay fees for the privilege of delivering programming to paying subscribers without having to navigate the maze of negotiated clearances.

Compulsory Music License

The granddaddy of compulsory licensing traces back to the 1909 Copyright Act. The license for making and distributing sound recordings has a simple premise: Once a composer has published a musical work, others should be allowed to record their interpretation of it for play on mechanical devices by paying a fixed fee. Therefore, after Liza Minelli introduced "New York, New York," Frank Sinatra was able to make his own version of it. To qualify, Sinatra and his recording company could have negotiated a mechanical license, but failing agreement, they could take the compulsory route by filing a notice of intention to obtain a compulsory license with the copyright owner of the musical work. Then, they would have to pay a royalty for every record, tape, or CD distributed to the public, based on a certain number of pennies per recording or a smaller number of cents per minute of playing time, paid directly to the copyright owner on a monthly basis. The rates change periodically, so it is necessary to check the current numbers. A key restriction is that the use must be for a recording that will be sold to the public for private use; the compulsory fee does not permit the public performance of someone else's music. Either the performer or the venue must obtain a performance license when rendering a work to the public.

Sound Recordings

Just as the compulsory license for making and distributing records does not sanction public performances, it also does not allow someone to duplicate the original sound recording and sell copies to the public. In the 1960s and early 1970s, the arrival of the tape recorder on the mass market spurred a booming (albeit underground) business in selling bootleg tapes. The tapes, copies from purchased originals, were sold on the street for half or less the price in the retail stores. Some clever bootleggers even registered with the copyright owner under the mechanical license of the 1909 Act and used a gap in copyright law that did not provide express protection for sound recordings. The underlying works (music and lyrics) were protected, but the actual LP or tape was not.

Despite the absence of legal protection under copyright, the U.S. Supreme Court in *Goldstein* v. *California* found that the duplication violated local laws of misappropriation. In other words, it was theft. The bootleggers were stymied. The practice drew such attention that Congress amended the Copyright Act, effective February 15, 1972, to make sound recordings separately protectable. The owners of sound recordings, however, were not granted the five copyrights of other owners. The law allowed owners of sound recordings only the right to control copies, preparation of derivative works, and public distribution.

The failure to acquire public performance rights in sound recordings has remained a contentious issue between the record manufacturers and broadcasters. Major record labels have pressed Congress for changes in copyright law to require that, when a sound recording is played in public, the composer and lyricist are entitled to royalties and, in addition, the owner of the record itself deserves some revenue.

The broadcast industry has opposed the payment of new license fees to perform music. The stations argue that the record labels receive bounty enough from the commercial sales that follow airplay. From the point of the record labels, those sales are welcome; but why not get extra compensation from a blanket license fee like the composers and lyricists?

The battle lines have been drawn even more clearly with the advent of digital sound recordings. The copyright interests in the music industry pressed very hard for a copyright interest in the public performance of digital sound recordings. They argue that, due to the superior ability of digital technology to copy music off the air, once digital sound gains a dominant market share, home taping will replace buying CDs. While home taping with older technology is enshrined, the digital domain has offered a new opportunity to revise the rules; and in 1998, Congress instituted a new digital recording compulsory license for webcasting.

The change was inevitable. In 1992, Congress passed what could be called the precursor legislation. It amended the Copyright Act to establish a royalty system covering the sale of digital audio recording devices. As a result, DATs and other digital devices are subject to tax at the source, a flat royalty of $1 or 2% of the transfer price, for every machine initially distributed in the United States. The money collected is divided between two funds (two thirds to the Sound Recordings Fund and one third to the Musical Works Fund) then distributed from the funds to those whose works are included in digital recordings. Of the money in the Sound Recordings Fund, 4% is reserved for nonfeatured musicians and vocalists and the remaining 96% is divided between featured musicians (60%) and the sound recording companies (40%). Money in the Musical Works Fund is split between music publishers and writers.

The digital sound recording compulsory license covers the use of musical CDs and sounds from digital media in Web pages. Whether the use is original to the website or a streamed version of a radio or television broadcast, the license can be obtained if a privately negotiated deal is unworkable. A hotly contested Copyright Office arbitration proceeding over rates marked the introduction of the license to the public in fall 2001. We discuss this license in Chapter 32.

Ephemeral Recordings

One of the more intriguing copyright concepts is the *ephemeral recording* limitation. *Ephemeral* means short lived or transitory. To the extent that a copy of a work is made, even if it is not retained, an author's copyright right is implicated. Therefore, when radio stations want to perform "10 hits in a row" without worrying about setting up each piece individually, they need to make a composite recording. The ephemeral recording exemption permits the station, provided it holds a performance license from ASCAP, BMI, or SESAC, to prepare the prerecorded tape or CD of songs it wants, making for a smooth, easy-to-follow program, without running afoul of the copying right.

The rule, however, applies only to "transmitting organizations," ones entitled to broadcast music to the public under a performing rights license. Without that safety net, there is no ephemeral exemption. Furthermore, the ephemeral recordings prepared for the transmitting organization must be (1) retained and used solely by the transmitting organization that made it, (2) used solely for its own local transmissions or archival purposes, and (3) destroyed 6 months after the public use or archived. The rule has occasionally been stretched to the limit by music format distributors who tape songs to license precisely organized formats, such as beautiful music, oldies, "middle of the road," and rock. Since so many aspects of the music business have been subdivided and licensed for copyright purposes, these distributors have escaped the scrutiny of the licensing sources. Nevertheless, this practice fits the mold of a use that requires clearance even though the habit of the industry is to ignore it.

The ephemeral recording limitation also comes into play in distance education. When an educational institution has a closed circuit performance of a classroom lecture that incorporates third-party copyrighted materials, the school is permitted to record up to 30 copies and reuse them for 6 months. The actual recording can be retained for archival purposes for as long as 7 years.

Recordings for the Blind and Visually Impaired

To accommodate the handicapped, Congress amended the copyright law to enable qualified nonprofit organizations whose primary mission is to educate and train the blind and other persons with disabilities to make copies of previously published nondramatic literary works. The copies can only be made into special formats—Braille, audio, or digital text to be used exclusively by the disabled person.

Computer Programs

A core principle of copyright law is that a work is covered if it is fixed in a medium of expression. Ever since piano rolls, interpretations have held that fixation does not have to be read only by humans. Machine-readable works can be copyrighted. So, when computer programs arrived on the scene, there was no doubt that they joined other copyrighted expression. This is especially fair because they are among the more complex and expensive works to create. As a result, all copyright rights flow to the owners of software programs, just like they flow to the owners of books and films.

At the same time, the nature of software has some unique elements that affect the way software is publicly distributed and also require accommodations within the Copyright Act. Most fundamentally, even though users receive a physical copy of software (in the form of a diskette, CD-ROM, or download directly onto a hard drive), unlike their print counterparts (books and magazines), the copy of software is usually distributed to the public by means of a license agreement, not by sale. This is a crucial distinction that permeates the whole context of digital content. If a user acquires access to a work by license, then the terms of the license may set conditions that restrict the ways in which the digital content may be used. Software upgrades (e.g., Version 1.0 replaced by 2.0; Windows 95, 98, 2000, and XP) constitute derivative works that not only extend copyright terms of protection, but also render earlier versions obsolete, even useless.

Nevertheless, copyright law has long had some things to say about the use of software. Most important, when a computer opens software, much of its content is automatically copied onto a user's hard drive. Also, most people who buy software like to have a backup copy of the original. Because the software is often expensive to purchase and its content can be compromised during usage, backing up copies of software is a standard practice. The Copyright Act, section 117(a), expressly provides that making these copies, automatically by a machine or as an archival backup, is not an infringement. The owner of the copy must keep these backups under tight control, but if he or she does, then no infringement occurs. The only time an owner can transfer the exact copy is in the context of disposing of the original software. Then, these exact backups should be passed on and not retained. Owners of copies are also permitted to allow the making of a copy for purposes of computer maintenance or repair. Often, the individual or an outside contractor has to copy the software used on the machine to troubleshoot problems in performance. Section 117 of the Copyright Act expressly allows that activity.

However, just because one has finished using software, one is not free to dispose of it any way one pleases. If software was obtained subject to a license (either within the boxed packaging, a so-called shrink-wrapped license, or online, a so-called click license), then the terms of that license rule.

Because software unprotected by technological measures that prevent copying is easy to reproduce, a fair question arises: Can that backup copy be given to someone else? The question is most often answered by the license, rather than copyright law. The law essentially gives the software creator the right to control copying. By the license, the copyright owner can impose (and usually does) conditions prohibiting the transfer of a copy to anyone else.

Chapter 5

Compulsory Licensing: Government's Helping Hand

A central part of the success of the cable industry was the creation of the *cable compulsory license*. This permission allows cable systems to deliver copyrighted programs to their subscribers; in exchange, they pay a fee set not by the marketplace but by the government. The payment is delivered to the Copyright Office, which then arranges for its distribution to copyright owners. This copyright policy compromise was essential in enabling the cable industry to move into the media big leagues. A similar compromise has, as we will see, helped the direct satellite industry assume a significant role in delivering content to the home (Figure 5-1).

To understand the tension in the compulsory license scheme, a brief bit of history is in order. In two important copyright cases in the 1960s and 1970s, the U.S. Supreme Court held that, under the Copyright Act of 1909, cable companies had no copyright liability to owners of copyrighted programs. During those days, cable principally retransmitted Federal Communications Commission (FCC)–licensed broadcast stations. The Supreme Court ruled that the cable operators were just like their subscribers; they were on the "viewer side of the equation." Since "viewing" did not violate an exclusive right of copyright owners (check Chapter 3 if you disagree), there was no liability for the system operators with regard to the copyright interests when they delivered signals to subscribers.

These decisions caused a firestorm reaction in the programming community. In an era when cable television served less than 20% of U.S. television households, the medium was considered by some of its most vociferous critics as a parasite on the broadcast community's very being. The local television stations paid hefty fees to acquire programs, while cable operators freely took those signals and made a buck, simply by delivering them, unchanged but with a clearer picture, to households in the market.

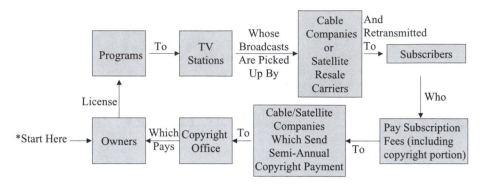

Figure 5-1 Cable and Satellite Compulsory Licenses

When the FCC changed its rules in 1972 to allow cable operators to bring in distant signals (e.g., New York City stations to Albany, Pittsburgh, or New England), local broadcasters and movie companies screamed. Not only was cable taking the broadcast station's very signal and programs and making money off the retransmission, it was draining audiences from local affiliates with no legal obligations. The criticism mounted and reached reconciliation in Section 111 of the 1976 Act. The compulsory license created by this section has five main elements.

Cable's Duty to Pay Programming Sources

The compulsory license system recognizes that cable systems owe a copyright duty to the owners of content. That duty is satisfied by paying a fee fixed by statute for the retransmission of distant, nonnetwork programming. The fees were originally set by statute and are subject to revision every 5 years. If the interested parties cannot revise fees by mutual agreement, any change is left to Congress's designated agent (first the Copyright Royalty Tribunal [CRT], a federal agency created by the 1976 Act to manage compulsory licensing, then beginning in 1994, the Librarian of Congress). In addition, because the original fees were based on FCC rules in place when the 1976 Act was passed, any material changes to those 1976 FCC rules, expanding the scope of retransmission rights, could also trigger royalty changes.

In fact, FCC rule changes involving leapfrogging rules and syndex rules have required important rate adjustments:

- *Leapfrogging rules* are geographical limits on which signals could be imported by cable operators. The FCC had required the cable system to pick a nonnetwork signal from the city closest to it. By eliminating the closest city requirement, cable systems could choose independent signals originating in more distant cities, thus "leapfrogging" over a signal from a closer city. The CRT imposed a fee of 3.75% of a cable system's gross receipts based on each leapfrog signal and system imported.

- *Syndicated exclusivity (syndex) rules* are standards that require a cable operator to delete a program from a nonlocal station when it duplicates programs broadcast on a local station to which the local station has exclusive market rights. In 1981, when the FCC eliminated the syndex rules, cable operators were freed of the obligation to black out duplicated programming. A syndex surcharge, a 20% boost in fees, was added by the CRT.
- In 1990, after many broadcaster complaints, the FCC reinstated syndicated exclusivity in 1990 (more on this shortly). The CRT reversed its course and canceled the surcharge.

All these changes were important because, coupled with the increased popularity of cable, annual compulsory royalties rose from $10 million in 1978 to over $200 million by 1990. Since its inception, the cable license has generated billions of dollars in fees. Compulsory licensing means real money.

Local and National Network Signals Are Free to Cable

The compulsory license mandated that cable subscribers are entitled to receive local programming and national network programming free of any copyright charge. The winning argument was that, when cable acts as a mere conduit of programming otherwise available off the air, only aiding in reception by boosting signal strength, no copyright fees are due. Also, the legislators reasoned that national communications policy was advanced by ensuring that all U.S. households had access to the national networks: ABC, NBC, and CBS. With the arrival of new networks, such as Fox, WB, and UPN, the definition of *network* is being tested, but for the time being, only the original big three are free under the compulsory scheme.

Intermediary Conduits, Including Telephone Companies and Satellite Resale Carriers, Pay No Fee and Have No Liability

When the copyright rules were originally developed, cable was an earth-bound system. Signals were picked up off the air by microwave relay operators or common carriers, which, through a system of point-to-point towers placed on tall buildings or mountaintops, retransmitted signals from the originating broadcasting station, via the towers to the cable systems' headends (central signal processing centers). The cable operator then delivered the signal into subscribers' homes by coaxial cable or wire. Although the terrestrial microwave links were instrumental in getting the signals to the system, they did not serve subscribers directly and made no change to program content. Because of this status, they were exempted from any copyright liability. Similarly, telephone companies whose facilities were also used to deliver signals to cable customers were defined as exempt under the compulsory copyright rules.

When Ted Turner, then owner of a struggling UHF station (WTBS, Channel 17 in Atlanta), looked at the compulsory scheme, he saw an opportunity to take his channel and make it available beyond Atlanta. At the same time, satellite transmission of broadcast signals—the microwave relay in the sky—had just become a reality. By uplinking WTBS to a stationary satellite 23,000 miles above the earth, the signal could be relayed down and received anywhere in the United States.

Elimination of the leapfrog rules led Turner and a few others to capitalize on a provision of the compulsory scheme that was developed with the old terrestrial and telephone technology in mind. Under Section 111(a)(3), a retransmitter that merely facilitated the delivery of signals to cable operators was exempt from any copyright liability. The resale carriers were viewed like truckers, who are merely consigned to pick up the programming from one place (say, Atlanta) and deliver it to another place (say, Los Angeles). When the FCC eliminated the leapfrog rules, a critical barrier to Turner's vision was eliminated. Within a few years, WTBS became a nationally distributed cable channel (along with WGN, Chicago, and WWOR-TV, New York), and the cable superstation was born.

The popularity of these signals did much to get cable into new homes. With the availability on these channels of programming different from or complementary to that available on local stations and the networks, television viewers saw a reason to subscribe to cable, more video choices. The attractiveness of cable increased as these superstation outlets became sources of unique programming. In the 1980s, Turner and his growing company bought sports teams such as the Atlanta Braves and the Atlanta Hawks and programming such as the MGM Film Library. This last acquisition, which cost over $1 billion, gave Turner more than 3,600 classic movies to use in developing programming choices on his expanding cable network empire.

The compulsory license does not apply at all to the hosts of nonbroadcast channels that developed during the past decade. Why? Because the movie channels (such as HBO, Showtime, Cinemax, and The Movie Channel), sports channels (such as ESPN and Home Team Sports), and variety channels (such as Discovery, The Weather Channel, Nickelodeon, FX, SciFi, USA, Lifetime, CNBC, and dozens of others) license programs directly from a few sources. Cable grew into the media force it is today because it established the ability to deliver something different, something more than three or four local channels. In the 1970s and

1980s, the capacity to deliver the distant off-the-air independent signals, thanks to the compulsory license, put cable on the map for good.

Royalty Distribution

Since its inception, the compulsory royalty scheme has generated several billion dollars for programming interests. The money is paid by cable systems to the Copyright Office twice yearly. Payments accompany a completed statement of account forms. For the larger cable operators, the form looks like a complex version of the IRS's 1040. Medium-sized systems file an abbreviated report, and tiny systems (with less than $300,000 in annual revenue) pay a fixed fee of about $60.

During 1978, the first year of the compulsory scheme, only about $10 million was collected. However, with the growth of cable subscriptions (from 20% of TV households in the early 1970s to almost 70% of such households by the year 2001), the royalty pool multiplied dramatically, reaching a high point of almost $200 million. Since 1998, with the change of WTBS's satellite service from a retransmitted broadcast signal to a full-time specialty cable network and the explosion of competing satellite service direct to homes (covered by its own compulsory license), cable compulsory royalties have slid to about $120 million annually. At the same time that cable fees slid by 40%, the satellite fees have grown to $75–100 million. In total, the cable-satellite royalties still generate more than $200 million a year.

This bounty is divided among a core of avid claimant interests (Figure 5-2) in hotly contested royalty proceedings. The principal interests have been

- Program suppliers: film and syndicated programming distributors (first run and off-network).

- Joint sports claimants: major league baseball, the National Hockey League, the National Basketball Association, collegiate sporting interests, and other sports programmers.

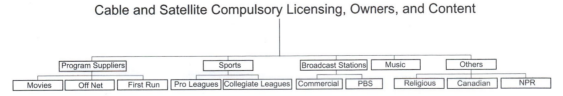

Cable and Satellite Compulsory Licensing, Owners, and Content

Figure 5-2 Cable and Satellite Compulsory Licensing, Owners, and Content

- Commercial television stations.
- Public television stations.
- Music performing rights societies.
- Religious programming owners.
- Canadian broadcast stations.
- National Public Radio (NPR).

When the CRT was abolished in 1994, the victim of a lethargic administrative system and a Congress looking to shave costs, the royalty distribution responsibilities were transferred to the Librarian of Congress, with the mandate to empanel Copyright Arbitration Royalty Panels (CARPs) if the parties cannot privately agree on how to divide the royalties. The procedure requires each CARP to conduct a hearing and issue a report to the Librarian. The Librarian may accept or modify the recommendations of the CARP. Any final decision may be appealed to the U.S. Court of Appeals for the District of Columbia.

Based on rulings of the CRT, the first CARP recommendation and the Librarian's ultimate decision awarded the majority of the royalties to the program suppliers, the film and television syndication industry. However, following a recent trend, the percentage award to the program suppliers dropped from almost three quarters to slightly over half. The biggest gainer during that period has been professional sports leagues, whose share has risen from about 15% to almost 30%. This reflects the strong influence of sporting events on cable subscriptions. The remaining share of royalties is split among the parties: commercial television receives about 7.5%, music performing rights societies 4.5%, public television 4%, and religious programmers and Canadian broadcasters about 1% each. NPR has been gifted 0.18% by the parties, who have settled on an award for noncommercial radio, even though it was decided in the first royalty case that commercial radio stations were not entitled to any compulsory royalties.

Cable Prohibited from Altering Programming

At the center of the compulsory scheme was the precept that cable operators could not alter content or sell ads during retransmitted programming. The statute makes very clear that, with regard to retransmitted signals, there can be no alteration of programming or substitution of commercials by the cable operator. Local and distant signals must be carried in their entirety, without change, for the compulsory scheme to apply.

This makes good policy, but it has been tested by the syndex rules. In 1990, after years of studying commercial television's complaints about loss of market share to retransmitted, distant signals, the FCC reinstated the right of local broadcasters to demand that a program on a distant signal be deleted if the local station holds the exclusive right to air the syndicated program in its market (the syndex rules mentioned previously). Initially, only one superstation, WTBS, had a "syndex-proof" signal, that is, national broadcast rights to all its programs. The other two primary superstations, WGN (Chicago) and WWOR-TV (New York) carried programs that local stations could force cable operators to delete. This created a real dilemma for many cable operators, who wanted to continue to deliver these popular stations to subscribers but did not want the hassle of deleting and substituting programs or, worse, carrying a channel with a blank screen during blackout periods. Such a situation would wreak havoc with the orderly scheduling of programs, impose a heavy administrative burden, and turn off subscribers.

To answer the problem, clever satellite resellers, firms in the business of picking up the broadcast signals off the air and relaying them to cable via the satellite, took advantage of a loophole interpretation of the compulsory licensing scheme. When WTBS became almost universally available to tens of millions of cable households, Turner sought to capitalize on the national reach by selling advertising on a national basis. Obviously, the charges for spot ads for a national cable audience of a million or more would greatly exceed the rates for a local Atlanta independent seen by only tens of thousands of viewers. To manage this two-tiered system, WTBS developed two ad rates, one for Atlanta only, and a second national cable rate. It then arranged with the satellite reseller to substitute commercials *before* the signal was uploaded on the satellite. If an advertiser wanted its advertisement seen only in the Atlanta market, Turner substituted a national spot when delivering the signal to the satellite firm. Because the substitution was done by order of the television station and not the cable operator or the satellite company, it did not run afoul of the compulsory license. And the U.S. Court of Appeals for the Eighth Circuit so ruled.

With that decision in hand, enterprising satellite resellers moved to solve the syndex or blackout dilemma, which was even more complicated than the goal of achieving a split advertising system. By taking the WGN and WWOR-TV signals and substituting programming at the uplink site (at the request of the station), the carriers were able to qualify for the compulsory scheme when the local, regular WGN and WWOR-TV programming aired. And when the syndex-plagued programming arrived, they substituted programs for which they acquired national rights. This activity rejuvenated many old programs unseen for years, such as *The Jack Benny Show* and *The Lawrence Welk Show*. In the intervening years, the cable superstations, relying on the advertising advantage of reaching millions of cable subscribers, cleared their own facilities to contain more syndex-proof programming.

Satellite Statutory Licenses

Another twist for the satellite resale carriers led to another compulsory scheme in copyright law. Since the satellite retransmitted signal is available everywhere in the United States and most channels of cable programming migrated to satellite retransmission as the preferred mechanism for delivery, an industry selling huge satellite receiving dishes directly to homeowners burgeoned in the 1980s. The dish sellers offered people the ability to get cable programming without paying the monthly cable fees. Simply buy the dish and point it to the satellite, no cable hookups required. The practice also had appeal to restaurants, bars, and motels, which saw a cheap way (once the dish was paid for) to deliver programming to customers.

Needless to say, the practice created copyright controversy. To respond, in 1988 Congress passed a compulsory license just for home dish owners, the Satellite Home Viewer Act (SHVA). Under the scheme, noncable private homes using satellite receiving equipment could be licensed by satellite resale carriers. The carriers were obligated to collect royalties from the homes and pay them into a pool, which was managed initially by the CRT and then the Librarian of Congress.

Unlike the complex cable formulation, satellite rates are set at a fixed amount of cents per month per subscriber, based on the kind of signal received. Satellite services pay $0.06 per subscriber per month for network and educational signals, $0.175 per subscriber per month for independent signals, and $0.14 per subscriber per month for "syndex-proof" independents (those for which no deletions are required). While initially the amount of money generated by the SHVA was modest compared with the cable compulsory license, the system enabled many neglected television households in "white areas" (places where no off-the-air signals could be received and no cable exists) to benefit from local and national programming.

With smaller dishes, less-expensive equipment, hundreds of signals utilizing satellite transmissions, and a compulsory license, satellite resale carriers became a viable challenger to cable service operators by the year 2001, serving over 17 million homes. With this growth came the desire to make the service as functional as cable; however, unlike cable, the SHVA set limits on the number of distant network signals that could be imported. Late in 2001, a U.S. Circuit Court of Appeals upheld an FCC requirement that, if a satellite service offered a station from one market, like its cable competitor, it had to offer all the channels in that community. The local-to-local service requirement is the last piece in the puzzle to make satellite service a true alternative to cable. In February 2002, as part of the proposed merger of the two largest satellite carriers (DirecTV and EchoStar), EchoStar announced plans to deliver every broadcast signal in the country. This is no small task, and EchoStar conditioned its promise on approval of the merger proposition. (More about that plan in the discussion of antitrust issues in Chapter 17.)

Intense controversy developed, moreover, because the satellite compulsory system does not cover commercial establishments, such as bars, restaurants, and motels, which want easy access to the satellite programming. Concerned about the high fees associated with retransmission, many businesses resist paying top dollar rates and try to opt into the SHVA scheme. However, no broadcast station and no satellite carrier can authorize retransmission of programming owned by another, even though they have the right to deliver the content locally. The Copyright Act construes these for-profit uses, such as attracting customers to a sports TV bar, as requiring direct licenses. They are usually available from the program owner, even though they may be more expensive to secure than under the compulsory license.

An issue that appeared to be of major importance during the high-flying 1990s but was placed on the back burner with the telecom bust by the close of the 20th century is the entitlement of new players, such as telephone companies and other utilities, to a compulsory license. If the Baby Bells and other telephone operators or OSPs are to compete on an even playing field with the cable systems and satellite television for delivery of programming to the home, they must have access to the compulsory royalty scheme. Otherwise, they would have to greatly reduce offerings to subscribers who like particular broadcast channels. As could be anticipated, denying access to the compulsory license could leave the phone companies and OSPs hopelessly behind in the race to secure viewers. Although the Copyright Office requested comments on whether the phone companies qualify for the compulsory license, so far it has not given the green light to these companies.

Nevertheless, if the telephone industry, OSPs, or any other segment of the economy is ever to compete with cable and satellite companies in delivering television programming to the home, direct participation in the compulsory licensing scheme is essential. The compulsory scheme is part of the body and soul of cable. While it is an artificial marketplace that has few content-owning advocates, it provided a helping hand at a formative time for cable and remains a force essential to cable's rise in public popularity. Denying rights to the emerging media would place a potentially insurmountable barrier on the road to their success. Look for the compulsory scheme to apply evenhandedly to all new media.

Another compulsory license added by the DMCA is the sound recording license. As previously noted, we have more to say about that provision in the discussion of digital music rights in Chapter 32.

Chapter 6

Penalties for Infringement: Paying the Price

Failure to comply with the rules of copyright can be very expensive. The law imposes a number of penalties for misuse of copyrighted works. Most important, the courts enforce money damage claims. The costs of noncompliance can be profits and actual damages, but sometimes these values are difficult to determine. To ensure that the copyright owner is compensated when works are infringed on, the law establishes *statutory damages*, which may be sought in lieu of the others. Statutory damages can be awarded in the range of $750 to $30,000 per work infringed; if the actions of the infringer are determined to be willful, these claims can balloon to $150,000 per work.

A copyright owner does not have to offer any proof of loss to claim statutory damages. That makes them a powerful remedy and a key disincentive to infringement. Once the determination has been made that there is an infringement, the owner chooses which form of monetary remedy to seek. For media users who violate copyrights, the statutory claim can have a multiplier effect. Since damages accrue to *each* work infringed, if a number of works are involved, statutory claims can be sought for each work.

For example, in the early 1980s when the right of a satellite resale carrier to retransmit broadcast signals under the cable compulsory license was tested in court, the carrier was well aware that every day about 20 programs were delivered to cable systems. Therefore, every day statutory damage claims (which then were $250 to $10,000 per work) accrued at the rate of $5,000 to $200,000. Similar exposure could occur if a new medium (such as an Internet provider) decided to deliver off-the-air signals to the public without clear entitlement under the Copyright Act's compulsory licensing limitation. If disputes linger in court while the alleged infringing activities continue, the statutory claims can be monumental.

Even claims of actual losses, as distinguished from statutory damages, can be huge. In the digital arena, film distributors and recording companies are frightened that copyright pirates can cause tens of millions of dollars of losses simply by posting copyrighted works on the Internet, thus allowing millions of people access to them for free. With digital copying as easy to accomplish as pushing a few computer keys, their fears are well founded. Napster, one of the dot-com websites that allowed copyrighted musical files to be exchanged, was sued for copyright infringement and lost. When the court awarded damages to the recording companies that initiated the case, the total award was in the hundreds of millions of dollars. Expect to see many more battles over digital use of copyrighted works in the coming years. The more works affected by the litigation, the higher the awards will be for successful owners.

In addition to monetary damages, the copyright law provides that infringement can be terminated and the infringing goods seized and destroyed. In one case of media copying, known appropriately by the call letters WPOW, an applicant for a radio station was found to have copied the engineering section from a competitor's file. A court later ordered the purloined portion deleted from the infringer's application. The result was potent—POW!—the stripped-down file was held to be incomplete and the application was summarily dismissed.

Such injunctive relief is vital when infringements occur at formal checkpoints as, for example, customs depots. Bootlegged copies of software and musical CDs delivered from infringement capitals in the Far East are routinely seized and destroyed by customs officials, since under copyright law, the Customs Service can be deputized to protect registered copyrighted works. However, in a world of satellite communication and e-mail, the capacity to enjoin the transmission is essential in maintaining control over the work because the transmission may be unstoppable once sent.

As a rule, injunctive protection proves more complex in online environments. With the anonymity often associated with online and Internet communication, it is cumbersome to locate and stop infringers. Even if a targeted infringing site is shut down, clever hackers can move to another location to continue illegal postings. Cyberspace offers the greatest challenge yet to the efforts to stop infringing activities. As a result, OSPs like AOL and the phone companies have been logical targets. Since any website that utilizes copyrighted materials without consent must, of necessity, pass its content through the OSP, these businesses are materially involved. And, since it is easier and financially more rewarding for a content owner to locate and sue a deep pocket like AOL than an individual user living (say) in the Philippines, OSPs sought changes in the copyright laws of the United States and many foreign countries to minimize their risks. We discuss the OSP Limitation on Liability, which was an essential component of the DMCA, in Chapter 8.

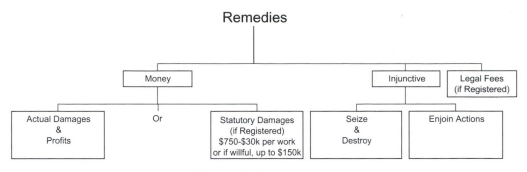

Figure 6-1 Remedies

Another dynamic feature of copyright remedies (Figure 6-1) is that the prevailing party in a copyright lawsuit can seek to be reimbursed for legal fees and expenses. In the U.S. judicial system, where parties typically pay for their own lawyers and the cost of bringing a case can be so high that some rights are never enforced, this provision makes copyright law very accessible to owners and, therefore, a credible threat to would-be infringers. It means that, if one risks infringing on a copyright and is successfully sued, the cost could include paying the fees of all the lawyers in the case, which is not a happy thought.

Therefore, we must be aware of four important limitations in the case of the statutory damages and attorneys fees provisions. First, if the owner is a U.S. resident or citizen, the work must be registered with the Copyright Office at the time of the infringement. Even though the old formality of registration was made permissive by the 1976 Act and cannot be required of any foreigner claiming rights under the Berne Convention, for U.S. nationals the requirement still has vitality. The balance struck encourages filing works with the Copyright Office by requiring that registration for the work must be completed prior to filing a lawsuit.

Second, infringements that occur prior to registration do not subject the defendants to statutory damages or attorneys fees with two exceptions. One exception is the case of infringements occurring very soon after publication, as in the case of live transmission of, say, a baseball game or daily newscast copied simultaneously with its telecast. In that event, the owner has 3 months to register and claim the special statutory benefits for infringements dating from the initial telecast. The second exception is for works of foreigners: *No* formality can impede their rights. In the absence of compliance with these rules, infringements still allow the owner to seek actual damages and accounting of profits, but the other benefits are lost. Bear in mind, however, that if the infringements are continuing, statutory entitlements are reestablished each time the infringing behavior is repeated.

Third, an exception applies to qualified nonprofit educational institutions (such as libraries and public broadcasters). If the qualified nonprofit user has reason to believe that the use of the work was allowed under the *fair use* doctrine, the court should not charge statutory damages. While the nonprofit defendant could still be required to pay actual damages caused by the infringement, statutory damages cannot be assessed. Finally, "innocent" publishers, which may include a broadcaster carrying an advertisement containing copyright infringement materials that it had no reason to believe was unauthorized, are granted an exception that limits the damages they might have to pay to $200.

This gives you an idea of the costs of missteps that attend copyright infringement. Since most people are voracious when it comes to content, the potential for large claims to develop is substantial.

Chapter 7

Ownership of Copyright: Keeping What Is Yours

In an era when content is prized as an asset of commerce, the claim to ownership of copyrighted works becomes more intense. Therefore, care must be taken in establishing the lineage of works. Failure to attend to the niceties of ownership could drive the careless to headaches or, worse, the loss of rights. The most practical moment to address these matters is *before the work is created*. Devise a plan for the ownership of a work and do your homework.

Keep in mind a handful of important points about owning copyrights. First, a basic concern is meeting the statutory requirements for creating a work, most notably fixation in a tangible medium. Perhaps the central issue of ownership involves the rules of authorship, especially the relationship between employer and employee. There is also the matter of acquiring or transferring rights and, of course, registration and term of copyright. Do not forget to get to know your friendly agency, the Copyright Office. Now, we take a closer look at the ownership manual.

Creating the Work

We already discussed the fact that the rights of a copyright owner come into being only when a work of creative and original expression is fixed in a tangible medium. As noted, the concepts of *originality* and *creative expression*, *fixation*, and *tangible medium* are fluid. Originality excludes direct copying of another's work and creative expression and involves a modicum of thought and sufficiency (15 words or more, for example). The fixation requirement is satisfied when the work is preserved even if it is later erased or destroyed. Thus, a copyright can be infringed even if the original author owns no permanent copy. As a tangible medium, almost any environment will do—paper, tape, disk drive, piano roll, film, negatives, microfiche, or even steel. As long as one can point to the object where the fixation occurs, copyright rights are assured. About the only thing that would *not* constitute copyrightable medium is unrecorded conversation.

Authorship and Work for Hire

Copyright rights belong to authors. The author of the copyrighted work is the one who created it. Sometimes the author is an individual, such as a poet or sculptor; other times, the author is a team of creators, such as in the case of a song, where one party writes the score and another the lyrics. When creation is joint, copyright law acknowledges the capacity of works to have more than one author. If their contributions are inseparable, then each may lay claim to the entire work and be entitled to all the benefits of ownership in that work. In that case, however, each joint owner owes a duty of accounting to the other if the work generates income.

When works are created by employees in their jobs, the copyright is usually owned by the employer. *Work for hire* is a time-honored copyright principle that allows the person or entity paying for the work to enjoy the economic benefits of the effort. If a number of creators are involved in the development of a work for an employer, then it makes sense to concentrate the copyright interests in a single party to facilitate exploitation of the work. For example, movies or television programs are described as a collaborative art form because dozens of individuals could combine to create them. When you see the credits roll, they include many people who individually created copyrightable elements that merged into the final picture. Directors, cinematographers, writers, set decorators, costume designers, even the performers—each lays claim to copyrightable elements.

Typically, the producer has each of these people sign a contract that grants the producer control of all the copyrights and related interests, such as rights of publicity and the authority to make sequels. The signing of the contracts is important, because in many instances, the producer does not employ these individuals in the traditional sense; they are not on staff but hired for the specific project. At the conclusion of their work, these artists move on to another job, often with a different producer. Under these circumstances, employees are like independent contractors (see the discussion later).

The copyright law specifies that, if the employee is not regularly employed, a written memo should be signed by the parties indicating that their contribution to a work is a "work for hire." In the absence of this magic language, the individuals may claim a right to copyright, which could seriously affect the way in which the rights of exploitation are implemented. Technically, copyright law defines a work for hire as one of nine types of works specially ordered or commissioned for use as

1. A contribution to a collective work.
2. A part of a motion picture or other audiovisual work.
3. A translation.
4. A supplementary work.
5. A compilation.
6. An instructional text.
7. A test.
8. Answer material for a test.
9. An atlas.

If the work is not one of these and the author is not an employee, work for hire does not apply. In such cases, a written document should clearly cover ownership or transfer of rights.

When one individual works for another and his or her job is to create a copyrighted work, the employer owns the product. Since most people are employed by some kind of business, the ownership of copyright rights usually does not belong to the individual creator. Any employee whose job is to create works becomes disenfranchised from his or her creations, but the copyright bargain is that the person is paid for that labor.

Sometimes, the bargain is complicated because the job one is hired to perform may not cover the creation of a specific work. For example, assume a sales manager at a television station is encouraged to write a jingle for a new station theme, but he is not employed as a composer. Unless the creative task is within the employee's *scope of employment*, that employee is the author for copyright purposes. If the music turns out to be popular, the employee, not the company, is the author under copyright law. Is there any way the company could claim ownership? Only if the task is within the scope of employment. Therefore, a clever employer would have to prove that writing the jingle really is part of the sales manager's job of selling the station. Of course, things could be simplified by making sure that the original employment agreement clearly covers the scope of work or is amended before a new task is undertaken.

Photographs can be another source of ownership dispute. Because taking pictures is easy and common, many people employed for one task may on occasion take a photo of people, places, and things for an employer. If the act of taking the photograph is not tied to an employee's responsibilities, then ownership of the work remains with the employee-photographer, even though the picture may be used by the company. A still or video photographer hired to take family pictures owns the copyright even though he gives the client copies of the pictures. This prevents the client from taking a photo to a local photo development store and ordering 40 copies for family and friends with no obligation to the photographer. Many photographers put a copyright notice on a picture or a legend on the back of the photo restricting such copying. Alternatively, the client and the photographer can negotiate a different fee for the services.

Matters are also ticklish if the creator is an independent contractor. The general rule here is that a nonemployee hired to create a work, such as an outside software developer hired to create a program to manage a cable company's subscriber database, owns the product. Unless a written contract gives the end product to the company paying the bill, the result is uniformly in favor of the independent contractor and may be a nasty surprise to the employer.

As it turns out, software development has been particularly contentious in many industries. If the software works, there may be annual fees to pay for maintenance or upgrades, and, most likely, it cannot be used by sister companies without express permission. Many misunderstandings are created when the paying party does not realize that, although it may have footed the bill to develop the copyrighted software product, paying the fee does not transfer copyright ownership. Remember, the right to use a copyrighted work is not the equivalent of the right to own it.

Acquiring and Transferring Copyrights

As companies are bought and sold, their assets, including their authorship of copyrights, trade as well. The media merger activity of the last 15 years was driven by a desire to lock in control over not only channels of distribution but also the elements of content. With every acquisition proposal, research concerning the employment agreements and outside contractor relationships is necessary to ascertain the assets of the parties.

When the Copyright Act was changed in 1976 to create a unified federal system, it made clear that copyright rights are divisible. An owner can license more than one party to the rights and can separate the rights or divide them any way it pleases. The right to control the making of copies can be granted to one party and the right of public performance to another. This is, in fact, quite common in the music industry, where ASCAP, BMI, and SESAC are authorized to grant public performance rights in songs but are not allowed to grant synchronization rights, that is, the right to copy works onto video.

Intellectual property, like real estate, can be passed to heirs. In fact, the successful effort to extend the term of copyright from 50 to 70 years after the death of an author (from 75 to 95 years in the case of entities) was principally designed to allow great-grandchildren of authors to obtain the benefit of their efforts. The children and grandchildren had been protected by the 50-year term, but the change enables an additional generation to reap the economic fruits of creativity.

(Remember to keep track of the term extension rule by checking out the Supreme Court's ruling in *Eldred* v. *Ashcroft*, due in 2003.)

One special limitation on assignment in the copyright rules is intended to help the struggling artist who has to part with his or her work prematurely in life. Under the termination of assignment, the author and his or her heirs may cancel the assignment between the 56th and 60th years. For works that are still worth something 56 years after they were sold, the copyright law gives extra bargaining power to the author or heirs of the original author. They can reclaim rights that might have been licensed away for little value when the author was young (and generally in need of money) and renegotiate license terms with the same or a new party.

Registration and Copyright Term

Copyright registration rules used to be a fixture of the U.S. system. However, in 1978, mandatory registration was eliminated in favor of a Berne-compatible legal system. Under the Berne Convention, no formality, whether registration or notice, can interfere with a copyright owner's full enjoyment of rights. Hence, registration, a system whereby every work had to be filed with the U.S. Copyright Office promptly after publication, was eliminated in favor of a permissive filing system. In other words, copyrights could not be conditioned on filing with the Copyright Office.

Registration, it must be said, is a good thing. Since it is often necessary for users to track down copyright owners to seek permission, registration affords them a simple and effective mechanism to know when works are published and who owns them. When copyrights are transferred, the assignment should also be noted. Even though we now have a permissive filing system, registration therefore remains important for several reasons:

- It allows the world to know how to reach you. That can be important when rights are being sought or when people want to contact the correct person when works are used, even on a fair use or other permissive basis.

- U.S. citizens need to file if their rights are to be enforced in court. And, if they are registered at the time of an infringement, the copyright owner may claim statutory damages and attorney's fees for infringing acts that occurred after registration.

- The practice of registering assignments of rights allows the public to track down current owners. Orphaned copyrighted works are a serious problem in the field of preservation and archiving. In particular, creators of photographs are often unidentifiable because the works have no source on them. A registered work must have a copyright notice that identifies its author and the year of its publication, two key bits of data that allow identification of the right parties in interest.

Renewal of copyright deserves a mention as well. Under the rules in place from 1909 to 1978, published copyrights that were registered were protected for 28 years. To claim a second 28-year term, a renewal application had to be filed. If the owner forgot to file or concluded that the work did not merit filing, the copyright fell into the public domain. Some famous works (including, as we saw earlier, the movie *It's a Wonderful Life*) met this fate. No amount of wishing can resurrect lost copyrights. Even though the copyright term was extended in 1978 (Figure 7-1), if a work was first published under the 1909 Act, Congress required that a renewal be filed in the 28th year to claim not only the additional 28 years, but the extra 19 (the new 75-year term minus the original 56) as well. However, as it developed, because copyright owners forgot or did not know about the renewal requirement, many works unintentionally fell into the public domain. That problem was rectified when Congress provided for automatic renewal in 1992. However, if a copyrighted author has a dispute with a successor-in-interest, the author could assist a claim by filing a renewal anyway.

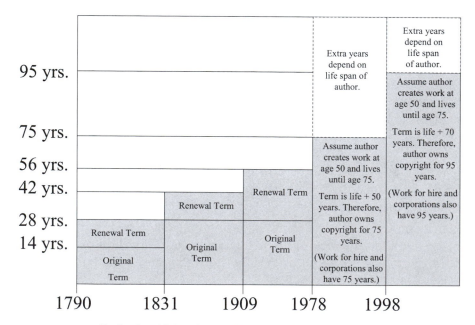

Y axis = Copyright Term in Years   X axis = Year Copyright Law Term Took Effect

Figure 7-1   Copyright Term

As we noted, the Constitution allows Congress to grant copyrights for a limited term, and in our history, the term of copyright has been extended many times. In 1978, the full term of copyright was increased from 56 years (28 years plus the 28 years renewal) to the life of the author plus 50 years or, in the case of works owned by entities such as corporations, 75 years from publication. Works in their original or renewal term were protected for 75 years, and works that were never published, and therefore existed only under common law copyright (which was to last forever), were granted an automatic term to 2002. If the author published the work before the end of 2002, the term advanced to 2027. In 1998, the Copyright Term Extension Act (CTEA) added an extra 20 years to all works whose copyright term had not yet expired and for all future works.

It had been a truism of copyright law that, once the term of a work expired and the work entered the *public domain*, all rights lapsed. The term extensions granted in 1976 and 1998 applied only to works still under copyright protection. Nevertheless, to relieve international pressures caused by several treaties, in 1994, Congress made a unique exception to this copyright term rule. The exception was derived from commitments in GATT and NAFTA and the Berne Convention principle that no formalities should bar rights of a foreign national. If a foreigner—this rule applies only to non-U.S. citizens and entities—did not comply with a U.S. copyright formality under the old copyright laws, and that person's work therefore entered the public domain, copyright could be restored. The restoration applies for the balance of the full copyright term, if newly established Copyright Office procedures are followed. Thus, anyone relying on the public domain status of foreign works is cautioned: Check out the restoration lists kept by the Copyright Office before you exploit foreign-owned works without consent.

Despite the clear mandate of the treaties and the amendment to the copyright law that implemented the restoration requirements, several challenges to the statutory scheme have surfaced. In Chapter 2, we discussed the *Eldred* case. In fall 2001, a group of musical conductors, led by a few from the University of Denver, initiated a challenge to the restoration requirement. Claiming that orchestral scores that had been in the public domain for years now enjoyed full copyright protection (including the extra two decades authorized by the CTEA), the group argued it was difficult if not impossible to afford licenses for musical compositions of long dead foreign composers. They argued that, if the restoration law and term expansion were not declared unconstitutional—as an unauthorized expansion of copyrights beyond the *limited term* imposed by the Constitution—then they and their patrons would suffer irreparable harm. The case, which is founded on a truism that once a work enters the public domain all rights cease, will work its way through the courts in the coming years.

So, to summarize, here is the copyright term sheet:

- 1790–1831: 14 years plus a second 14 years, if author was alive when first term ended.
- 1831–1909: 28 years plus renewal for 14 years.
- 1909–1977: 28 years plus renewal for another 28 years.
- 1978–1997: Life of author plus 50 years or, in the case of works owned by entities, 75 years from creation.
- 1998 onward: Life of author plus 70 years or, in the case of works owned by entities, 95 years from creation.
- Tack on 1, 1978–1997: All works in their 1909 term get an extra 19 years protection.
- Tack on 2, 1998–onward: All works in their 1909/1978 terms get an extra 20 years protection.
- Unpublished works: Copyright until 2002; if published between 1978 and 2002, term extended until 2047.
- GATT and NAFTA resurrected works: Public domain works of foreigners may be restored to the balance of their original terms if the loss of copyright protective status in the United States was due to failure to comply with formalities.

The Copyright Office

The agency that supervises this entire system is the Copyright Office. This user-friendly agency processes the registration of every work and retains a copy of every work in the archives of the Library of Congress. The Copyright Office also collects compulsory royalties and supervises arbitration panels. It has a host of informative reports and documents that make copyright life less complex. Check out its website at www.loc.gov. One thing it does not do, however, is issue advisory opinions applying and interpreting copyright law to facts, such as whether a use is a fair use.

As the recipient of copies of all published and unpublished registered works, it is unsurprisingly a rich treasury of American history. Its officers also serve as special advisors to congressional committees on copyright policy in public and private forums.

A 1996 bill threatened to merge the intellectual property agencies (Patent and Trademark Office and Copyright Office) into a new, superindependent organization, but there was a huge outcry against moving the Copyright Office out of the Library of Congress. As it turned out, the motion had few public supporters. Therefore, the Copyright Office remains a part of the Library of Congress and the legislative branch.

Chapter 8

Online Service Providers: Gateway or Traffic Cop?

As we noted, many OSPs—thousands of commercial companies as well as public libraries, colleges, and universities—have been exposed to a legal claim of copyright infringement without even knowing it. Under copyright rules if someone copies, distributes, or displays a copyrighted work publicly without authority of the copyright owner or its agent, then a violation of law has occurred. Even innocent infringements are subject to penalties. In Chapter 6, we saw that, in addition to injunctive relief, a copyright owner prevailing in an infringement action may be entitled to receive actual damages and profits of the infringement, or statutory damages plus attorney's fees.

One of the developments associated with the Internet has been that valuable copyrighted works, such as new musical CDs and movies, are posted at renegade sites for anyone to download without paying a fee. This practice has driven some copyright owners to the courts for relief. However, since the source of the infringements is often an untraceable site in cyberspace, an alternative defendant has been the Internet service provider that links customers to these sites (Figure 8-1).

Traditionally, common carriers have been exempt from liability for copyright infringement because they merely provide the facilities that link sender and receiver and have no control over the actual content of the transmissions. Many OSPs, both for-profit like AOL, WorldCom, AT&T, and Earthlink, and nonprofits such as libraries and educational institutions, feel this describes their function for subscribers, customers, patrons, students, and faculty in connection with the Internet. However, in their capacity as OSPs, the firms and institutions do more. Technically, they provide software to link users to sites as well as store information on their servers and facilitate recording and display by users or subscribers. Each of these activities is a function recognized in copyright law as an exclusive right of copyright owners. Copyright law also holds that helping someone else violate

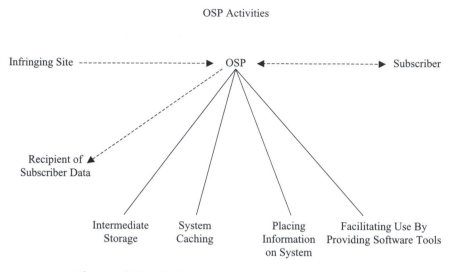

OSP Activities

Figure 8-1 Online Service Provider in the Middle

copyright rights is an infringement, a so-called vicarious or contributory infringement. Therefore, certain commercial OSPs have been held by some courts to be liable for copyright infringement. That an institution is "not for profit" does not eliminate exposure to the copyright infringement claim.

To remedy this exposure, commercial and nonprofit OSPs sought a limitation under copyright law. After 2 years of negotiations, the Online Copyright Infringement Liability Limitation was approved by Congress as part of the omnibus DMCA. The limitation greatly reduces an OSP's exposure to monetary damages; however, it does not exempt an OSP from legal action or injunctive relief. Nevertheless, it is a first line of defense against a claim of copyright infringement, in addition to other copyright defenses and limitations like fair use. The rules are complex and require strict adherence to rigorous deadlines. Unless in full compliance with the law, an OSP, even a nonprofit institution, faces loss of the exemption and exposure to potentially large copyright damage claims. Service providers must not only understand the rules, but also establish internal mechanisms for compliance and monitoring of these activities. Here is the OSP primer.

Definition of an OSP

The statute sets forth the following definition of service provider:

(a) An entity offering the transmission, routing, or providing of connections for digital online communications between or among points specified by a user, or material of the user's choosing, without modification as to the content of the material as sent or received; and

(b) A provider of online services or network access, or the operator of facilities therefor.

All entities whose services fit these descriptions, and the definition in (b) is intended to be very broad, may qualify with regard to those activities. However, to the extent the functions of the OSP involve the creation and posting of content, choosing recipients of messages or controlling users, the limitation does not apply; and regular copyright rules respecting proper clearance, as well as fair use and other defenses, are fully applicable.

Types of OSP Activities Covered

The OSP limitation covers most transitory digital network communications. Specifically, these are

- Intermediate and transient storage of materials (such as Web pages or chat room discussions) in the course of transmitting, routing, or providing connections
- System caching
- Placing information on a system or network at the direction of users
- Use of information location tools, such as directories, indexes, and hypertext links

To qualify for the limitation with regard to all covered OSP activities, a set of conditions for each specific function must be met. If a firm or institution performs all the OSP functions, as most do, then all requirements must be met.

The requirements fit into three key categories:

- *Material.*
    1. The material must be made available online by someone other than the OSP. The limitation therefore does not cover any content that the OSP creates and places online for its subscribers.
    2. The OSP cannot modify the material. If the OSP plays a role in changing content created by others, it loses the benefit of the limitation.
    3. No copy of the material during intermediate storage can be maintained longer than "reasonably necessary." When an OSP transmits information or content through its facilities, its systems keep a working copy of it

for some period of time. The law requires that this retention not be indefinite, rather it should be retained only as long as required by the technology.

4. The OSP cannot have "actual knowledge" that the material or the activity is infringing. What is more, the OSP should not even be aware of facts or circumstances from which infringing activity is apparent. If the OSP receives such awareness, it must act quickly to remove or disable access to the site. In short, a little knowledge can be a bad thing for the OSP. Since most OSPs do not monitor content for copyright ownership, in most cases they do not know much about a possible infringement. After all, a user might be an independent creator of the work, a licensee, or even a fair user. How is the OSP to know? We get to that in a moment.

- *Parties to the Transmissions.* The transmissions must be initiated by one party or at the direction of another person and sent to yet another. To qualify, the OSP must be just like a phone company, an intermediate link between points A and B, not an outputter of the message at either end. No copy of the material during intermediate storage can be made accessible to another person. In other words, as the Internet transmission is occurring, only the sender and recipient should have access to the content. The OSP should not allow strangers to the transmission to have access to the work. The OSP cannot select recipients; rather, whoever sends the message or solicits the work should be in control. The OSP cannot receive a financial benefit directly attributable to an infringing activity in a case in which the OSP has the right and ability to control the activity. Congress did not want the OSP to benefit from the infringement. Even so, the OSP may make reasonable charges for its services. Either the sender, the receiver, or both may have to pay for services. In short, a monthly subscription fee is not a benefit directly attributable to the infringing activities.

- *Procedures.* The transmission, routing, provision of connections, or storage must be carried out through an automatic, technical process. All these activities are typically performed through the use of highly specialized equipment. The OSP must follow rules relating to refreshing, reloading, or other updating of the material; and the OSP cannot interfere with technology associated with the material, such as software that controls access or use, like fees. In other words, the OSP must enable technology to work its ways without intervention.

The owner must also comply with *notice and takedown* procedures. This is a key concept of the limitation; if a content owner discovers an infringement in cyberspace and follows procedure by giving the OSP "proper notification," then the OSP must expeditiously remove or disable access to the offending material. In other words, it has to block access to the site and prevent content from flowing via the Internet to its subscribers. However, if the affected website owner properly objects and serves an appropriate "counternotice"—here's a twist—then the OSP must adhere to "put back" procedures. These procedures keep the OSP at arms length from the content dispute while allowing the copyright owner and the alleged infringer to work through the dispute by themselves.

The recent response of Google, the popular Web search engine, to receipt of an infringement notice points out some as yet uncharted aspects of the OSP provisions. Google was notified by the Church of Scientology that its search results for "Scientology" included links to copyrighted church material; the material in question was located on the website of Operation Clambake, an organization located in Norway that was critical of the church. Google complied with the DMCA by removing the link to the Scientology material (initially removing but then restoring the link to the Operation Clambake home page), but was besieged by free speech advocates who claimed that Google was censoring its search results. Google's solution was to adopt a new policy under which it informs users when it has removed a result and links them to the Chilling Effects Clearinghouse website (www.chillingeffects.org), where they can read the DMCA complaint, which Google supplied.

Obligations of Copyright Owners

As is apparent, the limitation places several key obligations on copyright owners. Among the most relevant are the following:

- When refreshing, reloading, or updating material, the owner must adhere to generally accepted industry standard data communications protocols.
- As a parallel to the OSP's obligation not to interfere with technology controlling access to the material (e.g., passcodes and fees), the owner's technology must (1) not significantly interfere with the OSP's system or network performance regarding intermediate storage of material, (2) be consistent with generally accepted industry communications protocols, and (3) not extract information from the OSP's system or network about the person initiating the transmission that it could not have acquired through direct access to that person.
- The OSP must comply with notification requirements in connection with *notice and takedown* procedures.

Notice and Takedown, Counternotice, and Put-back Procedures

Notice and takedown is an essential part of the protections sought by the content community and forms a new regulatory regime for both OSPs and copyright owners. If a content owner reasonably believes that a site misuses copyrighted matter and notifies the OSP according to statutory procedures or if the OSP independently becomes aware of the facts and circumstances of infringement, then the OSP must quickly and effectively remove the material or disable public access to the site or else face loss of the limitation.

Among the elements of the notice and takedown process are the following:

1. The OSP must have a designated agent to receive notices, and it must use a public portion of its website for receipt of notices.
2. The OSP must notify the Copyright Office of the agent's identity. The Copyright Office will maintain electronic and hard copy registries of website agents so that they may be easily contacted in case of infringement.
3. Proper written notification from a copyright owner to an OSP must include (a) the name, address, and electronic signature of the complaining party; (b) sufficient information to identify the copyrighted work or works; (c) the infringing matter and its Internet location; (d) a statement by the owner saying that he or she has a good faith belief that there is no legal basis for the use of the materials complained of; and (e) a statement of the accuracy of the notice and, under penalty of perjury, that the complaining party is authorized to act on behalf of the owner.

Any misrepresentation of material facts will subject the offending party to claims for damages and attorney's fees.

If the OSP complies in good faith with the statutory requirements, the limitation immunizes it from liability to subscribers and third parties; however, this immunity is conditioned on affording the affected subscriber notice of the action. If a subscriber files a proper "counternotice," attesting to its lawful use of the material, then the OSP must "promptly" notify the copyright owner and, within 14 business days, restore the material, unless the matter has been referred to a court. The counternotice must contain (1) the subscriber's name, address, phone number, and physical or electronic signature; (2) identification of the material and its location before removal; (3) a statement under penalty of perjury that the material was removed by mistake or misidentification; and (4) subscriber consent to local federal court jurisdiction or, if overseas, to an appropriate judicial body.

Special Rule for Higher Education

The OSP regime makes one special exception to the general rule that an institution is responsible for the acts of its employees. In a bow to academic freedom, scholarly research, and the practice of administrators of higher educational institutions of not interfering with classroom work, the statute provides that faculty and graduate students employed to teach or research shall not be considered part of the institution for OSP purposes. Thus, if a member of the faculty posts infringing content, selects recipients of infringing matter, or knows of an infringement, the school where he or she teaches would not automatically lose its right to the limitation.

The higher ed exception has three important qualifications: First, the faculty or graduate student's activities cannot involve online access (including e-mail) to materials that were "required or recommended" within the preceding 3 years for a course taught by the employee at the institution. Second, the institution cannot have received more than *two* notices of actionable infringement by the faculty or graduate student. Third, the institution must provide all users of its system or network informational materials in compliance with U.S. copyright laws. It is important to note that the policy should not only spell out the rights of ownership but also the limitations on those rights, most noticeably fair use and educational exceptions.

If properly followed, the higher educational institution will not be tainted by the actions of its teaching and research employees. As an institution, it should qualify for protection against money damage claims and should not be required to block access or terminate a subscriber's use. It could still be subject to other injunctive remedies, such as those involving preserving evidence.

OSP Limitation and Privacy

The statute also recognizes the importance of protecting the privacy of a user's identity on the Internet. Procedures are laid out by which a complaining copyright owner may obtain the identity of individual subscribers from the OSP. The principal safeguard involves the content owner's compliance with a formal court request that can be issued by federal court clerks. If followed, this process protects the OSP from liability under federal or state prohibitions respecting release of information regarding individual subscribers.

In addition to all these rules, the OSP must develop and post a policy for termination of use by repeat offenders and accommodate and not interfere with "standard" technical measures used by copyright owners to identify and protect their works, such as digital watermarking and access codes. The act makes clear that the OSP is *not required* to monitor its services for potential infringements. It need not seek out information about copyright misuse; however, it cannot ignore obvious facts.

These rules took effect in October 1998. Almost immediately, the Copyright Office swung into action, establishing a procedure for accepting OSP registrations. Today, thousands of companies and institutions have registered their services with the Copyright Office. This registry is the first place to go when a copyright owner knows about website infringements. Putting OSPs on notice and demanding take-downs are the orders of the day. It is also important for unregistered OSPs to review the statute and practices with their administrators. Ignoring the benefits from the limitation on OSP liability leaves the unprepared exposed to potentially huge copyright liabilities.

Chapter 9

Right to Control Access: The Trump Card

When the history of copyright law is written, the digital debate of 1998 will be primarily about access or, more specifically, about the right to control access to digital works. From time immemorial, authors sold copies of their works to the public and that was how they made money. The individual who purchased the work owned the copy but not the copyright. The purchaser could place the book in a personal library, read it at leisure, loan the copy to a friend, or give it away. For the person who possessed the hard copy, it was always there to review and research if the spirit moved him or her.

But in a digital world, works are less frequently sold and more often licensed. Combined with the fact that, in an online environment, works are placed on remote servers and users pay a fee to access them, licensing and access are the core concepts of copyright exploitation in the digital millennium.

When a user employs a computer and the Internet to access a work on a remote site, several things of copyright importance happen. The computer receives an electronic transmission via a modem or similar device and makes a copy of the work in the random access memory (RAM) of the computer. That process enables a user to view the work. With the aid of the computer, a user can transfer the document from RAM to a file on a hard drive. Once on a hard drive, a user can send a digital copy of the file via e-mail to friends and family or simply keep a copy for future reference. That digital copy can be viewed as text, graphics, sound, photographs, or motion pictures. Also, that copy can be a perfect clone of the original.

However, as many know, ingenious computer programmers can create instructions and barriers to the performance of many tasks. Some instructions can require information like a passcode, a word, or phrase so exact that failure to provide it will leave the user unable to open a file. In other instances, a computer user may be able to copy a work onto a hard drive, but embedded in the work may be a set of instructions that make the file unusable. Alternatively, the file may be coded to be accessible for a period of time, for example, a week, and then, it can be ordered to vanish. Now, some wizards (a.k.a. hackers) can decode or countermand these instructions. When these talented hackers overcome barriers, copyright owners feel vulnerable, and their control over their works is subject to the whims of the programming experts, who can take works and treat them without regard to any limitations, even reasonable ones. These concerns were at the center of the DMCA debate over technological protection measures and restrictions on access to works.

As a precursor to the digital debate of 1998, copyright owners (primarily representatives of major movie studios, record labels, software and book publishers) asked U.S. representatives negotiating updates of international copyright laws to add certain treaty obligations covering these digital issues. They did so, and when the delegates returned to the United States, Congress was urged to change U.S. law to satisfy the mandate of the Berne Convention. (See Chapter 19 for more details on the Berne Convention.) At the top of their agenda was a statutory change that would declare anyone unlawfully accessing a digital copyrighted work protected by a technological protection measure (TPM) to be civilly and criminally liable for infringement.

Their argument was that bypassing these devices was akin to breaking into a locked house. If one was not authorized to access a work, then one should not be allowed to circumvent measures that a copyright owner lawfully placed on the work. The ban on circumvention that owners sought had two parts to it. First, the owners wanted to prevent the manufacture and sale of devices that could technologically open the digital locks. Second, the owners wanted to make an individual's action of circumvention unlawful as well.

Opponents of a ban on circumvention suggested the changes would decimate the balance that existed in copyright for decades. If one cannot access a work, then there would be no opportunity to engage in independent criticism, scholarship, and teaching. There can be no fair use of works that cannot be lawfully accessed, it was argued.

Equipment manufacturers sought a standard for the creation and dissemination of equipment consistent with the standard adopted by the U.S. Supreme Court in a seminal case in the 1980s debate over the videocassette recorder (VCR). In an important copyright fair use case named for the Sony Betamax machine, the Supreme Court held that the VCR was a lawful device (*Sony Corp. of America* v. *Universal City Studios, Inc.*). Even though the Betamax machine facilitated widespread, unauthorized copying of movies and other audiovisual works, it had a legitimate fair use purpose. The VCR permitted people in their homes to record programs off the air, in case the telecast was at an inconvenient time, and shift the viewing to a better time. This "time-shifting purpose" was a fair use, in the Supreme Court's view. Because the VCR had an important noninfringing purpose, its manufacture and sale did not violate copyright law.

By analogy, computer device manufacturers sought a similar standard with regard to digital content. If a computer or software program could bypass a technological measure designed to prevent unauthorized access (for example, a passcode or encryption formula) to permit a noninfringing use (e.g., a fair use for educational purposes), then the access limitations would be rendered harmless as far as that equipment or device was concerned.

In the end, Congress sided with the copyright owners. It concluded that the threat of digital theft facing copyright owners was far greater than any they faced in more than a generation. Prohibition on the manufacture, importation, sale, or trafficking in any technology, product, service, device, or component was decreed. The ban affects equipment, devices, processes, and services whose "primary purpose" is to be used in defeating technology that limits access to copyrighted works. The new law prohibits any equipment or services that (1) are primarily designed or produced for the purpose of circumventing a TPM, (2) have limited commercially significant purposes or uses other than circumvention, or (3) are marketed for use in circumventing TPMs.

At the same time, Congress grappled with what to do about individuals who bypassed TPMs. Again, the breaking and entering analogy to the locked digital warehouse was raised. Even though one can engage in fair use under copyright law without having purchased a work, the affirmative act of using someone else's passcode or disabling encryption code to access a work that one has no license to see was deemed unacceptable behavior. Therefore, the DMCA includes a key provision that prohibits unauthorized circumvention: "No person shall circumvent a technological measure that effectively controls access to a work protected under this title." That is strong medicine in a digital world.

However, in two modest bows to those concerned about the broad sweep of the anticircumvention rules, Congress crafted two compromises.

Copyright Office Periodic Rulemaking Proceeding

In the first instance, on a periodic basis, the Librarian of Congress (principally through the Copyright Office) is instructed to review how the law is being or should be implemented and determine whether persons are being prevented from exercising fair use and other privileges set forth in the limitations to copyright rights. If the results are too restrictive of fair use and other copyright limitations, the Copyright Office is allowed to fashion limited relief: It can carve out those particular classes of works for which the limitations are being unduly restricted and exempt those works from the rule entirely. As part of the phase-in approach to the DMCA prohibition, Congress delayed implementation of the prohibition on persons accessing protected works without authority for 2 years (until October 28, 2000) while the Copyright Office conducted its first study of the new rules.

The DMCA instructed the Librarian of Congress, in doing this study, to consider several factors including (1) the availability for use of copyrighted works; (2) the availability for use of works for nonprofit archival, preservation, and educational purposes; (3) the impact of the prohibition on circumvention on criticism, comment, news reporting, teaching, scholarship, or research; and (4) the effect of circumvention of TPMs on the market for or value of copyrighted works.

After the initial 2-year study by the Copyright Office, completed in October 2000, the Librarian of Congress determined that only two specific classes of works should be exempt from anticircumvention restrictions:

1. Compilations consisting of lists of websites blocked by filtering software applications.
2. Literary works, including computer programs and databases, protected by access control mechanisms that fail to permit access because of malfunction, damage, or obsolescence.

Since the first study was initiated before the prohibition on user circumvention took effect, little empirical evidence of harm to users could be found, which was the hallmark test for the Copyright Office. Once TPMs become standard elements of more digital content, the true impact of the DMCA reform will be felt and the question whether users have reasonable access to the digital works or viable alternative works will be answered. The next study must be concluded by October 28, 2003.

Exceptions to the Prohibitions

In the second instance, Congress adopted a group of explicit exceptions (Figure 9-1) to the anticircumvention prohibition:

- *Nonprofit libraries, archives, and educational institutions: browsing right.* Qualifying public institutions are permitted to circumvent TPMs to gain access to a copyrighted work *solely* to make a good faith determination whether to acquire a copy of the work. This accessed copy cannot be retained longer than necessary to make the determination and may not be used for any other purpose, and the work must not be otherwise reasonably available in any form. Violations of the limitation subject the nonprofit organization to civil damages, and repetitive violations can result in loss of the exemption. The exemption is *not* a justification to traffic in prohibited equipment.

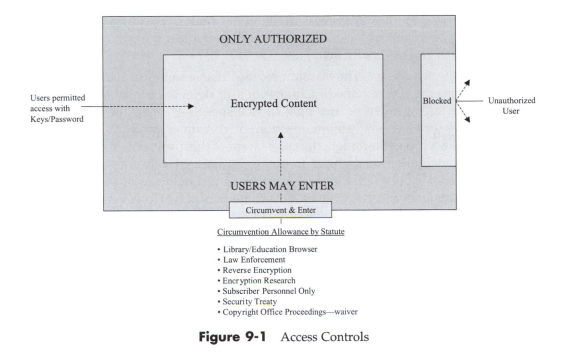

Figure 9-1 Access Controls

- *Law enforcement, intelligence, and other government activities.* Federal and state government law enforcement authorities are not restricted by this statute.
- *Reverse engineering.* A lawful user of a computer program may circumvent TPMs to ensure that the program can work with other programs (interoperability), provided there is no readily available commercial alternative for that purpose. The research may be shared with others, as long as it does not constitute a copyright infringement of the original or related work.
- *Encryption research.* Circumvention is permitted in the context of "good faith encryption research" with respect to copies lawfully acquired. Persons availing themselves of this exemption must have tried to get permission from the original owner and cannot engage in practices deemed a violation of computer fraud laws.
- *Personally identifying information.* Circumvention is permitted to detect and disable technology that collects and then distributes information about an online subscriber that was not authorized by the subscriber.
- *Security testing.* Circumvention is permitted for good faith efforts at accessing a computer system or network (with permission of the owner) to investigate and correct a security flaw.

- *Analog devices.* The law requires compliance by analog recording device manufacturers with anticopy technologies that do not affect the playability of the machines or restrict lawful activities.

- *Other rights not affected.* The statute provides that nothing in the new access rules affects the rights, remedies, limitations, or defenses available in cases of copyright infringement or any right of free speech or press for persons using consumer electronic, communication, or consumer products. While this sounds like a broad limitation, the clear intent of this provision is to recognize the prior obligation of the user to obtain authorized access to work. Once lawful access is obtained, the other limitations and defenses of copyright law (such as fair use) and the Constitution come into play. However, if a person who lacks lawful access cannot assume that fair use or free speech will apply if he or she chooses to circumvent a TPM. Moreover, any subscriber whose paid online subscription has expired should not presume a right to circumvent a TPM to make fair use of content in the period of the original subscription. Indeed, a strict reading of the law says he or she cannot.

Sidebar to the DMCA Debate: Judiciary and Commerce Committees Clash over Jurisdiction

An interesting sidebar in the DMCA debate that told much about the way laws are made was a jurisdictional tussle over congressional authority to regulate matters affecting the Internet and its transmissions. While copyright jurisdiction lay with the Judiciary Committees in the House and Senate, the Commerce Committee in the House wanted to participate in deciding how Internet communications were regulated. The dispute helps explain why the final structure of the DMCA incorporated participation not only of the Copyright Office (which reports directly to the Judiciary Committees), but also the National Telecommunications Information Administration (NTIA), which is within the Department of Commerce, an agency overseen by the Commerce Committees.

Copyright Management Information

In an attempt to ensure the integrity of any information included with digital works that the owner intends to use for management purposes, the DMCA prohibits the removal or alteration of copyright management information (CMI) or the dissemination of false CMI. CMI is defined in the law to include

- The title and other information identifying the work.
- The name and other information about the author.
- The name and other information about the copyright owner.

- The name and other information about performers, writers, and directors of qualifying works.
- Terms and conditions for use of the work.
- Identifying numbers or symbols.
- Other information that the Register of Copyrights may appropriately prescribe.

Law enforcement, intelligence, and other information security activities, as well as certain public performances by radio and television stations, are exempted from portions of these prohibitions.

Penalty Provisions

The DMCA added new, substantial penalties for anyone caught violating the prohibitions on unauthorized access, manufacturing, or trafficking in banned equipment and devices. Persons who violate the access prohibitions are subject to awards of actual damages and profits or statutory damages of no less than $200 nor more than $2,500 per act of circumvention or per device sold or service offered. Violators of the CMI rules can recover statutory amounts ranging from $2,500 to $25,000 per violation. A nonprofit library, archive, or educational institution can escape damages if it can establish that it was not aware and had no reason to believe that its acts constituted a violation. These institutions are also exempted from any criminal sanctions, which include fines up to $500,000 and imprisonment for up to 5 years (doubled in the case of repeat offenses). As with other copyright laws, injunctions against certain practices can issue and the prevailing party can be awarded attorney's fees.

Early Decisions Uphold the Anticircumvention Rules

A few early cases tested the constitutionality of the DMCA access rules, and so far, the validity of the statute has been upheld. The most notable decision involved DeCSS, a computer program designed to bypass TPMs and allow DVDs to play on Linux-based operating equipment. We have more to say about this decision, but for the moment it is important to note that the important Second Circuit Court of Appeals upheld a decision that the DeCSS software violated the DMCA and was not an instrument of fair use or free speech.

So the copyright law moves into the 21st century with a new twist. The grant of rights covering uses of works has been extended to the right to control access in digital formats. The power to restrict who can see a work has enormous educational and social implications. Those effects will be felt for decades to come.

Moving On

We presented the broad framework of copyright—the outer layers of law—and discussed its practical applications. Now, it is time to approach another wing of IP rules important for content—trademark law. Once we have a grounding in the philosophy of this sister body of rules, we can appreciate the shading and nuances necessary for better understanding of media content rights.

But, before we move on, let's summarize the core premises of copyright law.

Core of Copyright

1. Authors are entitled to exclusive rights in their works for limited times.
2. The copyright rights are broadly defined to cover copying in any format, creating derivatives, and publicly performing, displaying, or distributing a work.
3. The rights are subject to crucial exemptions, including fair use, compulsory licensing, and educational uses.
4. The law provides powerful remedies to enforce the rights.
5. There are no longer any prerequisites to claiming copyright; the original work need only be fixed in a tangible medium.
6. The term of copyright is for an author's life plus 70 years (95 years if an entity).

Now, on to trademarks.

Part Two

Trademarks

Chapter 10

What Is a Trademark?

While copyright law defines the rights and responsibilities regarding works, trademark treats the subtle arena of words, names, phrases, and symbols. In many ways, these linguistic and visual elements are the linchpins of relationships in the minds of people to the products and talents of creative professionals. Serving as source identifiers, trademarks allow the consumer to relate to a product or service based on a body of experiences or images. They are most fundamentally distinguished from copyrights by their brevity. While copyright law requires the element of originality and generally applies to works of at least 15 words, trademarks are often short and pithy. One word (Paramount), a string of letters (ABC), a short phrase ("All the News That's Fit to Print"), a visual design (the CBS eye), sounds (the melody of "When You Wish upon a Star"), colors (pink for fiberglass), or smells (high-priced perfumes) all constitute trademarks. They identify a source and embody a reputation.

Thus, TVs that say GE, movies stamped Universal, Internet access from AOL, clothing from Dior, bags from Gucci, gems from Tiffany, cable services from Comcast all have meaning to the public. The consumer relies on the information to help make choices in the marketplace; the trademark serves as the identity of the enterprise or individual. Picking a trademark is a way of defining who and what a business is all about.

Sometimes, marketplace competitors, searching for an advantage, play off the reputation of others. Whether by comparative advertising (Pepsi tastes better than Coke) or tricks to simulate logos, trademark issues dominate the efforts of many who seek to create a specific niche. Being savvy about trademarks smoothes the operation of any business enterprise.

The Internet and digital communications opened a whole new area for trademark exploitation. Domain names, metatags, and keywords are often shorthand for someone's trademark. We are constantly being bombarded with new uses of old marks. Even the right to use one's own name is being regulated in the interest of trademark protection.

Before delving into the key issues of trademark law, we look at the principal concepts that dominate this discipline.

Trademarks, Service Marks, Trade Names, Trade Dress, and Product Design

While we shall use the word *trademark* to cover all the types of elements, there are actually five terms that need to be distinguished. A *trademark* is a word or phrase physically stamped on a good or a label attached to a good. It is a unique identifier as to the source of the product. The product itself is tangible and can be held, lifted, eaten, or worn. Sometimes, the product is too big to fit into your pocket, like an automobile or airplane, but the word or symbol by which it is distinguished from competing articles is clear. Therefore, whenever the product is tangible, the relevant legal term is *trademark*.

A *service mark* is the word or phrase associated with the provision of services. Like a trademark, it is a unique source identifier. Since services are not tangible, you cannot touch them, eat them or wear them; yet, they are crucial to commerce and living. So, even though you cannot touch a communications service, you know the firms that deliver those services by these symbols: Verizon, AT&T, NBC, AOL–Time Warner, and KABC-AM and -FM. All these are service marks for the entities that provide communication services. Of course, the same symbol could serve as a trademark and a service mark: In the phrase *AT&T long distance services*, *AT&T* is a service mark, but when you reach for an AT&T telephone, the letters *AT&T* function as a trademark. In terms of legal treatment, there is no difference whatsoever between trademarks and service marks. This was not always the case, and indeed some portions of international law retain the distinction, but the practical effect for U.S. law is merely semantic.

Semantics, however, does not characterize the difference with *trade names*. A trade name is the actual name of a business, and it is readily identified by additional words, such as *Company*, *Corporation*, *Ltd.*, *LLC*, or *Inc.* A trade name often comes attached to a street address, a phone number, or an e-mail address. Unlike a trademark or service mark, which is linguistically an adjective that modifies a type of good or service, a trade name is grammatically a noun; it identifies a particular person or business. A trade name can be converted into a trademark, as it is when AT&T Inc. stamps *AT&T* on one of its telephones.

Trade dress is a concept that has taken on great significance in recent years. Trade dress refers to a product's packaging or a business's overall image. The U.S. Supreme Court explained that the marketplace appearance of the Mexican restaurant Two Pesos (from the novel architecture of its building, to the uniforms worn by its wait staff, and the design of its menus) constituted the company's trade dress. In another case, the label on a bottle of booze was held to be distinctive trade dress. In short, trade dress is the total, unique image of a product or the enterprise providing services. While it may include individual elements that themselves are trademarks (e.g., a bottle of soda may have the mark *Coca-Cola*, along with the red stripe or a well-known bottle shape), it is the totality of the elements that makes trade dress. As with other source signifiers, trade dress can be exclusively claimed by its owner.

Product design is a related concept that became the subject of a more recent U.S. Supreme Court decision. In a case involving a clothing designer's stylistic line of children's garments that were imitated in low-priced outfits sold at Wal-Mart, the Supreme Court was asked to pronounce whether the design of a product was inherently distinctive (i.e., a source signifier) and functionally a trademark. Despite its declaration a few years earlier that trade dress could be inherently distinctive, the Supreme Court said that that could not be the case with product design. Even though the design of a product might become a trademark if it achieves great public familiarity (in trademark parlance *secondary meaning*), the Supreme Court explained that a product's design could never be inherently distinctive.

In this case the product design was clothing, but the potential kinds of product designs—particularly those made by creative artisans—are actually infinite; if you doubt this, just wander around a craft fair and look at the various practical creations, salt and pepper shakers in the shape of a dog and cat or a pair of chopsticks with a connecting flexible bridge. For the Supreme Court, the bottom line is a bright-line test: While the trade dress of a product or business can be inherently distinctive with no special legal showings, a product's design never can be. The decision requires that public association of a product's design with its designer as a unique source must be shown; however, the creator may turn to other bodies of law for some relief. If a product's design has original, expressive elements, copyright law may grant relief. Thus, even though the children's clothing designer may have a hard time proving that the public readily identified her as the sole source of the garments, if she had registered the clothing design as copyrighted work, then at least she could claim protection against direct copying.

As you now know, both a trademark and a copyright can be owned exclusively. However, the nature of the legal rights differs in two key respects, and those differences have important implications for competition. First, even though the term has been extended several times in recent decades, copyrights are granted for "limited periods of time." At the conclusion of the term, the rights cease. Trademark rights, by comparison, need never end. As long as a mark is in use in commerce, the owner's interest continues. If the owner stops using a mark for a number of years, then the rights may be extinguished, but even short periods of inactivity do not terminate trademark rights.

Second, the copyright law is designed to prevent copying. If two people independently create the same work, with minor variations or even none at all, each can hold a copyright in his or her work and use it to the full extent of the law unless copying is proven by one or the other. While fair use and other limitations sanction certain uses of a copyrighted work without consent of the owner, the similarity of those works, in and of itself, is not dispositive of the legal question of infringement. Trademarks, by contrast, are monopolies on a word or phrase, with no regard to the independent creativity of a second comer. The key requirement is *first to use in commerce*, and the test for infringement is *whether there is a likelihood of confusion between two marks*. If the originator establishes his or her field of commerce, then the law will prevent anyone from infringing directly or in a way that creates a likelihood of confusion as to source.

As the owner of an exclusive right, a shrewd trademark owner can foreclose competitors from exploiting a word or phrase and thus gain a competitive advantage. When launching new product lines, popular trademarks can also bring enormous market presence and value to something new, even if the product or service is untested. Sometimes, the best laid plans and trademarks can disappoint if the new product itself does not measure up.

In the late 1980s, the national newspaper *USA Today* used its reputation for colorful newspaper pages, encapsulated news features, and its market familiarity to launch *USA Today—The Television Show*. A newly conceived first-run program, the show was to be produced by Grant Tinker, a television producer of great renown. Tinker, husband of Mary Tyler Moore, had produced a string of hit television series, including *The Mary Tyler Moore Show*. The combination of *USA Today* and Tinker proved to be a dynamic team. The program was offered to television affiliates without so much as a pilot. What could go wrong with such firepower? Over 170 stations signed on to carry the show in prime TV time. Syndication deals to carry the show made big news.

Despite the success in establishing affiliations and garnering choice air time, which are normally the toughest things for a new program to achieve, the show itself failed to meet its own hype. After critics panned its "too fast-paced" programming and audiences stayed away, *USA Today* tried to remake its image. Grant Tinker was replaced by another producing wunderkind, Steve Friedman, fresh from success at NBC. Still, the program never quite developed a formula for television. Ironically, had the program been able to develop with less hype and more experimentation, say, if one or two pilots had been utilized to test the approach with the viewers, the advantage afforded by the extension of the *USA Today* brand might have paid off in a big way. As it turned out, the advantage earned by the trademark franchise was squandered. Had the show reached its potential, it would have been a powerful demonstration of the persuasive brand extension of trademarks. As matters played out, it illustrated the risks of associating a valuable trademark with an underachieving product.

A similar fate befell Coca-Cola when it launched its highly promoted drink New Coke, only to discover the public loved the old Classic Coke taste. Nevertheless, successful trademarks will always inspire a spin-off. The launch of MSNBC, the cable channel merging Microsoft and NBC, underscores the never-ending search for the effective brand extension. In sum, the proper handling of trademarks from their inception can provide lasting benefit to the owner.

Another important thing to know about copyrights and trademarks is that many important copyrights can be protected as trademarks as well. Cartoon characters, such as Mickey Mouse, fit this mold. Originally conceived as a drawing (that is, a copyrighted work), this friendly rodent has become one of the symbols of the Disney empire. Decades hence, long after the copyrights in the original films are in the public domain, Disney will prevent third party misuse of its works by trademark protection. Even though the original animated works will be freely available for recirculation by anyone in the public, no one will be able to commercialize the Mickey character alone without Disney's approval. And the same can be said for Minnie, Donald Duck, Daisy, Goofy, Snow White, and all the animated folks. While the storylines may be free to be developed, the names, animation, appearance, even voices, of the Disney characters will be independently protected as trademarks of the company.

Trademark Continuum: Fanciful, Arbitrary, Suggestive, Descriptive, and Generic

Think of trademarks existing on a continuum or a ruler, as in Figure 10-1. At one end, there are *fanciful marks*, terms that have no dictionary meaning. These are coined terms, like *Kodak*, *Polaroid*, and *Exxon*. They are invented, then invested with an image. Based on the success and breadth of the products and services, they become unique identifiers that are granted significant trademark recognition.

Continuing along the ruler, we find *arbitrary marks*, those that contain words or phrases that are commonplace but applied in an uncommon way. There is no dictionary connection of the word *Eagle* to potato chips or *Sable* to cars. However, the words themselves connote images that the commercial users decided to capitalize on. Choosing an arbitrary word and associating it with a new good or service usually requires substantial effort in marketing and image building. It entails creating word associations that never existed before or purposefully using words that have no logical connection with one's products or services; needless to say, this is not an easy task. When done successfully though, the identification

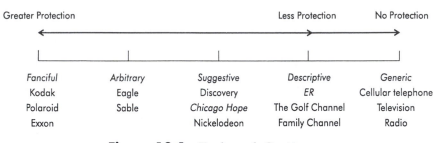

Figure 10-1   Trademark Continuum

of fanciful and arbitrary marks with products or services establishes the most useful and long-lasting bonding of all trademarks.

Most people gravitate to familiar words or phrases; creative types therefore try to use familiar words in inventive ways, suggesting what their product or service is about. Sometimes they seek to exploit words or phrases that already have an association in the consumer's mind and thus create *suggestive marks*. Titles of cable channels and television shows fit this bill routinely: Nickelodeon, Discovery, and *Friends* are but a few examples of titles that function as media service marks because they are suggestive of their content.

Nickelodeon is a particularly clever illusionary mark because it conjures up associations with entertainment and children without explicitly saying "children's channel." Discovery is similarly intriguing because it suggests programming fare that is about science and nature without expressly stating so. In trademark terms, these titles are invested with greater potential for protection against competitors or others who would try to trade on their reputation. For example, when a video store shelved children's videos in a section called the *Discovery Zone*, the cable network raised some flack. It argued that the use either implied an association with or endorsement from the Discovery Channel. The matter concluded when the video store ended the practice.

As a program title for a weekly drama set in a medical emergency room, the CBS series *Chicago Hope* did not tell you much about the show's content, other than that you might expect it to be set in the city of Chicago. By contrast, a prime time competitor's title, *ER*, leaves little doubt about its medical emergency theme. In trademark terms, *ER* is a *descriptive mark* for a TV series about a hospital emergency room. The distinguishing feature of a descriptive mark is that it specifically states the essential element of the product or the nature of the service. One way to characterize the key ingredient is as follows: If you know what the product or service is about without ever coming into direct contact with it, the mark is descriptive. When one hears The All News Channel or The Golf Channel in connection with cable services, it requires no mental gymnastics to understand what programs these channels will feature.

The phrase *generic mark* is really a misnomer, because a generic word or phrase identifies a category of goods or services, rather than a source. The terms *television*, *radio*, and *cellular telephone* are generic. They cannot function as trademarks because they are inherently incapable of helping a consumer distinguish one source from another. Sometimes, a fanciful mark becomes so successful in the marketplace that the public and competitors treat it as generic. It happened to *aspirin* and *cellophane*. That is death to a trademark. Concern about a fanciful mark turning generic is why Xerox, Inc., has worked so hard over the years to inform consumers that *Xerox* is a trademark for photocopy machines. As the ads say, one does not make a Xerox, one uses a Xerox photocopy machine or creates a Xerox photocopy.

A variant of concern may also affect Microsoft's ownership of the Windows trademark. In March 2002, a Seattle judge denied Microsoft Corporation's request for a preliminary injunction to prevent a little company called Lindows.com, Inc., from using that name for a Linux-based operating system. The court's initial order suggests it believes *Windows* may be generic. Although there is a strong likelihood such a ruling, if issued, would be overturned on appeal, the preliminary scuffle presents an interesting question as to whether the mighty Microsoft Windows trademark could possibly be considered generic.

The possibility of a mark becoming generic underscores the grammar of trademark law. When developing trademarks, think *adjectives*. Properly used, trademarks qualify a type of good or service and, in sentences, should serve to modify a noun. Often, the noun is elliptical, but that does not mean it does not exist. While *Cheers*, the title of the television show, is a suggestive mark for a program about a bar, it is also a thriving trademark enterprise. The word and logo are associated with T-shirts, mugs, calendars—you name it. Any kind of product can bear the trademark, but the proper placement of the mark is always as that little old adjective.

The Strength of a Mark

After the trademark continuum, another continuum should be mentioned, the "protection continuum." This concerns the strength of a mark. Fundamentally, there are strong marks and weak marks (Figure 10-2). The stronger the mark, the more legal protection it is entitled to receive.

Marks gain strength in two ways: First, they are conceived with strength, because they are fanciful, arbitrary, or suggestive terms. The more a mark is removed from generic and descriptive terminology, the stronger it is. Second, a mark can be invested with strength by advertising and promotion. Even a weak,

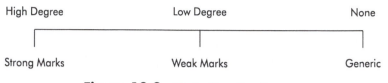

Figure 10-2   Protection Continuum

descriptive mark can become so well known to the public and the identifier of a unique source that it is entitled to a high degree of trademark protection.

Cable News Network describes what it names quite simply. However, because it was the first cable news network, over 12,000 systems serving nearly 70 million subscribers carry it, and its prominent news-gathering success has made it a household name, Cable News Network and its acronym CNN are strong trademarks. Had several cable networks specializing in news been launched at the same time and had each tried to use the phrase that connects them most simply to the viewers, then Cable News Network might not be a strong trademark for anyone. The competitive use of phrases like The Game Channel, Game Network, and Game TV for new startup channels evidences the dilemma CNN would have had with direct competition in its early years.

Unique Identifiers in Specific Lines of Commerce

The most important feature of a trademark is that it stands for a unique source. Provided it does, the mark is protectable as a monopoly for its owner; if it does not, then it may not be a useful trademark at all. However, while trademark law grants a monopoly, allowing its owner to remove the mark from the commercial vernacular of competitors, it does so only with respect to the particular classes of goods and services actually associated with the mark. Because there are a finite number of words or phrases and consumers have certain expectations about the relationship between marks and services or goods, not all uses are restricted. Therefore, even though a new television series could not consider calling itself *ER*, no hospital in the country is prevented from using the label *ER* on account of the television series. Similarly, if a pharmaceutical firm produces an ER line of medicines, it will not be stopped from employing the phrase; there is little likelihood of public confusion about medicines and a television production.

Sometimes, even popular trademark owners carry their case too far. During the early years of the Reagan administration, a proposal to launch a network of "killer satellites" that could target and destroy enemy forces was proposed. The plan was dubbed Star Wars because of its futuristic, out-of-this-world theme. As press reports trumpeted the project, the owners of the popular *Star Wars* film trilogy took offense. A trademark dispute arose, in which the film company tried to shoot down the government's use of the phrase. The attack failed, a victim of the old "different class of services" defense.

A similar issue surfaced for the food maker Hormel, known throughout the world as the creators of Spam. Spam is a venerable trademark, and in the middle of the Internet craze Hormel discovered its carefully nurtured trademark became synonymous with one of the evils of e-mailing. *Spamming* is Internet-speak for sending unsolicited e-mail to millions of addresses. After much reflection and debate, Hormel developed a policy, now posted on its web page at www.hormel.com, in which the company accepts the unflattering nomenclature as a sign of the times, but urges all other uses of the trademark be true to its proper origins.

The misfiring of trademark phraseology can harm even presidential aspirations. During the 1996 presidential race, trying to echo former first lady Nancy Reagan's antidrug theme, "Just Say No," Republican candidate Bob Dole exclaimed, "Just Don't Do It." Unfortunately for Candidate Dole, a shoe company called Nike, known for the theme "Just Do It," emerged to complain.

In sum, *trademark law protects words or phrases, images, and trade dress, even designs and colors, in specific lines of commerce.* When one moves into an unrelated field or endeavor, trademark legal protection *may not* follow. Thus, the word *Eagle* may be used for potato chips by one company, a car by a different company, a hand stapler by a third, and a TV production business by a fourth. Each can use the same trademark without violating another's trademark rights because consumers can readily distinguish the different sources of the marks. The strength of a mark is vital to this determination and so is the nature of the mark on the trademark continuum. If the NBC network challenged Newark Banking Company (NBC), it would lose. Even though it owns one of the most famous trademarks in the nation, the public's familiarity with acronyms is such that the marketplace can accept both titles. By contrast, a strong and fanciful mark like Kodak is in a much better position to prevent other uses even in unrelated areas. If it existed, Kodak Bank or Kodak Television Company would find the venerable film company on its back ASAP.

Likelihood of Confusion

These principles lead to the crucial legal test in trademark law: *likelihood of confusion*. The landmark case that explains this principle is *Polaroid Corp.* v. *Polarad Electronics Corp.*, known as *Polaroid* for short. Since the law grants monopolies in trademarks and a limited number of words or phrases are available in the lexicon to describe goods and services, the *Polaroid* test looks at a variety of elements to determine if the two marks in question are likely to cause confusion as to source in the minds of a relevant consuming or purchasing public. If there is a likelihood of confusion, usually the first to have used the mark will prevail, and the second owner will either lose its rights to the mark or find its market severely restricted. If confusion is unlikely, the two marks can coexist.

The elements of likelihood of confusion, explained in the *Polaroid* decision, include

- *The nature and strength of the marks.* Are the marks fanciful, arbitrary, suggestive, descriptive, or generic?
- *The similarity of the marks.* How close are they in sight, sound, and meaning?
- *The nature of the goods or services.* Are they sold in the same channel of commerce?
- *The gap to be bridged.* Are the channels of commerce different, and, if so, how likely is it that the first user will bridge the gap?
- *The sophistication of the buyers.* Are they specialists, able to discern small differences in marks that can identify different sources?
- *The intent of the second comer.* Was the second user aware of the first, and is there any evidence of intentional copying?
- *The evidence of actual confusion.* Is there documented evidence that someone has been confused already?
- *The quality of the defendant's product.* Does it measure up to the original? Is there potential for negative publicity for the first?

Anytime the trademark of another is used, these issues must be considered. If a second comer cannot satisfactorily explain its use under each of these criteria, then its wisest course would be to choose another word or symbol. We take a closer look at this all-important issue in Chapter 13.

Secondary Meaning

Although a descriptive mark (such as *60 Minutes* for a 1-hour television show) is usually deemed weak and unprotected, if the mark becomes well known to the public as originating from a sole source, it can gain status as a protectable trademark. When a mark achieves this status, it is said to have gained *secondary meaning*. In such cases, the word or phrase's secondary meaning points to a unique source.

Secondary meaning is secured through the expenditure of two precious commodities: time and money. The longer a mark is used by a sole source and the greater the public's awareness of the mark as originating from the source, the more likely it is that secondary meaning will attach. Therefore, a television program about cooking by European master chefs called, ingeniously, *The Master Chefs*, can gain secondary meaning by virtue of being the only such program so titled, by achieving solid ratings, and by having significant public exposure, through advertising and other publicity. In fact, many television programs readily fit this category: *Touched by an Angel*, *The Tonight Show*, *Friends*, *Monday Night Football*.

The issue of who is entitled to secondary meaning can spark debate. When David Letterman switched from NBC to CBS, the transfer was embittered with public wrangling. Among his television signature items, Letterman wanted to continue using his "Top 10" on CBS. NBC resisted, claiming the logo was theirs. The legal dispute was a small subplot in the larger issue of his departure, but CBS ultimately relented and came up with a close, albeit slightly different title, "The Late Show's Top 10 List." Certainly "Top 10" is descriptive, but NBC claimed for television purposes it had achieved secondary meaning. No one else was doing it, and Dave had been using the phrase for the better part of a decade. The mark was identified with Letterman, because he created it during his employment by NBC, but the network used its status as his employer to claim ownership over his work. However, the addition of the phrase *Late Show*, which was CBS's alternative to *Late Night*, further separated the marks and gave Letterman's new network a viable trademark claim that the titles were distinguishable.

Ten years later, The "Top 10" dispute is something of a distant memory. However, a new battle may be brewing. One of the popular innovations of *The Tonight Show* is Jay Leno's reading and commenting on newspaper headlines and classified ads sent in by viewers. The routine has become so popular that David Letterman has taken to reading his own headliners. While no legal battle ensued, if *The Tonight Show* producers had taken the time and effort to invest the segment with strong trademarks, it might have formed the basis for a serious claim. As the matter now stands, it is symbolic of the common phrase, "imitation is the highest form of flattery."

Use in Commerce and Intent to Use

A necessary characteristic of a trademark is that it be *used*. If a trademark is not used in commerce, no rights attach. Talking about a mark to friends does not create any trademark rights; sitting at a computer and composing a business plan does not create trademark rights. By contrast, marketing a product or telecommunicating a program creates rights. Prior to 1988, the use need only have been token;

merely sending a mock-up of a magazine to a colleague in a different state was sufficient to support "use."

However, since 1988, the use must be more than token, although that does not mean it must be very extensive. The change in 1988 came when Congress added the concept of *intent to use* into law. The new law states that as soon as one has an idea for a title or mark, one can file a request with the U.S. Patent and Trademark Office (PTO) and effectively reserve the mark. Once the application is approved, the mark can be held in reserve for up to 3 years, provided there remains a bona fide intent to actually carry out the plans to use the mark in commerce. That can be a valuable asset against a competitor. This generous opportunity altered the trademark landscape. Now, the race is on to file for a trademark.

Geographic Coverage of Marks

An important limitation on use of trademarks is geography. Unless the user of a trademark has applied to the PTO for federal registration of the mark or intention to use a mark, then the owner of the trademark is entitled to protection only in the geographic area where the mark has actually been used. Typically, trademark protection for nonregistered marks runs on a state-by-state basis. Thus, the same trademark can be owned by someone in Oregon and another person in Massachusetts. In broadcasting, this occurs frequently; for example, when a local radio station develops a format theme (Mix, Cool Jazz, or Hot Hits) and another station in a distant market picks up the same image. Unless protected by federal registration, the phrase can seep into many markets. Even though a station may be able to stop a local competitor, a broadcaster or business legally related to that local competitor but in a remote region may still be free to use it.

Concurrent Use

One balancing act of trademark law is the decision to let more than one party use the same mark. *Concurrent use* recognizes the fact that two local firms separated by geography or operating in different businesses can coexist as trademark owners. Their uses do not offend consumer sensibilities or business realities. Hence, one Sharper Image store can sell gadgets and another can cut hair. The original Holiday Inn can carve out a geographic zone in Myrtle Beach, South Carolina, while the national franchise can operate everywhere else. Concurrent uses and even registrations on a split basis are essential to the fairness and balance of the trademark system.

These are the core principles of trademark law, but keep in mind that trademarks are regulated by a complex system of federal, state, and common laws. For example, a federal agency like the FCC assigns all sorts of identifiers, such as call signs and telephone numerators, which can have trademark significance. On top of this, there is a 50-state system of trade name registrations and, with the arrival of the Internet, a system of allocated domain names. We take a closer look at the trademark systems in the United States.

Chapter 11

The Trademark Systems: How to Protect Your Mark

There are three trademark legal systems in the United States: common law, state, and federal. The abiding basis for trademark protection in the United States is "use in commerce." If a word, phrase, or image has been used, then common law rights attach. *Common law* refers to the legal decisions of judges based on equity or simple fairness. A common law system based on use is our departure point.

Trademark rights are acquired whenever and wherever a mark is adopted and affixed to a good or service employed in commerce for sale or given away. Even if you are unsuccessful in selling the product, trademark rights exist in connection with that good or service; the fact that the offer is made is legally significant. Sometimes goods are not sold but rather given away. Companies promote services with all sorts of giveaways, such as T-shirts, mugs, and hats.

In the radio business, stations guided by PR consultants trumpet new slogans heralding changes in formats or new services: think of "WHRX—Miami's Hot Rock," "KSSS—Seattle's Starlight Station," "WIOF—Wilmington's Island of Fantasies." Not only the call letters, but also the slogans, are trademarks for the operations. Promotional products emblazoned with slogans are designed to identify the station and fix it as a source in the public's mind. Therefore, the words or symbols are trademarks, and common law protects them as well.

One does not have to "do" anything to acquire common law trademark protection other than *use the mark*. Once the mark appears in commerce in connection with the good or service, common law rights attach. In simplest terms, common law rights mean that a degree of exclusivity is secured in the mark. This ensures that neither a local competitor nor a national enterprise can later displace a prior trademark owner merely because it is a bigger or richer company and wants the same mark. The common law rights can be used offensively or defensively in the trademark owner's market.

Still, since common law rights are local and many enterprises want a broader protection for the mark, common law status is often inadequate. For example, when a radio station or magazine enters the national advertising or programming markets and seeks to be uniquely identified, local common law protection will not cut it; regional or national protection is a must because the enterprise is reaching audiences in many states. Therefore, many entities concerned with the names and slogans that identify them, and especially those that spend a significant part of a business budget promoting a mark, need to turn to the state and federal systems of protection.

State Registration: A Quick and Inexpensive Start

All states operate a trademark registration system for those firms that do business in their state. As a practical matter, state registration offers only a few advantages over common law protection. Since common law is usually defined on a state-by-state basis, a media outlet is protected in areas where it operates as soon as it uses a mark. A radio station in Atlanta has rights throughout the state of Georgia, whether or not it is registered with the Secretary of State. So, you might ask, what are the advantages of state registration? First, there is *notice*. The state trademarks are published in a registry, which constitutes effective notice to those doing business in the state. Second, in some localities state registrants are granted certain procedural advantages in the case of disputes, such as a legal presumption that the mark is valid, which is of course a good thing. Third, experience shows that judges who rarely deal with trademark disputes are impressed with a state registration. It turns out the formal paper the registration is printed on can make a difference.

State registrations are inexpensive and quick to obtain. Filing fees vary from $20 to $50 and are often processed in 2–4 weeks. That speed, however, underscores the weakness of the state system: The state registries look to determine only whether an identical mark is already registered and whether the request meets the barest definition of a trademark. No assessment is made as to the appropriateness to register under any standards that affect the legal validity of a mark. As a result, the state registrations are given limited credence by knowledgeable courts.

Federal Registration: If You Really Care About Your Trademark

In contrast to state registration, federal trademark protection is what most trademark proprietors need. Once a trademark is registered with the federal government, protection is nationwide. You can go from coast to coast, preventing interlopers from stealing your theme. Whether you care about uses a thousand miles away is another point; if you are a federal registrant, you have the right to stop such uses. Since a core requirement for federal registration is that a mark be used in interstate commerce and *communication* is legally defined as interstate commerce, all media enterprises can assess their marks and consider them ripe for federal protection. The same is true for firms in one state with customers in another. Webcasters whose subscribers or product purchasers reside across state lines can satisfy the interstate commerce requirement.

The federal registration system is staffed by trademark lawyers (examiners) trained in the legal standards. Processing a federal application can take 1 year or more to complete. With that laborious process, however, comes a host of rights that make federal registration the only system to consider for important trademarks. A federally registered trademark is entitled to

- *National protection.* As noted, you can defend your rights anywhere in the country and stop infringers in distant markets, even if you do no business in those markets.
- *Prima facie protectable status.* This means that a plaintiff in a trademark dispute can point to the registration as legal proof that the mark is valid and entitled to protection. While courts occasionally reject that conclusion, registration is powerful proof in most lawsuits.
- *National notice.* The federal records provide constructive notice to the world of the registrant's rights.
- *Use of the official registration notice,* ®. Only a federally registered mark can be associated with the notification, which places legal burdens on anyone misusing marks with such notice.
- *Special penalties.* In special cases of infringement, penalties, including triple damages and attorney's fees, are awarded.
- *International status.* Under international trademark treaties, federal applicants are granted special filing status in many foreign countries.
- *Special protection for domain names on the Internet.* Under the system of registering domain names, only federal registrants can be readily assured that third parties do not steal marks.

Steps in the Federal Registration Process

With all these advantages, you might want to know the steps in securing a federal registration. First, conduct a search. Whenever a company identifies a new trademark that it intends to exploit, it is simply foolish not to research its availability.

Because developing a trademark means investing time and resources into creating a public connection between the mark and the company and a mark once established is a headache or worse to change, failure to attend to this practical step leaves one vulnerable to forces unknown. Just ask NBC.

The dispute seems to want biblical terms for its description—a David and Goliath trademark affair. And Goliath should have known better. In the mid-1970s, NBC tried to lift its image. The once mighty network had fallen on some rocky times and slipped behind CBS and upstart ABC. NBC hired a Madison Avenue PR firm, which designed a new logo and market-tested it. It concluded NBC should shelve the long-used peacock and N-B-C chimes in favor of a sleek, cool block letter *N*. The network announced the shift in closed-door meetings with staff and affiliates and rolled it out with much fanfare on a bright and hopeful New Year's Day amid football hoopla and huge audiences.

Unbeknownst to NBC, one viewer of that New Year's Day initiation was a station executive at a public television station in Nebraska. The new NBC logo sure looked familiar; indeed, it was identical to the University of Nebraska's Educational Television Network logo, developed by an art designer for about $30 and in use for over 6 months. When NBC was warned about the similarity of the marks, the network rebuffed the Nebraska station brusquely. Soon after, a trademark infringement suit was filed, during which it was learned that NBC never had conducted a search. Despite a multimillion dollar budget, not one penny went into checking the availability of the block *N* for broadcasting. Based on its priority of use, Nebraska had the upper hand. NBC soon recognized its legal vulnerability and settled the case, sending a fully loaded mobile van with a fortune in equipment to the university. Oh, and NBC paid Nebraska's legal fees—all because someone forgot to conduct a search.

In a more recent variant of the David and Goliath tale, a big company with a big name, Bliss World, failed to do a common law search before it rolled out its line of Bliss cosmetics. Bliss Salon Day Spa, located in a Chicago suburb, tried to stop Bliss World from using the name Bliss for cosmetics within a 100-mile radius of Chicago. The only way Bliss World could prevail was to argue that the word Bliss was too weak to justify relief for the first user. The net result was a trademark with a permanent blemish, a word so weak that it can be imitated, even within the world of beauty care. Certainly not a blissful result, one that might have been avoided if a proper search had been done and its results skillfully exploited.

Trademark searching is like digging a hole looking for something that may not exist—a confusingly similar mark in an overlapping area of commerce. How deep should one dig? The simplest answer is as far down as possible, based on the firm's finances and comfort level, as well as the importance of the mark to that business. For most uses, a search of federal and state trademark registries and pertinent databases of articles from newspapers and magazines, corporate name listings, domain name registries, and phone directories should suffice. Trademark specialists and research firms can do the trick for under $1,000. However, if the mark selected is commonly used and the costs to launch it are substantial, then more extensive digging is appropriate. When Exxon Company was looking for the right word to replace its collection of Esso, Humble, Standard Oil, and others, it spent tens of thousands of dollars searching and clearing title. That research was reported to be so extensive it turned up a garage owned by the Exon family of Nebraska, and Exxon bought the name rights. That was a good thing, because one of those family members became a U.S. senator from Nebraska.

The second step in securing a mark is to file for federal registration. While state registration will do for strictly local uses, only federal registration should be considered for marks of importance. Filing with the Trademark Office (part of the PTO within the Department of Commerce, www.uspto.gov) involves preparing a two-page application, paying the filing fee ($325 per mark per class in early 2002, but better check for any fee hikes), and attaching some examples of material showing the mark in use ("specimens" in PTO parlance).

If the mark is not in commerce yet, the 1988 Trademark Revision Act allows filing an application for an "intent to use" (ITU) mark. This filing permits the reservation of a trademark that the applicant has a good-faith intent to exploit. One has up to 3 years after the initial grant to actually start using the mark. The rules require notice to the PTO every 6 months after the mark is "allowed," showing that plans are still progressing, to maintain the ITU.

The importance of these federal filings cannot be understated. Once a first user registers a mark, that firm acquires national protection and has a virtual monopoly on the right to use the mark for its products or services. The monopoly can be enforced in any federal court in the nation. Also, the federal process allows a registrant to apply for protection in other countries under the rules of certain treaties. One scam to be aware of, however, is that some savvy foreigners register popular U.S. trademarks in their own territory and then lie in wait for U.S. companies to export goods or services into that land. When they do, the foreigners inform the U.S. company that, to use their own mark, they have to pay a license fee. The threat can be avoided by a trademark owner if it has the foresight to register the trademark in other countries as well as the United States. In particular, media moguls, who make much of their income from overseas licensing, should be especially attentive lest their names and reputations be pilfered by unscrupulous competitors abroad.

The third step is to be attentive to the federal trademark family tree (Figure 11-1). Registration is neither automatic nor immediate. The PTO assigns all applications to an examiner, who scrutinizes the application for proper form and compliance with legal standards. Here, the most crucial test is whether the mark could

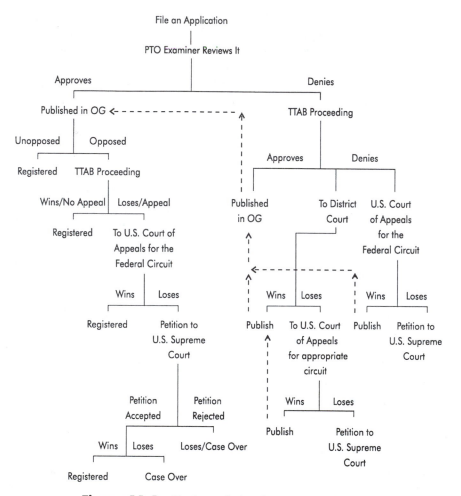

Figure 11-1 Trademark Application Family Tree

be confused with another registered mark. Although the same mark can be used for unrelated goods or services (e.g., KOOL is both a radio station's call letters and a brand of cigarettes), if the services or goods are related and the marks closely resemble each other (e.g., KOOL for a radio station and Kool Jazz for a radio program), then the PTO might reject the application.

Before denying an application for registration, the PTO issues an *action letter*, to which a response is required within 6 months. The sooner an action letter is responded to, the faster the application is processed. Sometimes, responses can be provided in a short phone call. After final action, an application is either approved (and published in the PTO's weekly publication, the *Official Gazette*) or denied. If published, there is a 30-day period in which parties who believe they will be harmed by registration can file an opposition to the registration. (The 30-day opposition period can be extended for up to 90 more days on request.)

Opposition forces a legal proceeding before the PTO's Trademark Trial and Appeal Board (TTAB). The TTAB conducts a hearing, during which the parties engage in discovery, much like in formal court cases. Discovery includes the process of asking for written answers to questions (interrogatories) and taking oral testimony from witnesses under oath (depositions). The TTAB has a second stage or testimony period, during which each side files the key information it intends to rely on for its arguments. Briefs are filed and the TTAB rules on the opposition.

If registration is denied by the examiner, the applicant can give up the quest or file an appeal with the TTAB. If the applicant appeals, the TTAB either sides with the examiner and denies the application or permits it to be published for opposition.

In any instance in which a litigant is unhappy with the TTAB's final decision, a further appeal process is available. In cases of opposition, the losing party can head to the U.S. Court of Appeals for the Federal Circuit. In application cases, the rejected applicant can appeal to the Federal Circuit Court or file an action in federal district court, which basically starts the process all over again.

The last resort, after the Federal Circuit Court, is the U.S. Supreme Court. It is very, very (you get the point) unlikely that any appeal to the U.S. Supreme Court would be heard, much less emerge victorious. Trademark rulings by the highest court come once every few years.

Even if the applicant is successful in obtaining a registration, a potential hitch remains. The trademark law allows a challenge to a registration within the first 5 years after registration. In particular, a prior user can ask the PTO to cancel the registered mark. A cancellation proceeding is rather like an opposition and handled similarly by the TTAB. After the fifth year of registration passes, a registered mark becomes "incontestable." While this does not mean there is no basis whatsoever to challenge a mark—if a mark was obtained fraudulently or if it becomes generic, it can always be questioned—it is very hard to overcome an incontestable mark.

The fact that one's priority to national registration can be extinguished by a second comer underscores the importance of vigilance in caring for trademarks. Not only can one lose important benefits by discontinuing use in commerce, if one fails to keep on top of what the Trademark Office approves for registration, superior rights can be materially diminished.

Another important thing to understand about the federal trademark registration process is that there are two registries. The *Principal Register* is the place where all protectable marks end up. There is also a backup registry, called the

Supplemental Register. Trademarks that examiners believe are descriptive but not generic can be enrolled in the latter. While the Supplemental Register has a "second-class citizen" feel about it—descriptive marks cannot succeed in many claims of infringement or confusion—there are two good reasons to consider it as an alternative to simply abandoning the quest for registration. If a mark is registered there for 5 years, its owner can petition to move it to the Principal Register and claim full trademark rights. It is a way of establishing secondary meaning by longevity. A Supplemental Register mark will also be used by an examiner as a basis to reject someone else's application. Together these are sufficient reasons to view the Supplemental Register kindly if it is just not possible to secure registration on the Principal Register.

If you make it this far, don't forget to *maintain* and *renew* the registration. Trademarks are registered for terms of 10 years; however, during the first term of registration, the owner of a trademark is required to file an affidavit of continued use in the fifth year after registration to maintain it. Once the affidavit attesting to the fact that the mark is still in business for the applicant is filed, the mark is deemed incontestable and kept on the registry for the full term.

After 10 years, all trademarks must be renewed by filing a renewal application. The 10-year rule took effect in 1988; previously, registrations were granted for 20 years. As legal reform, the Congress sought to clean up "deadwood," marks that stayed registered long after the owner discontinued use.

Two other parts to this system deserve mention, particularly for all creative professionals. First, for all radio and television stations, the FCC is the "call letters" gatekeeper. Whenever a new station is licensed or an existing station wants to change its formal name, the FCC must approve the choice of call letters. From the 1930s until the mid-1980s, the FCC acted like a mini-PTO and heard complaints by competitors who believed an assignment of call letters was too similar to another assignment in the market. In this way, radio station KLUB could challenge the assignment of KLUG to a station in its market. As competition over call letters became more intense, the FCC abandoned its mediator role and adopted a rule that encouraged stations with a dispute to work the matter out privately or to go to court. As long as the letters are available, they can be assigned. But such a trademark, like any other, can be challenged by a party claiming likelihood of confusion.

A related change implemented in the 1980s coincided with the FCC's breakdown of certain of the ownership limitations. The agency's rules were relaxed enough to allow unrelated radio and television stations to share common letters. While previously radio station WRAD-FM and television station WRAD-TV had to be owned by the same company, the FCC decided to let the parties work the call letter assignment out among themselves. If the two independent owners did not object, the FCC's rules would not prohibit the overlapping call letter assignment. However, if WRAD-FM objected, trademark principles could be called on to prevent the assignment of WRAD-TV to an unrelated owner.

Second is the matter of domain names, the words or phrases that precede *.com*, *.org*, and the like, in Internet addresses. In Chapter 15, we have a lot to say about trademarks and the Internet. For the present time, note that issues of trademark use and misuse are cropping up in cyberspace. Federally registered trademarks are granted special protection when it comes to the assignment of domain names, the key element in an Internet address. An amendment to the trademark law, adopted in 1999, was designed to squelch cybersquatters before their dot-coms become too common.

Foreign Systems also Come into Play

Just as "no man is an island," so, too, no trademark system exists in isolation. The U.S. trademark law, like its copyright cousin, is part of a larger world scene. As every state has its own system of regulating trademarks, every country in the world does as well. In a few instances, most notably in Europe, a number of countries banded together to permit the filing of a single application with coverage in European Community nations. More frequently, an application must be filed in each country where a trademark is in use or use is anticipated. Sometimes, even if a mark is not used, an application is appropriate because unrelated petitioners may apply for and acquire rights to another's U.S. trademark without approval.

Another important international consideration to ponder is language. Under the U.S. and most foreign systems, words can be subjected to a variety of tests to determine whether they create impermissible confusion as well as whether they may be registered. Translations of words can be a crucial part of this analysis. Therefore, one does not avoid confusion as to source by utilizing a phrase in a foreign language. The Big Blue for IBM is protected against similar phrases, including Le Grand Bleu. Now that domain names may be applied for in more than 70 languages, multilingual determinations will be more and more common. One of the first tests involved the successful protest by the Japanese owner of Sankyo.com against a requested domain name assignment in Chinese characters that translates to sankyo.com.

As conventions and institutions are an important part of the copyright legal structure, treaties and world organizations are vital to an effective functioning international trademark system. In trademark law, treaties helped establish a common system of classifying marks. In the early 1970s, the United States abandoned its convoluted system of classes of trademarks, which numbered over 100, in favor of the streamlined international classification system. The remnants of the U.S. system may still appear on some older trademarks, which are registered in class 101, for example. But thanks to the Paris Convention for the Protection of

Industrial Property (more on this later), trademarks have common elements in most countries in the world.

As it helps to administer copyright, the World International Property Organization (WIPO) plays a crucial role in trademark law as well. Most recently, WIPO established a mediation and arbitration center to address international domain name disputes. Resolving to place such matters in the hands of an international organization was a major step forward in the orderly transition of the Internet from rogue to reliable media.

Well, you have the overview of the various trademark systems. Now, we move on to the acquisition of trademarks.

Chapter 12

Strategy for Acquiring Trademark Rights: A "How-to" for Branding

Trademark law has the goal of protecting two interests: those of the investor, who spends resources to create words or symbols identifying the business as a source, and those of the consumer, who relies on a mark as a symbol of quality and an association with a known source. Unlike copyright law, which secures protection only against copying, trademark law grants a monopoly to use a word or symbol in commerce. In other words, trademark law provides that, even if a second user is *unaware* of the original use, it may be forced to stop an infringing use.

As already noted, the nature of the rights secured by a trademark depend on a number of factors. Sometimes, the trademark proprietor has a master plan, an elaborate strategy for identifying and securing trademark rights. For example, when Exxon consolidated all its public images (Esso, Humble, Standard Oil, etc.) into a single brand, it followed a branding approach marked by a grand scheme to acquire rights and alert the public in a conspicuous and organized campaign. It carried out its stratagem methodically and diligently. But then, there are times when a product, like a toy or a film, becomes a phenomenon beyond anything one could have imagined. Cabbage Patch dolls and Mutant Ninja Turtles became sensations far greater than their creators could have anticipated. Pet Rocks were a Christmas sensation a number of years ago. Each success translated into markets for products and services not anticipated at inception. Because the Cabbage Patch dolls and Ninja Turtles scenario is common, it is useful to do a periodic inventory of the key words and symbols a business actually uses to determine which symbols, if any, are really important assets. The most important ones should be protected by federal registration; those of lesser importance could be protected by state registration.

Deciding Which Marks to Register

To determine which marks to register with the PTO, consider the five "hows":

1. How distinctive is the mark?
2. How much has the owner invested in the mark?
3. How well is the mark known to consumers?
4. How diverse are the goods or services offered by the owner under the brand?
5. How likely is it that another's trademark use will confuse the public as to source?

As you answer these questions, it will become clear which marks are important to your operations. With that essential determination in hand, a strategy for ensuring protection for the mark will then develop.

How Distinctive Is the Mark?

Some images and phrases endure for decades, others disappear overnight. The CBS eye is of immense value to the network. It is a suggestive mark made strong by unique usage that indelibly stamps the program's source. When CBS finally chose to enter the cable market, it developed an "Eye on People" logo and look. By contrast, many radio stations have developed descriptive, weak trademark themes for their formats, such as "Beautiful 98" for an easy listening station on FM 98.3. On the trademark continuum, this title is doubly descriptive. *Beautiful* describes its music, and *98* is its geographic address on the dial. Given the radio allocation assignment rules, the Beautiful 98 format may be repeated in many broadcast markets. Therefore, radio station owners should be cautious when they invest primary identity in phrases of limited trademark distinctiveness.

Another interesting story involved the Fox television logo. When the owners of 20th Century Fox made their foray into broadcasting by acquiring the Metromedia television stations in the top broadcast markets, one moniker under consideration for the network was Fox Broadcasting Company, FBC for short. This acronym was designed to make the upstart appear like its established competitors, National Broadcasting Company (NBC) and American Broadcasting Company (ABC). However, FBC was already an acronym for a New York advertising company with ties to broadcasting. When the owners of FBC made a fuss, they forced the new network to be creative. This helped the Fox organization realize it had an even more useful and distinctive trademark already groomed for television. Hence, Fox Television was born.

How Much Money Is Invested in the Mark?

Look at expenditures over time. Promotional advertising is often a hefty chunk of any operation's budget. The more money invested in repeating thematic images to the public, the more important those images are. Trademarks are at the core of the imagery. With newspaper and magazine ads, flyers handed out on street corners, online and highway billboards, radio and television ads running many times an hour, the investment in a phrase can be substantial. This underscores a truism of trademark law: *Every business has a name and an identity.* Make sure that the ways you are known to the public justify the expenditures you have to make to compete. The more distinctive is a mark, from a trademark law perspective, the better. Be inventive and clever. Remember the trademark continuum: The more fanciful or arbitrary the mark, the stronger is the protection.

Take the Beautiful 98 example. It is a simple and informative phrase, but hardly one that can be hailed as inventive or fanciful. It may more than serve the purpose of helping the listener in a search for a specific sound while driving in steady traffic; however, it will win no uniqueness awards and will not prevent competitors in neighboring towns from adopting the same phrase. In sum, the amount invested in this phrase should be commensurate with its lack of trademark strength.

By contrast, when a firm wants the public to know it has a new name, it can go all out. Launching products on Super Bowl Sunday, with the largest viewing audiences of the year glued to their sets, affords the well-healed the opportunity to bring trademarks instant recognition. Monster.com had such a campaign during a recent football classic. Telephone companies in the business of merging and adopting new logos are also known for investing hugely in corporate images. Verizon, born from the merger of Bell Atlantic and NYNEX, remains one of the biggest national advertisers. So too does BellSouth's switch to Cingular. In the end, when the amount invested is big, the trademark payoff can be equally large.

How Much Consumer Awareness?

Heavily promoted marks are known to consumers. Also, events can make marks more popular. It is often surprising that, while a trademark owner may decide to drop a mark from its advertising, the consumer may nevertheless maintain a favorable association for many more years. The power of consumer awareness was brought home when Duracell announced plans to pull its slogan CopperTop Battery off the retired shelf after learning that the phrase still resonates favorably with consumers. If a campaign works, it is not surprising that, years after it has concluded, many consumers still fondly remember it. Checking through the trademark attic can result in discovery of some valuable assets.

How Diverse Are the Products?

Brand extension is often a fundamental strategy. We start with the understanding that some trademarks are the signature for a company; for example, Disney's rendition of Mickey Mouse's ears are world renowned. If one sees this symbol on any product or service, the connection is instantaneous. Disney owns that image in the marketplace as one of the trademarks signifying its company. Not only can it stop others from confusing the public to the detriment of the company, it can also leverage the mark to extend into new markets and diversify. When Disney launched a cable channel or when it opened a chain of stores, the logo for the company was used front and center. In short, Disney is able to attach the mark to a wide variety of goods, capitalizing on its brand's popularity, and diversify the products associated with Disney to make more money.

How Likely Is It That Another's Mark Will Create Confusion?

As we often repeat, the key issue in trademark law is the likelihood of confusion as to source. When a strong trademark is used in connection with certain goods or services, it can be said to have a "penumbra effect," a halo around it that translates into an association with other goods or services. Even if a trademark owner does not sell certain goods or offer certain services, the public may be led to believe it does. Kodak does not own movie theaters, but if a theater chain opened with that name, the film manufacturer might object. How likely is it that consumers will be confused, even without direct competition? That is always a pertinent issue.

Answering the five "hows" leads to a crucial practice of trademark law for the 21st century, *branding*. When a mark is important, claim it and let the world know it stands for you as the source. Even if the public does not *really know* who H-P, Handspring, or Intuit is, the constant and aggressive use of branding establishes trademark imagery in the public's mind.

Key Hints for Branding

Here are the key hints for branding:

- *Do that search at the very first opportunity.* If any significant financial investment is going to be put into a mark, start out with a search. The wisdom of clearing titles early is proven by the bitter disappointment of many who learn well after the fact that third-party use of the same mark is an insurmountable barrier to plans. In some cases, if the early search discloses a prior use, the first user may be willing to sell its rights, and to do so for a lot less than after a trademark is launched. If you doubt this, just compare Exxon's handling of the Exon name with the NBC–Nebraska N logo dispute.

- *If the mark is clear and you think it will be useful, register it.* Once cleared, if the mark is important, register it with the PTO. If the plans do not call for initiation of the goods or services for a period of time (more than a few months), file an ITU application. The filing establishes rights fixed by law, and the modest fees associated with the effort repay themselves over and over again during the ensuing years.

- *Brand all uses of the mark.* Until a mark is registered, one should not use the federal registration notice ®, but by all means use ™ or ℠ anytime you can. These lay symbols for trademarks and service marks put the public on notice and bring instant recognition that a trademark is afoot.

- *Go for the domain.* We live in the Internet era, and a prudent trademark owner should never forget that. Reserve the domain names needed to extend your communications to the Web.

- *Plan domestically, but think internationally.* Business occurs across national borders as readily as across states. With scores of U.S. companies earning over $1 billion in foreign sales and thousands more receiving significant percentages of their revenues from international customers, no one should miss the opportunity to take one's product or services abroad if feasible. This means being alert to the various international implications of all trademark uses, from trademark registries in other nations, to translations of words that mean the same or confusingly similar things in English.

- *Be alert to third-party mischief.* Keep a watchful eye in your immediate marketplace and elsewhere for third-party uses that create confusion. Remember, even though copying is a sign of flattery, each unauthorized use that continues unimpeded in the marketplace dilutes the distinctiveness of a mark and can lead to loss of rights.

- *Take action when necessary.* Failure to stop known third-party infringements can result in the loss of rights vis-à-vis that entity and may, over time, seriously diminish all trademark rights. The law gives a monopoly to aid in the orderly working of the marketplace for the consumer and the business. If the business fails to protect its interest, the consumer may come to rely less on the marks as a sign of unique source identification. At that point, any trademark rights that might have been claimed could be lost forever.

Chapter 13

Likelihood of Confusion: The Acid Test

Protection of trademarks has a very concrete meaning. Under federal law, common law, and state statutes, a trademark owner can prohibit the use of the same or a confusingly similar mark. Injunctive relief can be secured to order the cessation of use and the destruction of offending merchandise. The trademark owner is also allowed to trace profits of the infringer and obtain lost revenues. Sometimes, the monetary elements are hard to determine; however, if a sale has been made by the infringer or the trademark owner's ongoing business has suffered a decline in funds, then the connection is arguably there. It would be up to the infringer to justify that the relationship to its gain and the owner's loss does not exist. The more egregious the trademark theft, the less likely the court will be willing to hear the rationale.

As copyright law sanctions certain uses as "fair use," trademark law also has a corollary, even though the statutory language does not expressly set it forth. Take *Twister*, for example. While Universal Pictures may register the word as a trademark for its popular film and spin-off video game, action figures, and theme park, the storyline of weather chasers is not exclusively anyone's. Would a film called *Tornado* or a theme park ride the Hurricane infringe the trademark rights of Universal? Could a television station launch a series of news inserts called "Twister," along with the station's own images and thematic music?

The answers lie in trademark analysis; the questions to which we always return bear on the likelihood of confusion: Is there likely to be confusion as to source? Would a consumer be confused into thinking the origin of the program or the theme ride is the same as the familiar title? Proving confusion is fundamental to establishing trademark rights.

Key Issues in Likelihood of Confusion Analysis

Whenever a trademark analysis arises, these are the questions to ask.

Are the Words or Symbols Used Identical?

If they are, the most crucial part of the case is established. However, even identical words do not make a trademark infringement claim a certain winner. For example, *Twister* the movie and Twister the toilet bowl cleaner share the word; nevertheless, since the word has dictionary meaning, it starts out as "weak." For the toilet bowl cleaner, the notion of "twister" has suggestive qualities. How strong is the association of the words to the products? How much advertising or publicity has been put into developing associations between the word and source? Remember, judgment calls are going on in assessing the likelihood of confusion.

A few years ago, courts did flip-flops on the question of whether the phrase *Here's Johnny* was well enough identified with *The Tonight Show* host Johnny Carson that it could be infringed by a toilet bowl cleaner called Here's Johnny. Carson lost in district court but won on appeal, establishing the important principle—don't mess with Johnny.

If Not Identical, How Close Are the Words in Sound and Meaning?

If the words are not identical, then the analysis becomes more subtle. For example, assume the movie *Twister* spawns its own enterprises, including a syndicated television series and merchandise such as lunch boxes, notepads, T-shirts, and soft drinks. All of these uses, on products and services, can be registered as trademarks for the movie studio. Now, also assume that some competitors want to tap into *Twister* mania and start a similar enterprise, Tornado, Inc., with similar business lines. The two marks are distinguishable both aurally and visually. However, their meanings are virtually identical. If the competing project were dubbed Hurricane, it would be a few more steps removed. For trademark confusion purposes, the chances of the public being confused and thinking that the source of Twister and Tornado are the same would be reasonably high, but less so for Hurricane because the word means something else and does not begin with the letter *T*.

How Similar Are the Goods or Services?

In the Twister–Tornado example, we are considering the same goods or services—TV shows or films and spin-off merchandise. In the case of "Here's Johnny," the products were very dissimilar—a TV personality and a toilet bowl scrub brush. The closer the products or services are in their lines of commerce, the more likely the public is to be confused about source. Even if the products are dissimilar, if there is a reasonable consumer expectation that the different product line might have originated from the complaining party, then the first user will generally prevail. Whether a Sprint long distance phone company sells branded telephones or not, consumers could believe it does. But could a consumer believe the same thing if he or she saw a Sprint brand of running shoes? Probably not.

Are the Marks Strong or Weak?

If the mark in question is fanciful or arbitrary and rates high on the strength meter, then there is a greater likelihood that, even with dissimilar products, confusion will be found. Strength can be a vital factor in reaching a favorable conclusion for a first user. Remember that red light we flashed when thinking about using Kodak on a chain of movie theaters. A red light would not go off if one wanted to manufacture pairs of gloves under the logo Palm. Despite the popularity of the handheld organizer that fits in the palm of one's hand, the word *palm* has suggestive qualities. Those same qualities apply to gloves. The word is not arbitrary or fanciful with respect to either product.

What Is the Intent of the Second Comer?

In some instances of confusion, a problem materializes accidentally. The parties do not know each other and the crossing of paths in commerce is unplanned. Certainly, NBC did not deliberately try to rough up the University of Nebraska when it adopted the block N logo. However, in the case of "Here's Johnny," the fame of Carson was not in doubt, and the toilet bowl company wanted to be cute and play off of the familiar phrase. While parody is respected in copyright, there is less leeway in trademark law for one to parody another's mark. Because controlling market image is crucial to effective use of trademarks, the law is less tolerant when commercial use is made of a famous phrase or mark, even if the intent is parody. Trademark cases also reflect a concern about tarnishment—negative imagery about a mark and its product or service. Knowledge of the original and a plan to copy can be a decisive factor in a finding of trademark infringement.

Is There Any History of Confusion?

Actual confusion is easy to measure. Have there been any misdirected phone calls or letters? Did someone pay a bill from Company A by sending it to Company B? In a radio slogan dispute, a small town station showed evidence that local merchants had complained that the station was going to raise advertising rates to support a big media blitz. It turns out the expensive promotional campaign was for a larger market station whose service area overlapped the small town station's zone. The smaller station was on the periphery of the large station's market, and proof of actual confusion was persuasive on the issue of likelihood of confusion.

Despite this result, a basic tenet of trademark law is that actual confusion is only evidence of likelihood of confusion, not conclusive proof that confusion exists. Why? Because even though some folks may be confused, that does not mean that marks are likely to confuse *reasonable* consumers. This is a variation on the old saying about fooling some of the people some of the time.

Are the Consumers Sophisticated?

Defining the market for the goods or services and knowing the level of sophistication of the customer are important facts in trademark disputes. In many trademark disputes, the consumers are professionals who, it can be argued, should readily distinguish between the sources of the services or products. For example, most television station engineers who buy a station's technical equipment know that Jerrold is a respected brand name for electronic devices. Would an equipment manufacturer that named its new products Jerry create confusion among seasoned engineers? Probably not; however, if the products made their way into the mass marketplace and ordinary consumers were purchasing them, the conclusion would be different.

What About the Quality of the Goods or Services?

If the quality of the second product is clearly inferior, that fact can raise additional sympathy for the first trademark owner. Even sophisticated consumers might be disinclined to the first brand if they believe two products are related by source and one is clearly inferior. In all likelihood, they will have concluded that the respected name failed to maintain acceptable standards.

Interestingly, even if the second comer's products are superior, trademark law still holds that the second user is an infringer. The original owner is entitled to define its goods and services the way it chooses and not have the product image made by another. If Motel 6 wants to be known for low cost lodging, being associated with a high-priced venue could spoil its reputation.

Is There Any Survey Evidence?

More and more, courts want to see some survey research when it comes to proving the likelihood of confusion, especially if the case does not involve identical marks in similar product or service lines. Polling a responsible sample in support of a claim of confusion is good form in trademark disputes.

Survey research, which must be disclosed to an opposing party in litigation, should be handled very carefully by professionals. The wrong results can doom a case quickly, so it is important for the research to be done with a view toward results. A good rule is to plan a survey in stages. For example, a professional firm may start with a small telephone sample or mall intercept of 25–50 consumers to help refine the research and confirm the broad outlines of a claim of confusion. If these preliminary results suggest that confusion is likely, then a larger sample (in the 200 range) should be conducted. If the small survey produces surprising results, then a different tactic or an alternative form of inquiry may be needed. If a larger sample were undertaken with no preliminary results, the findings could be revealed during the course of discovery and the negative results utilized by an opposing party to the detriment of the one taking the survey. This also underscores the importance of consulting with professional survey firms from the outset of cases for which surveys are critical. The firm's analysts should be prepared to serve as witnesses in the event of a trial. The demeanor and credibility of the dueling expert witnesses are often decisive in survey-laden trademark litigation.

But any trademark litigant should be forewarned that survey results can be surprising.

In one radio dispute over the dial address 99 (short for the dial position 98.9), the survey showed some listeners could correctly source the station, while others thought 99 was generic for any of five other radio operations. Making sense of this survey nonsense proved impossible even for a professional market analyst.

Chapter 14

Trademarks and Licensing: Follow the Money Trail

Reputation Counts

Trademark licensing is often spelled with dollar signs. That is because licensing is big business. Whether it is transferring logos to merchandise or granting franchise rights to third parties who make their business by using a popular mark, well-managed trademarks can generate substantial revenue. While the film trilogy *Star Wars* netted almost $3 billion in box office and home video sales, licensing and merchandising Star Wars characters and products grossed over $4.5 billion. For colleges and universities, licensing can be a vital source of supplemental revenue. With large student bodies and loyal alumni, state universities garner millions of dollars by simply putting school colors and mascots on T-shirts and coffee mugs and almost anything else that is not nailed down.

Collegiate licensing was not always that way. Until about 1980, state schools had no organized licensing programs because it was believed that state school logos were public property. Not until the University of Pittsburgh challenged and defeated Champion (famous for making college T-shirts) did collegiate licensing get under way in an organized manner.

For many schools, preexisting deals left them little opportunity to develop a licensing program. In 1981, one large Midwestern state university had an unusual contract with a major clothing manufacturer written before the Pitt case was concluded. The license agreement did not provide for rights in a straightforward way; rather, the agreement was styled "a covenant not to sue in perpetuity." That is a legal promise that the school could never sue to overturn the deal. What is more, the license provided for a flat fee of $1,000 a year, while the T-shirt company grossed hundreds of thousands of dollars annually. Knowing that state judges would not look kindly on such an onerous deal and betting that the one assigned the case could be a grad of the university's law school, the institution unilaterally canceled the deal and threatened to sue. The gambit paid off and translated into a fair license settlement. Today, that Midwestern university garners millions of dollars for scholarships and other programs through proceeds from its extensive licensing program.

Trademark licensing also offers savvy owners ways to expand a brand's reputation. Take, for example, the extension of cable channels such as Discovery and ESPN. Not only have these networks created clearly defined programming niches for loyal audiences, they have also been able to sell videocassettes and other merchandise branded with their logos. Whether they created the product, acquired someone else's works, or gave another manufacturer a license to use their logo, placing their trademarks on the tapes increases market presence and permits a higher price to be charged for the goods.

Similarly, when Discovery bought The Nature Stores in 1996, it did so with the realization that selling nature-oriented products was a "natural" fit and that the most practical way to achieve brand extension was to move into the retail market. For the Public Broadcasting System (PBS), licensing is viewed as a potential supplement that can cushion drastic cuts in federal funding.

Characters are important elements in media trademarks. Mickey Mouse is a Disney franchise, and ET is a symbol for its creator, Steven Spielberg, and Universal Studios. Today, nary a major movie is made without consideration of the vast potential for character licensing and extension of the mark into unrelated goods or services (but related revenue streams). As a result, virtually every children's film coming out of Hollywood has planned associations with fast-food chains as well as products such as dolls, action figures, lunch boxes, notepads, and, sometimes, amusement park thrill rides. In winter 2001, every conceivable form of merchandise bearing the name or image of Harry Potter simply flew off the shelves. The same phenomenon occurred with characters from *The Lord of the Rings*. The extension of the copyrighted work into products developed by a theme or character is essential to justifying the unimaginable costs of creating and marketing major motion pictures and other big-time media programs. Even as film editing of *Jurassic Park*, *The Lion King*, *Harry Potter*, and *The Lord of the Rings* was being completed, plans for exploiting catalogues of merchandise were well under way. An interesting footnote relates to *The Lord of the Rings*: There are actually two distinct lines of products in an unusual "divided licensing" plan. One company owns the rights to merchandise related to the film (and its future sequels), while another company owns the rights to products related to the underlying books.

Another intriguing development is the interest in items appearing in fictionalized stories. In the 2001 Harry Potter film, the young wizard coveted a Nimbus 2000 broom, a perfectly designed spin-off product. Sometimes, the market values of the product lines are appreciated by outsiders even before the program's creator. An example of the need for creative programmers to be watchful of their own inspirations involves the television series, *The Simpsons*, where characters drink Duff Beer. An enterprising Australian took the animated series' product and began selling Duff Beer locally. Fox Television, the program's producer, was forced to bring a trademark infringement action in Australia, seeking an injunction to prevent the misuse of the trademark. Fox won, but the expense of litigating to preserve rights for Homer Simpson's crowd might have been avoided altogether had the producers taken several appropriate steps when the show became a worldwide sensation.

Tips for Planning a Licensing Campaign

When planning trademark licensing, whether as a licensee or licensor, there are a number of key things to keep in mind (Figure 14-1).

Attend to Trademark Research and Federal Registration

If an item is going to be a part of a licensing campaign, it should be treated with respect. This means that, at the earliest possible time in the creating process, before the licensing program is formalized, the creators should conduct a search regarding the availability of the words, phrases, and symbols that they intend to exploit. If a word or phrase is identified for an object likely to have commercial value—such as *Nimbus* for the Harry Potter broom or *Duff* for beer—it should be cleared from a trademark perspective as part of the creative process for the film. Particularly, if one is creating a work of fiction, failure to attend to the trademark clearance process can result in embarrassing conflicts down the road if it develops that someone else has preexisting trademark rights. It is no excuse that one did not know about a product already in commerce. Once cleared, an application for federal registration should be prepared and filed. If the mark is not going to be used for some time, as will often be the case, an ITU application should be filed. If the mark is in use, then a regular trademark submission is appropriate.

These filings should be broad in sweep and function. Even if one is not sure whether a particular product line will have value, it pays to protect it at an early date. A creative professional can always decide not to proceed with licensing or merchandising a product and phrase, but if protection has been secured, it will be much easier to stop others who would attempt to steal the franchise.

As already explained, registered marks are entitled to the strongest legal protection. Registered owners and authorized licensees can use the official registration notice, ®, which not only provides public notice but very often adds value to the marketing campaign and the worth of the item. It translates into "original" or "official" merchandise.

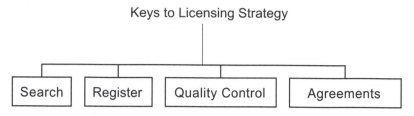

Figure 14-1   Keys to Licensing Strategy

Develop a Reasonable Plan to Cover Likely Uses

When considering the initial structure of a licensing campaign, develop a thoughtful plan before the product lines are established. It is best to take a broad view of the content being created and identify as many elements as one can that would be suitable for protection. Once you have identified the important images and phrases, it will be possible to narrow those deserving of a higher degree of protection based on a reasonable budget. One advantage of an effective licensing campaign is that many of the obligations of a strong program can be passed onto the licensee as part of its requirements in the contracting process. Nevertheless, at the early, creative stages, it is better to identify more trademark elements and potential uses, rather than fewer, to achieve maximum valuation of the creative works. So when thinking of clothing items to be manufactured or licensed, do not stop at the obvious ones, like hats and T-shirts. Thinking more broadly may identify ties, socks, shorts, sweatshirts, shoes, gloves, and so forth. The registration process allows an applicant to identify a limitless number of goods in a single class all for the same filing fee. Particularly at the ITU stage, one is not obligated to actually create all the objects identified to assert a valid claim.

Part of the plan includes selection of the licensees, the firms entrusted with actually making the products. Here, it is essential to do marketplace research, talk to others who serve as references for companies and accept competitive bids. If several companies emerge as possible candidates, consider whether nonexclusive deals work better for you or territorial divisions make sense. Assessing the strengths and weaknesses of licensees is vital business. They carry your reputation into the market.

Provide for Quality Control

The most essential element of a properly devised trademark licensing program is quality assurance. It is the duty of the licensor to be satisfied that the way the mark is used is compatible with its own standards. Every agreement should spell out precisely what constitutes acceptable standards, both with respect to the products being licensed and the way the mark appears on the goods and services. It may be desirable to preapprove certain samples or indicate in the agreement that use in a recognized fashion meets the standards of the licensor. The easiest way to lose a valuable trademark is to license without quality inspection. Quality control is the sine qua non of trademark licensing principles.

Rely on Written License Contracts

Confusion reigns when licensing agreements are not in writing. The agreement need not be a legal treatise, but there should be a written understanding covering the vital elements of the licensing, including

- *A definition of the mark or marks covered by the agreement.* Samples of the marks should be attached to the agreement, particularly if typeface, size, or stylization is relevant to the proper exploitation of the mark.
- *The term of the license.* A reasonable period of years typically identifies the term of the license. Setting beginning and end points also permits both the licensor and licensee to assess whether the transaction meets mutual expectations. If the term is too short (a year or two), the licensee may not have adequate opportunity to create the products, introduce them into the market, and develop a substantial consuming public. If the term is too long, an underperforming licensee could rob the licensor of valuable marketing potential in a mark. The nature of the goods and the mark itself also bear on the term. Some products, like merchandise associated with an event or a program, must be ready for sale at or prior to the day of the event or commencement of the program. Failing to adhere to a strict schedule can doom the success of the licensing program and hurt the long-term viability of a trademark. Therefore, licensor and licensee must have a clear schedule for production and launch of a product line. If the merchandise is not acutely time sensitive, it is still necessary to have a common understanding of the way in which the products will be planned, produced, and marketed.
- *Quality control.* As already discussed, quality control is an absolutely essential element of any licensing campaign. Failure to define what is acceptable quality and establish a mechanism to assure compliance with its specifications may not only result in poorly designed and marketed products but render a trademark legally useless. The quickest way to lose a trademark infringement dispute with a competitor who has taken your mark and exploits it without your control is to permit a licensee to operate without any standards. This means that the mark exists without proper source identification, which renders the mark meaningless.
- *Fundamentally, quality is what the licensor defines it to be.* There is no legal requirement that products emblazoned with a trademark meet a specific standard;

however, it is incumbent on the licensor to describe what is acceptable from its perspective in sufficiently clear terms that a licensee can understand and enforce the specifications and standards.

- The quality control term has at least four principal elements:
  1. The look and feel of the trademark itself; in other words, the physical appearance of the mark on the products and promotions, including typeface, placement, color, size, and shape.
  2. The quality of the products themselves; ingredients, cost, manufacturing process, durability, and shelf life are but a few essential elements.
  3. The manufacturing and inspection process; the more sophisticated the quality control, the more detailed the licensor will be about how the goods are to be produced and the greater the insistence on an adequate process of inspection to assure continuing quality control.
  4. The packaging and marketing of the product; even though the licensor may have a lot to say about this element or it may leave it in the hands of the licensee, chosen for its expertise in this area, as long as each of these elements is addressed in a quality control process, the licensor has satisfied its legal obligations at a level sufficient to maintain its rights to its trademarks.

- *Licensee fees.* Every licensing transaction has a monetary motive. The fees are the essence of the deal for the licensor, and they set the standard by which the licensee knows whether it is entering into a wise business venture. Typically, license fees for the privilege of placing a logo on a product produced by another range from 5 to 15%, with most fees falling in the 5–10% range. If more than one logo is to appear on a product (like a New Years Bowl collegiate T-shirt with the name of the game and the two competing teams), the royalty rate rises to the high end (15%), even though each team and the tournament directors fall in the lower end of the spectrum (5% each).

- *Termination procedures.* It is essential for the licensor to establish a way to get out of a bad deal. While a licensee can simply stop performing—an act that may be a violation of a contract requirement to continue to produce even if the results are not as anticipated and thus create some exposure to liability—the licensor may not have an equivalent option to intervene in the middle of a contract term, unless a specific process permits termination for failure to perform. Termination for good cause, such as failure to produce according to agreed-on specifications (part of the quality control process), is very appropriate. Other bases may include failure to provide adequate reports and financial accounting. But, under any circumstance, some termination provision should be required by the licensor.

- *Exclusive vs. nonexclusive.* A key decision that a licensor must make is whether the grant is to only one company. Exclusive deals tie the trademark owner to a particular producer of goods without recourse to other competitors. From the perspective of the licensee, an exclusive deal allows it to invest in the brand without fear that a competitor will reap rewards it does not deserve. Since marketing expenses—advertising, buying shelf space, creating themes, hiring famous spokespersons—mean financial risks, a licensee does not want a competing producer to siphon off sales meant for the one who created the market to begin with. For licensors, limiting a product line to one licensee usually means it can charge a higher license fee, but if the firm does not deliver results, it may have a smaller profit. Nonexclusive deals hedge the licensor's commitment to one producer but usually come with lower license fees. If multiple licensees each produce their fair share, the net result can boost licensor revenue. In the end, knowing the typical market deals and the parties you are contracting with are the keys.

- *Monitoring the marketplace.* Both parties to a license agreement should have a means of determining whether the product is reaching the right market and whether the market is satisfied with the trademarked merchandise. This feedback is another essential ingredient for a licensor properly assuring quality control over its product and a licensee properly determining the success of its program.

- *After the end of the license.* At the end of the license term, one of two things can happen. The license can be renewed or extended on the same or new terms or all rights can revert to the licensor. In that case, there should be some understanding about goods already produced. A licensee may need a shoulder period to get rid of unsold merchandise, or it may need a way of transferring that merchandise to its successor. It behooves the parties to think through the arrangement for the end of the term, just as they have to plan for the initiation of the program.

Licensing can take on a life of its own. It is a complex process that requires careful planning and forethought. Effective exploitation of trademark rights can be a lucrative supplement to any business and in some cases it can be the whole business. Whether a business is successful depends on some unpredictable factors and hard work, but do not lose the licensing opportunity.

Chapter 15

Trademarks in a Digital World: Domain Name Games and Other Fun

To the world, it seemed as if the Internet, that interconnected tangle of thousands of networks and millions of host computers, was born one day in 1993 or 1994. Even Microsoft master Bill Gates ignored it until then. By the mid-1990s, from daily news stories to hot stock offerings, a new mass medium arrived.

In truth, the Internet's roots date back several decades. Started as a U.S. government plan to coordinate super computers, it extended to university research institutions and their networks. When the means of sending graphic images was designed, it turned public. In its early days some enterprising hackers took advantage of public ignorance, adopting famous names as their own. That action had a trademark corollary that reverberated years later, as we shall see.

Now the Internet's commercial potential is being plumbed in every corner of the globe. As Internet technology ushers in a new era of mass communication, with emphasis on *mass*, the single most critical ingredient in finding your way along this information highway is knowing the sources of data you want to locate. While copyright law guides the use of content, trademark law provides the means by which the sources of the content are properly identified and the commercial reputations respected. To understand the importance of trademarks for this new medium, here is a quick Internet trademark tutorial.

The Address System of the Internet

In its early decades, the Internet's defining feature was a complex routing system. Interconnected networks were identifiable by a unique string of numbers or names. Today, the Internet contains thousands of computer networks and millions of "host" computers that share information. Locating a network and communicating with a specific computer on that network is the electronic equivalent of sending a letter to a specific address somewhere in the world. No two locations can be the same anywhere in the system.

For many years, the task of establishing electronic mailing addresses, called *domain names*, was regulated by national voluntary organizations. In the United States, the Internet Network Information Center (InterNIC), an organization funded by the U.S. National Science Foundation and managed by Network Solutions, Inc., of Herndon, Virginia, performed the function. In Europe, the task has been coordinated by RIPENCC and in Asia by APNIC.

Domain Names

A domain name is a unique combination of letters, numbers, and dashes that route packets of information among computer users. The domain name consists of both the arbitrary identifier chosen by the Internet user and a generic abbreviation that categorizes users (.com for commercial, .edu for educational institutions, .gov for U.S. government agencies, .org for organization, .mil for U.S. military, and .net for network). To locate an individual at an organization, a clause (including a person's name and the symbol @) precedes the arbitrary identifier. Combining all the elements, the address and name would read: john.smith@chrysler.com.

Another section of the Internet is the *World Wide Web.* The Web became the inspiration for the explosion of the Internet in the 1990s because this section is capable of transmitting pictures as well as text. The Web, identified after the @ sign by the letters www, transformed the Internet from a static collection of words to the colorful visual display everyone now knows.

Commencing in 1999, the domain naming system was privatized. During the latter part of the 1990s, one firm that had an agreement with InterNIC to assign names, Network Solutions, Inc., was acquired by a company called VeriSign. With that acquisition, VeriSign became the primary registry for millions of domain names. Furthermore, another organization known as ICANN (Internet Corporation for Assigned Names and Numbers) was designated to accredit private registries that in turn allocate domain names. Along with several other international groups, ICANN helped redesigned the big picture for Internet naming procedures in 2001. The combined effort resulted in several important changes, including the creation of a dispute resolution procedure and the creation of several new "top level domains" (including .biz, .name, .info) to ease pressure on the race to claim a name in cyberspace.

Domain Names May Be Used Like Trademarks

While Internet addresses are not trademarks per se, domain names function as a source of identification, much like a telephone number. Some telephone numbers, like 1-800-AMERICAN, 1-800-MATTRESS, and 1-800-BLUEBOOK, have been held protectable as trademarks.

As a general proposition, for a trademark to be protected in commerce and registered with the PTO, it must be *affixed* to a good or label and *used* in commerce. Placing a mark on a box or other consumer item sold to the public or incorporated in advertising is sufficient. But what about cyberspace communications? The Trademark Office has said that a mark displayed on a computer screen is acceptable as evidence of use. Therefore, displaying logos on a computer screen establishes trademark rights. Since the PTO registers on-screen identifications when used in connection with the provision of services, domain names and their related home pages may also serve as marks for the viewing public.

Trademark Disputes Flourish on the Internet

When famous marks are used as arbitrary identifiers, trademark conflicts arise. In the mid-1990s, there were a spate of Internet trademark litigations. One case involved use of the name *Kaplan* (famed for SAT review courses) by archcompetitor Princeton Review, Inc. (PRI). Although the registration of kaplan.com by PRI was allegedly a prank, the dispute over its use reached the courts and arbitration. In addition to taking its name for the competitor's address, Kaplan accused PRI of "urg[ing] prospective customers to e-mail 'KAPLAN horror stories' to us at kaplan.sucks@review.com." For its part, PRI claimed registration of kaplan.com broke no law or rule of the Internet. Its objective was to create an electronic brochure and comment on its competitor. The arbitration panel found for Kaplan and forced PRI to relinquish the name.

Kaplan and PRI were not alone. Although initially only a small fraction of the Fortune 500 companies claimed their name as an Internet address, as businesses awoke to the importance of Internet sites, parties began fighting to protect their names, including

- *MTV*. The cable service challenged a former employee, a VJ (video jockey), who registered mtv.com as *his* Internet address to promote music services related to his work for MTV. In the case, which was subsequently settled, the VJ asserted that he used the name with full knowledge and permission of MTV, after MTV saw no need for the address identifier.

- *Better Business Bureau*. In a case filed in federal court in Kansas City, Missouri, the Better Business Bureau claimed that the assignment bbb.com and bbb.org to Clark Publishing violated its long established trademark rights.

- *Knowledgenet*. Another trademark complaint involved Knowledgenet, Inc., an IBM subsidiary, against Boone and Co., which requested and was assigned knowledgenet.com for computer-related services, a business already occupied by the plaintiff. In an additional twist, Knowledgenet named Network Solutions as a co-defendant, asserting that its role in assigning the domain name without consideration of trademark law made it contributorily liable for infringement.

In response to the trend to assert trademark rights in domain names and to prevent becoming embroiled in trademark disputes, Network Solutions propounded a domain name policy in July 1995: When anyone seeks a domain name, it would have to affirm that it had the right to use the mark for interactive purposes and that, if a dispute were to arise, it would indemnify and hold Network Solutions harmless from any claims. Further, if a *registered* trademark owner challenged a domain name assignment, the party to whom the name was assigned would have to justify its use. Failure to satisfy Network Solutions would result in the domain name being withheld. If an objecting party were not registered but had trademark rights and the dispute could not be equitably resolved, Network Solutions could withdraw the name assignment and await a court order or arbitration decision. Network Solutions made clear that it did not believe it had any legal obligation to evaluate trademark rights before making domain name assignments, nor did it have the resources to conduct responsible trademark searches. It believed the domain name assignment process would be unduly burdened by any such effort, increasing costs and materially delaying name assignments.

Nevertheless, as an entity making such allocations, Network Solutions found it difficult to extricate itself from the trademark morass and was regularly joined as a material party to disputes. Coming to Network Solution's (or VeriSign's) aid was ICANN. Taking control of the naming dispute issue, ICANN developed a Uniform Domain Name Dispute Resolution Policy (the awkward acronym UDRP for short). The UDRP, which took effect in April 1999, was imposed by ICANN as a condition in its agreements with firms authorized as registries of domain names. The registries, in turn, required any party seeking a domain name to accept the UDRP process. In brief, whenever a domain name is assigned, the registry making the allocation reserves the right to cancel, transfer, or change a domain name based on resolution of a legitimate dispute. A mandatory administrative proceeding before an "administrative-dispute-resolution service provider" sanctioned by ICANN can be initiated by a party complaining that it, not the domain name assignee, owns the name. The party assigned the contested domain name must participate in the proceeding if

- The domain name is identical or confusingly similar to the complaining party's trademark or service mark.
- The party assigned the domain name has no rights or legitimate interest to it.
- The domain name has been registered in bad faith.

All three elements must be proven by the complainant. In particular, *bad faith* is defined in the policy. *Bad faith* means circumstances indicating that the registrant acquired the name to (1) sell it to the complainant, who is the owner of a trademark or service mark or a competitor of that owner; (2) prevent a trademark owner from acquiring it; (3) disrupt the business of the complainant; or (4) create confusion for commercial gain. For more details on UDRP check out http://www.icann.org/udrp/udrp-policy-24oct99.htm.

UDRP is a sensible answer to a nagging policy. It was also dictated by a federal law, adopted in 1999, that is designed to bring an end to the unfair taking of domain names rightfully belonging to more prominent parties. The Anticyber-squatting Consumer Protection Act (ACPA) amends the Lanham Act (the center-piece of U.S. trademark legislation) and prohibits the practice of cybersquatting, a word coined to cover all the sins of those who take domain names in conscious derogation of the rights of trademark proprietors. Simply stated, ACPA decrees that the bad faith exploitation of domain names infringes federal trademark rights. Anyone who adopts a domain name with the intent to take advantage of another's trademark, create confusion, or dilute the value of the mark will be liable for cybersquatting. That activity can result in an injunction ordering the cancellation or transfer of the domain name. Also, a complaining party may seek actual damages and profits, or a statutory claim of $1,000 to $100,000. Domain name registries can be contributorily liable; however, if they adopt the UDRP, they can escape liability. So that lawyers do not go too hungry, ACPA has a savings clause that allows a domain name registrant to defend its squatter's rights on grounds of fair use or free speech. Many of the initial cases involve so-called suck-sites; that is, uses of a trademark in a domain name designed to attract people complaining about the goods or services of the trademark proprietor, à la kaplansucks.com.

Yet, disputes on the Internet will not go away simply because an administrative resolution is feasible or a statute prohibits bad faith acts.

Trademarks on the Internet: Legal Quicksand

Trademarks on the Internet pose a legal quicksand for other reasons as well. While famous brand proprietors may have a strong claim to ownership of unique words, owners of a trademark known in a narrow specialty, such as Kaplan, may find their trademarks claimed by similarly named but unrelated parties, quite possibly by total strangers. Because domain names are granted exclusively and nationally, the trademark principle of *concurrent use* cannot apply in cyberspace.

A related issue is name depletion. Since there can be but one address kaplan.com, the list of available names can be quickly allocated, forcing firms desirous of using a specific name to seek alternatives. Although simply adding one letter, for example, skaplan, creates an entire *different* domain site, it may not relieve the trademark problem of likelihood of confusion as to cyberspace sources.

Another issue waiting in the wings is that of trade dress protection for computer screen images. The "look and feel" questions, which have been analyzed in copyright infringement claims, have a trademark corollary. With the U.S. Supreme Court holdings that trade dress and color are each entitled to trademark protection, creators of computer screen images may try to protect their display images and screen colors. Core questions raised when seeking to protect screen images will be whether the screen images are functional, whether they establish a distinctive visual impression, and whether they have achieved secondary meaning.

In one of the most ironic trademark proceedings in PTO history, two nonprofit groups that were organized to promote the Internet, the Corporation for National Research Initiatives (CNRI) and the Internet Society, brought a trademark cancellation action to recover public use of the word *Internet*. Robert Kahn and Vint Cerf, visionaries who worked for the U.S. government during the 1960s when the jumble of federal computers was being organized and personally coined the term *Internet* from their "internetworking" computers, discovered somewhat by chance that the Trademark Office had granted a federal registration for the word *Internet* for banking and publishing services to a company called Internet, Inc. Internet, Inc., was owner of the MOST automated teller network, and it sought dominion over the word in connection with all banking services.

So as not to paint the Trademark Office in a negative light, it should be noted that the registration was granted in 1989, before the word became publicly synonymous with the international computer network. On the eve of the mark becoming "incontestable," and thus subject to fewer bases for legal objection, the CNRI and Internet Society petitioned the PTO to cancel registration of the mark. At the same time, these two opposers, as well as hundreds of other parties using the word *Internet* in their business activities, filed applications for registration. Pending the resolution of the dispute, whenever the PTO granted a trademark or a service mark to a company whose business involved the Internet, it could not define the goods or services offered as relating to the Internet. That was the trademark of Internet, Inc., and trademark policy and law prohibited the use of a registered mark in the definition of goods or services. So the PTO required all Internet-related applications to utilize the neutral phrase *global computer network*. Moreover, hundreds of other applicants who sought to register a mark that incorporated the word *Internet* were put on hold pending the dispute.

After 5 long years of wrangling, dozens of pleadings covering procedural and administrative claims, and numerous preliminary rulings by the PTO, Internet, Inc., finally wearied of its plight and agreed to withdraw its registration. Thus, the men who coined the word *Internet* and made it part of intellectual property history saved it for all to use.

The Geography of the Internet and Trademarks

Another important trademark phenomenon of the Internet is its international aspect. Electronic communications are not bound by traditional geographic considerations. Because the Internet can be accessed with the touch of a keypad and it stretches across oceans to foreign lands, trademark proprietors find that the territorial integrity of their marks may be breached.

Although traditional trademark law allows different trademark proprietors in New York and Florida to use the same mark, defending exclusive geographic zones in a digital world is difficult. People can communicate as readily with colleagues or customers residing thousands of miles away in foreign countries as with those in the same building.

The degree to which trademarks relating to new services on the global information superhighway can coexist is becoming clearer. The World International Property Oganization, the international organization that administers treaties (mentioned in the copyright context), is also important for trademarks. With the support of many nations, WIPO initiated its own administrative dispute resolution process. Whenever trademarks have international conflicts, a complainant can initiate a WIPO review of the conflicting assignment.

Transborder communications, whether across state or national lines, also raise the legal issues of jurisdiction choice of law. For example, is an Internet user liable to be sued anywhere its home page can be displayed? When cases arise, what governing law applies—the jurisdiction where the transmission originates, where the transmission is received, or somewhere in between? In one decision, a California couple that operated an "adult" bulletin board was found guilty of transmitting obscenity via interstate telephone lines under Tennessee law and sentenced to several years in prison. In another case, a New York court dismissed a trademark suit against a Missouri business because its only contact with New York was the fact that its home page could be accessed online.

The company eBay became embroiled in an international dispute when a German court determined that the posting of Nazi paraphernalia on its auction site violated German law. Even though the order originated outside the United States, because eBay does business worldwide, it could not let the order stand unchallenged. It went into U.S. court and obtained a decree setting aside the German order on the grounds that the U.S. Constitution's First Amendment guarantees allowed it to maintain the material on its website.

Colonel Sander's Kentucky Fried Chicken franchise, now utilizing the more dietetic acronym KFC, discovered that a company in China registered www.kfc.com.cn using Chinese characters. When KFC challenged, alleging it was already a famous mark in China, the erstwhile domain competitor resisted, denying that the mark was really prominent in China. That dispute persists in

Chinese court, as does a comparable claim by Rolex, which is embroiled in a claim over www.rolex.com.cn against a company utilizing the native Chinese language.

For serious trademark owners and users, the message is clear: It is obligatory to pay attention to the details of foreign laws as well as those in the United States, lest they be in for a big surprise.

Moving On

We now have an overview of trademark and many of its practical applications. Trademark and copyright are two of the key pillars of laws governing content rights. But others come into play, most notably Unfair Competition, Privacy and Publicity, Antitrust, Patents, and Trade Secrets. Detailed discussion of these laws is beyond the scope of this book, but a general grounding is necessary to avoid unexpected pitfalls. As we turn to these disciplines, here is an encapsulation of trademark law (Figure 15-1).

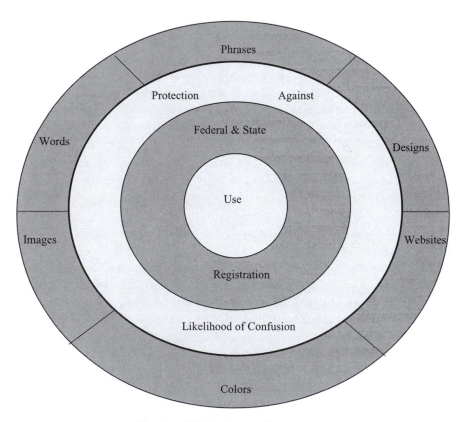

Figure 15-1 Core of Trademark

Core of Trademark

1. Words, phrases, designs, images, and colors are protectable by common law, state law, federal law, and the laws of foreign countries. Use of a mark is essential, but plans—intention to use—can form the basis for protection.

2. The key legal concept is that marks should be protected against the likelihood of confusion as to source. Protection can last for as long as the mark is used.

3. Trademark law has two key purposes: to enable consumers to trust the source of goods or services and to protect individuals and entities that spend resources to build a brand reputation.

4. Federal and state registrations systems offer greater protection and public awareness of trademarks and service marks. Every foreign country offers its own system of protecting marks that enter its commerce. All serious trademark owners should register wherever their marks are actively employed.

5. Domain names are the digital equivalent of trademarks and the latest arena for battling confusion as to source.

Part Three

Collateral Concerns: Things You Cannot Ignore

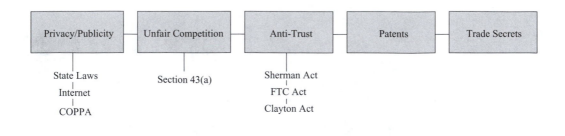

| Privacy/Publicity | Unfair Competition | Anti-Trust | Patents | Trade Secrets |

State Laws
|
Internet
|
COPPA

Section 43(a)

Sherman Act
|
FTC Act
|
Clayton Act

WIPO: International Treaties

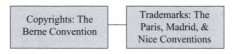

| Copyrights: The Berne Convention | Trademarks: The Paris, Madrid, & Nice Conventions |

Part Three   Collateral Concerns—Overview

Chapter 16

Unfair Competition, Publicity, and Privacy: Filling in the Holes

We have just been through a tutorial on trademarks and copyrights. However, as one radio commentator teases, "now here's the *rest* of the story." Copyrights and trademarks are the core issues in content, but you cannot overlook an important legal triad: unfair competition, publicity, and privacy.

The Rules of Unfair Competition

Buried in the Lanham Act, the federal trademark law, is a real surprise, a special provision characterized in simple terms as a *national unfair competition law*. Section 43(a), as it is known, provides that any misrepresentation in commerce is actionable (susceptible to a lawsuit) by someone who is "aggrieved." That person can be a consumer or a competitor. It covers not only active misrepresentations but also false designations of origin and misuse of names and trademarks. In fact, this rule also functions as the national trademark law for unregistered marks.

When most of the baby boomers were growing up in the 1950s and 1960s, the rule of thumb was this: Don't mention a competitor's brand by name. Comparisons were always between the one household term and Brand X. Then, in the early 1970s, sparked by some lawsuits and the impact of Federal Trade Commission (FTC) rulings, the notion of referring to a competitor's actual mark was encouraged, as long as the representations were truthful. To back up the potential problem of misrepresentations, Section 43(a) became a touchstone for protection.

Little appreciated when it was first passed in 1946, Section 43(a) is now a standard marker in most lawsuits involving trademarks, copyrights, competition, and consumer fraud. Its principles play out in several ways:

- In the media, advertising sparked these initial debates. Comparing one's product with a leading competitor, everything from soap to autos, meant representing one's goods in relation to another's. To determine whether the statements were inflated and permissive puffery or deliberate fraud, Section 43(a) was called into play to help mediate. As the publisher of potential misrepresentations, radio, television, print, and other media outlets must be satisfied that the hype is not fantasy. Although an "innocent publisher" clause can be invoked to reduce the sting of false claims, good publishing practices mean knowing what you are disseminating and being satisfied that extreme claims that identify competitors have a credible rationale.

- Section 43(a) is also a sword in the competitive battles in other marketplaces. If a material false statement is made in connection with a promotion, or if an unregistered trademark is used by a competitor, this provision opens the door to the federal courts. For example, when Stephen King complained that his name was used in promotion and on screen for the film, *The Lawnmower Man*, he sought action. Even though he sold the film rights to his early storyline, the movie that was finally produced bore no relationship whatsoever to his plot. The only elements in common were the title and the use of Stephen King's name. He sued, successfully, to have his name stripped from the title, and all videocassettes had to be reworked to replace his name in the title. All thanks to Section 43(a).

- The rule is also employed whenever one's name, voice, image, or likeness is taken without consent. Celebrities as diverse as Woody Allen and Jackie Kennedy Onassis have used this provision to challenge look-alikes from mimicking them in advertisements, thereby confusing the public as to endorsement of a product. Tom Waits and Bette Midler have protected their distinctive voices against commercial imitation, and any attempt to imply that Casper the Friendly Ghost is mean to kids could spark an action.

What makes this provision special is its breadth. It relies on the notion that merely presenting a false statement about another in commerce can create a claim by anyone who believes he or she is harmed.

Here is another example. Consumers Union, publisher of *Consumer Reports*, the monthly magazine that prides itself on unbiased reporting about products, sued under Section 43(a) when an advertiser, Regina Vacuums, used television commercials to tell the world how well *Consumer Reports* rated its product. From the magazine's perspective, the ad falsely implied it endorsed the product, which could have unfairly damaged its reputation for unbiased reporting. In this way, the law protects entities who are hurt when the public is misled. In the hands of clever antagonists, the provision is a powerful weapon.

But be warned, not every use of a name or image is a violation. If the use is a parody, it may be upheld. When Ginger Rogers sued to stop a movie from being called *Ginger and Fred*, the court reasoned that there was no impression that the legendary actress was endorsing the film. It was a fair and artistic use of the names to create an image essential to the story of the film. In contrast, Princess Stephanie of Monaco won a lawsuit against a Swiss magazine for a photomontage that showed her and the director of the Swiss national circus in sexy positions, the court having rejected the claim that the montage was a harmless joke.

Another intriguing twist involves the concept of "reverse passing off." When a spate of charges of plagiarism hit the news in 2001, one involving famed author Stephen Ambrose, another involving Doris Kearns Goodwin, and a third involving a prominent explorer-scientist, Bradford Washburn, each was characterized as writing a book that took too many facts and too much information from prior sources. While the charges involved potential claims of copyright infringement, they also raised issues of reverse passing off—claiming personal credit for someone else's research.

Publicity Protection for the Famous

As if Section 43(a) were not enough to think about, a whole body of rules covers famous people and the use of their names and images. Anyone who is a celebrity or has commercially exploited his or her own name, voice, or likeness may lay claim to this protection. Generally, the rules of publicity are set forth in state statutes. Sometimes, they are found in judges' decisions of fairness or equity. This means consulting the specific rules of the states where you are doing business to confirm what obligations are afoot.

However, if you want to develop content with a national reach, you must adopt an approach that respects the most restrictive rules. These usually apply in states such as California and New York. In general, the following are the key points to bear in mind.

What Is the Nature of the Use?

Is it commercial? Is there any element of public interest, such as news reporting or commentary? Would it qualify for fair use under copyright law? The more public the interest in the content and the less commercial the status, the better is the opportunity to use the image.

Who Is Involved?

Is the person famous? Is he or she recognizable by voice, image, likeness, or rendering? Is the person alive or dead? Is the person a minor? The rules help the famous keep what is theirs, the commercial exploitation of their persona. If the person is recognizable in any fashion, the rules may apply. Even if the person is dead, rights may be held by the heirs. In 2002, the Supreme Court declined to hear a case (*Comedy Three Productions, Inc.* v. *Gary Saderup, Inc.*) involving posthumous pictures of the Three Stooges on T-shirts and lithographs, letting stand an appeals court ruling that sided with their heirs, who claimed that their right of publicity outweighed any First Amendment rights of the artist. What is more, Elvis Presley's estate is one of the biggest licensors of images. Watch out especially for minors; unauthorized use of their images can be double trouble.

In short, even though a copyrighted work may be in the public domain and free to use by that set of rules and even though there may be no recognized trademark, the rules of publicity might come into play. The harm from misusing this right can be costly: You may have to pay a penalty, lose a profit, or destroy an infringing product.

Even if the person involved is not famous, there may be another headache.

Right of Privacy for the Less Than Famous

The privacy right is the other side of the coin. Most people have a legal entitlement to anonymity. State rules and common laws protect ordinary folks from

- Intrusion into their private affairs.
- Public disclosure of embarrassing facts.
- Publicly being placed in a false light.
- Misappropriation of a name or likeness.

For those who create content, these rules create some bright cautionary yellow lights. With Minicams capturing images right and left, private people are finding their private lives suddenly public. Unlike the paparazzi's pictures of royalty, photographs of unknowns should be carefully reviewed before publication. Clearance may be needed unless there is a rationale that supports a public purpose. Since talk is cheap and it is common for guests on radio or television to rant and rave about all sorts of things, especially the private lives of unknown people, a wise producer gets a release from every guest and has a ready finger on the so-called kill button when in doubt. The releases should cover not only the right to use the images of the guests but place responsibility on the guests for the accuracy of the aired statements. There is no 100% guarantee against a privacy violation, but the release gives you a firm footing on which to press your case.

The telling of some intimate and private details by the author Arthur Golden placed one of the most popular books of recent time, *Memoirs of a Geisha*, in an awkward limbo. While more than 4 million copies of the 1997 novel were sold and rights for a film deal acquired by none other than Steven Spielberg, Golden and his publisher became embroiled in a lawsuit with a former geisha. The woman, who recounted many stories to the author in taped interviews, claimed that Golden improperly breached their agreement about confidentiality, revealing her identity while fictionalizing many elements of her life. The case has elements of copyright infringement, invasion of privacy, and defamation as well as breach of contract. Needless to say, it is a complex story in its own right that may take years to unravel.

Privacy and the Internet

A whole new body of law is developing around privacy and the Internet. Because digital data is easy to organize and deliver to others, because servers can be hacked and precious information taken without knowledge of the creator, and because children are primary users of Internet websites, the level of concern about preserving one's privacy in digital communications is at heightened levels. The Children's Online Privacy Protection Act (COPPA) was passed in 1998 in response to a hue and cry, not only about the invasion of children's privacy, but the sadistic exploitation of youths via Internet communications.

COPPA applies to the online collection, after April 21, 2000, of personal information (such as full name, home address, e-mail address, telephone number, or any other information that would allow someone to identify or contact the child) from children under age 13. It covers operators of websites or online services directed toward children and other operators who know that they are collecting personal information from children. The law and the implementing regulations promulgated by the FTC spell out what such an operator must include in a privacy policy, when and how to seek verifiable consent from a parent, and what responsibilities an operator has to protect children's privacy and safety online. The operator must post a clear and prominent link to the policy on its home page and at each area where it collects personal information from children. The act directed the FTC to review and approve guidelines proposed by industry groups or others that would serve as safe harbors for compliance with the law. COPPA also authorizes the FTC to bring enforcement actions against violators, and, in fact, the FTC has already done so.

In addition to information about children, other types of information, much of which is collected online, has been the focus of recent legislative activity in the area of privacy; for example, information collected by financial institutions (Gramm-Leach-Billey Act), medical information (Health Insurance Portability and Accountability Act), and information from citizens of the European Union (EU Directive on Data Protection). These disparate laws and regulations have led to a recognition of the need for businesses to establish privacy policies that disclose the nature of the personal information they collect and the use they make of this information, and, in appropriate cases, provide for opt-in or opt-out customer consent to data collection. On the horizon is an effort to enact legislation that will create a comprehensive federal Internet privacy law.

Existing federal law on government, as opposed to private, rights to access personal information is grounded in the Fourth Amendment, which requires the government to secure a prior judicial warrant issued on probable cause. Internet communications and storage of electronic communications via networking have presented difficult Fourth Amendment questions. The events of September 11, 2001, triggered a frenzy of legislative activity intended to enhance the government's ability to combat terrorism, resulting in the passage of the Patriot Act of 2001. Some of the activity leading to this legislation was controversial, as civil liberties watchdog groups identified adverse implications for protection of individual privacy. The Patriot Act expands the ability of the federal government to conduct surveillance via "pen/trap orders" of electronic communications to capture potentially substantive "routing, addressing, and signaling" information and erodes privacy protection for electronic communications. In the wake of reports that the hijackers may have communicated with each other by using computers at public libraries, the legislation has serious implications for libraries and higher education institutions that traditionally feel bound to protect the privacy of patrons using library equipment to access the Internet and send and receive e-mail.

Chapter 17

Antitrust Laws: Keeping Competition Alive

Here is the dilemma. Copyright law grants to authors certain exclusive rights regarding their writings. Trademark law grants to owners the exclusive right to use a word or phrase in commerce. Both these bodies of law are premised on the notion that, by granting these exclusive rights—monopolies, if you will—individuals and businesses will be given the incentive to create and those creations will be good for the overall health and vitality of our economic system. But consumers can suffer when competition is restrained, when there is only one source for commodities. Hence, antitrust laws govern fair competition and are relevant to our understanding of content rights.

The antitrust laws are complex and worthy of a completely separate treatise. Yet, some familiarity with the principles designed to protect consumers by preserving competition is essential to appreciate the interplay of content rights in the digital world of the 21st century.

Key Concepts of Antitrust Law

Antitrust has several key concepts, which are evaluated not only when a company's conduct is being assessed as a violation of antitrust laws, but also when a proposal to merge two companies or sell one part of a business to another is being reviewed:

- *Monopoly, market power, and extension of power to new areas of commerce.* A monopoly exists when a business can control prices to consumers or prevent entry by competitors. You can determine the existence of a monopoly by calculating what is known as market power, the degree to which one entity controls a line of commerce. The greater the percentage of the business in an industry that a company controls, the greater is its market power. Market power in an industry may be diluted if alternatives not controlled by the monopolist exist. For example, if the government were trying to decide if the two largest companies that deliver programming to homeowners via satellite should be allowed to merge, the analysis would be greatly affected by a decision to count dozens of large cable companies as part of the same industry. If you ignore the cable companies, the combined satellite company might look like a colossus controlling more than 90% of the business, whereas if the cable firms are added to the mix, the net share of the satellite companies might not even break 15% of the market. Thus, the definition of *market* is crucial to an understanding of a company's power and whether consumers are helped or harmed by the combination. Also, the matter of extending market reach is always important. If a company naturally grows from one product line to another, it may be perfectly good for competition and consumers. However, if a company that has a monopoly in one line of commerce tries aggressively to utilize that power to buy control over another area, then competition may be unfairly harmed and consumers may suffer. As we shall see, this issue dogged the world's largest software company for the better part of a decade.

- *Combinations or conspiracies that unfairly restrain trade.* An important antitrust principle is that what an individual company decides to do on its own may be just fine; however, if that decision is made, not independently, but as the product of two companies working together, then competition is harmed and consumers can suffer. The good act of one can be a bad act of two. If the action restrains trade in any fashion, it is called a *combination* or *conspiracy in restraint of trade*, and the antitrust laws prohibit it.

- *Mergers and acquisitions that effectively destroy competition.* When does a joining together of two competitors make for an unlawful combination? That is the issue often posed by the plans of big business to get even bigger. As noted regarding the satellite and cable industry, the analysis may hinge on the definition of *market*. A company's behavior or market conduct is also relevant. Most big business plans to combine or acquire companies are carefully reviewed by the federal and state agencies that regulate competition.

Federal Antitrust Laws

The antitrust laws of the United States have twin processes, criminal and civil actions. The criminal laws are administered primarily by the Department of Justice and the FTC. The civil laws are enforced by private companies harmed by the actions of their competitors. There are also antitrust laws at the state level. In the interconnected, ever-shrinking world we live in, the decisions of U.S. firms with multinational business may be reviewed by foreign officials and governments. Altogether, these laws are designed to guard against the abuses of economic power. In the federal system, the key legal provisions include

1. Section 1 of the Sherman Act prohibits contracts, combinations, or conspiracies that unreasonably restrain trade.
2. Section 2 of the Sherman Act makes it unlawful for a company to monopolize or attempt to monopolize trade or commerce through unreasonable methods.
3. The Federal Trade Commission Act bans unfair methods of competition.
4. The Clayton Act prohibits mergers or acquisitions where the effect may be to substantially lessen competition or tend to create monopoly.

States and foreign governments have laws that provide similar restraints. In rare cases, even though a merger of companies or an assessment of conduct may pass muster in the United States, it may fail under the tests applied by foreign countries. This was the fate of the proposed merger of General Electric and Honeywell in fall 2001. A planned joining of the companies, deemed to be the crown jewel in the illustrious career of GE Chairman Jack Welch, was torn apart, not by U.S. or state law enforcers, but by the antitrust sleuths of the European Union.

Antitrust laws credit the notion that the behavior of a monopolist, even one with market power, does not have to be anticompetitive or anticonsumer. What counts is the nature of the conduct, and conduct that harms consumers and competitors is illegal. As a result, antitrust laws often require balancing facts and claims and a careful assessment of the impact of the proposed behavior and goals, in effect a "rule of reason." Justifications for actions are as important as the actions themselves.

Behavior Targeted by Antitrust Laws

In principle, therefore, antitrust laws and the exclusive grants of rights to copyright and trademark owners are compatible. However, certain behavior raises red flags, signs that careful review of the actions of entities must be considered. These activities, which traditionally have been deemed the seeds of abusive business practices, include

- *Agreements among competitors about price.* The essence of a market economy is the ability of competitors to price goods and services to maximize public appeal. When competition works effectively, prices can be affected by factors such as supply and demand, costs of production, promotion, quality, and service. However, if competitors reach side agreements on how to price their products or services, the law is violated. Price similarity is not the same as price fixing; an agreement to set a price by competitors is the difference.

- *Agreements among competitors to limit product.* Anytime two or more companies reach an understanding on how to control output, the antitrust laws are violated.

- *Boycotts.* A joint decision not to deal with another person or business is unfair if the intent is to force others to pay higher prices. The telltale sign of such an agreement is a plan to use their joint involvement as a way to limit a mutual competitor and thereby exact a higher price from a consumer.

- *Dividing markets.* An agreement among competitors to subdivide territories or allocate customers is an agreement not to compete. While it may have a rational basis, such as the desire not to overspend when getting into a new business or moving to a new location, if it is made by two or more competitors jointly deciding how to behave, that is not okay.

- *Tie-ins.* Linking the sale of one product with another is not per se a problem; however, if the effect harms competition, then the practice may be illegal. The annals of copyright include many stories in which authors tried to tie acquisition of one product to another. In essence, this is what Microsoft was charged with doing in making Internet Explorer inseparable from Windows 98. Decades earlier, major movie studios were charged with illegally bundling the licensing of certain films, one to another, without adequate opportunity for the customers to reject undesired titles. When the effect is detrimental to competition, the federal government will step in and rely on the antitrust laws to prevent the practice.

- *Mergers and acquisitions play a special role.* When a company seeks to add a new division or extend its control of a line of commerce by merging with or acquiring a competitor, both the Department of Justice and the FTC take a very close look at the impact of the action on the marketplace. Too much concentration of power or consolidation in the hands of fewer players can wreck a vibrant industry. The cable and telephone industries in recent years, like the newspaper and broadcast industries before them, have seen mergers or acquisitions reduce the number of major players from many to a few. The impact of these business developments on competition, price of services and goods, and standards for new entrants into the business, all must be considered by the government before such deals can close.

Microsoft's Antitrust Dilemma: A Case Study in Copyright Rights and Wrongs

At the height of its power and influence, at a time when the net wealth of its principal shareholder, Bill Gates, soared to $85 billion, the Justice Department launched a lawsuit to break up Microsoft, the most successful software company in history. The claim was that Microsoft had improperly used its copyright monopoly in Windows desktop computer software to attempt to control the market for Internet browser software. By embedding Microsoft's Internet Explorer as an essential and inseparable operating part of Windows 98, by issuing copyright licenses controlling how desktop icons are to appear, the original equipment manufacturers were materially constrained in utilizing an Internet browser other than Internet Explorer. In short, the charge was that Microsoft was utilizing its Windows copyright monopoly to make users adopt another Microsoft product by default, to the detriment of competitors (Netscape in particular and other Internet browsers in general) and the consuming public.

The case, which was initiated in the 1990s and decided in 2001, involved the Department of Justice, attorneys general from dozens of individual states, and an army of witnesses from many affected Internet companies. In one of the most dramatic legal decisions of American jurisprudence, a federal judge ordered a breakup of the world's richest company. The decision to split Microsoft into two independent companies was partially reversed on appeal.

The Appeals Court ruling kept in place many key elements of the District Court's antitrust decision. Nevertheless, the appellate decision required a reconsideration of the remedy imposed by the district court. In an extraordinary personalization of the proceeding, Microsoft charged, and the U.S. Circuit Court of Appeals agreed, that the district judge showed bias, stepping outside his role as dispassionate jurist by granting interviews with the press while the case was going on. That behavior forced the court to appoint a new judge to hear the case after it was sent back to the lower court.

When the matter was returned to the district court, in the aftermath of the September 11 World Trade Center attack and at the urging of the new judge assigned to handle the case, the Justice Department and Microsoft reached a compromise that promised to keep the company intact. That compromise was challenged by state attorneys general, who were parties to the complaint, and the case remained alive.

Then, in January 2002, AOL Time Warner filed a private antitrust lawsuit against Microsoft. Before the AOL–Time Warner merger, AOL had acquired Netscape and made it the service provider's preferred Internet browser. The AOL-TW antitrust complaint relied on the findings in the Department of Justice case and raised the specter of Microsoft owing billions of dollars in damages for anticompetitive behavior. The antitrust laws allow the court in a civil case to exact punishment against a losing defendant by trebling the money award.

Whatever the final outcome of these cases, they underscore the importance and relevance of the antitrust laws, not only for the world's largest company, but for all owners of copyrighted works and trademarks. As the Circuit Court, citing another appeals court ruling, pithily explained, "Intellectual property rights do not confer a privilege to violate the antitrust laws."

Chapter 18

Patents and Trade Secrets: Powerful Partners

For some, the words *copyrights*, *patents*, and *trademarks* are loosely interchangeable. To them, every creation, be it a word, a book, or an invention is a "copyright." Others speak about "patenting" a movie, or "trademarking" a new clothespin. For us, the distinguishing features of copyrights and trademarks are now better understood. With certain exceptions, the focus of content rights is not the patent law; nevertheless, patent law cannot be ignored by creative professionals who want to identify and protect their interests.

For example, take the first 15 years of Microsoft's existence. Bill Gates and his colleagues focused on copyright and trademark laws as the basis for legal protections. Then, suddenly, they realized that many software competitors were exploiting patent laws in ways that gave them legal advantages. In the early 1990s, patent litigation or even threats of patent litigation affected software development and exploitation. Microsoft went on a filing spree, applying for patent protection for many of its newly copyrighted software programs. Why this interest in patent protection? The answer lies in the power of the patent.

Short Course on Patents

Like copyrights, a patent is a government-granted right, also rooted in the Constitution and covering entitlement for a limited time. Unlike a copyright, however, a patent does not ensure that a patent holder can exploit the invention; rather, a patent enables the inventor to exclude others from making, using, offering, or selling the invention in the United States. Like trademarks, patents are issued by the PTO after a detailed review of an application.

A patent application consists of two elements:

1. *A written description of the invention.* Usually this includes drawings and enough detail to explain in everyday terms how to make and use the invention. A model of the invention is not required but may be requested by the PTO.
2. *A series of claims.* The claims describe how the invention works. Clearly the claims are crucial because they define the scope of protection.

Patents can be issued for machines, manufactured items, new ways of doing things (processes), compositions of matter (such as drugs, proteins, viruses), living organisms (plants and animals that have been genetically engineered), computer programs, and business methods. Improvements on an existing invention can be patented as well. In such cases, if the term of the original patent has not expired, then the new patentee may need permission from the original creator in order to exploit that invention.

Among these categories, computer programs and business method patents are particularly important for digital content. Business methods are sometimes controversial, because the PTO has granted patents to what appear to be common practices, such as web advertising, mutual fund financial analysis, one-click Internet shopping payment procedures, and menu options using a telephone keypad.

If the invention is new, then the application will be granted and the right to prevent others from exploiting the claims assured for a limited period of years. *New* has special legal meaning in the case of patents, including not known or used by others in the United States, not patented abroad, or not described in a printed publication more than 1 year prior to filing.

If a prior invention contains the same claims, then the PTO will deny the request. Also, the relevant literature of the industry is searched for clues to establishing whether the claims have been made public prior to the filing of the application. If so, a patent will not be issued. Patentees have 1 year from the time they first reveal the nature of their invention to make a filing. Failure to file within the 1-year period can result in a loss of entitlement.

In 1995 the patent term was changed to 20 years from the date of filing or 17 years from the date of grant, whichever is longer. When more than one person works on a patent, the rights are shared. When a patent is created on the job, either the employer or employee may own it; however, employers usually have a "shop right," that is, the right to exploit the patent in the company's business, even if the company does not own it.

Because patent applications take several years to process and denials can be tied up in appeals for several more years, a clever company attaches the phrase *patent pending* to many new products. Such a notice has no legal effect, but, like ™ or ℠, may discourage competitors from their new invention. Once registered, the law requires the inventor to mark the goods with the word *patent*. Failure to do so prevents entitlement to damages, unless the infringer was properly notified.

While a patent application receives careful scrutiny by a team of professionals at the PTO, sometimes the expert agency makes a mistake. Such errors may be so prominent that they cannot escape the wrath of editorial writers. In the early 1990s, well after the start of the digital revolution, the PTO made such an error. Compton's Encyclopedia applied for and was granted a patent for the technology involved in making CD-ROMs. Even though CD-ROMs were already a staple of the computer industry, the PTO failed to determine accurately when the technology became public knowledge. In an unusual move, the Tribune Company, venerable publisher of the *Chicago Tribune* and owner of several broadcast stations and the legendary Chicago Cubs baseball team, purchased Compton's and announced it would soon charge all exploiters of the technology a license fee per disk. The pennies-per-CD charge could convert the patent acquisition into a multimillion dollar bonanza for Tribune and more than justify its foray into patent ownership. All seemed headed in the right direction for Tribune's new venture when a cry arose from CD publishers around the nation. This technology was already in vogue before the application was filed, they assured the PTO, so granting the patent was a major mistake. While such challenges are normally heard in court in the course of a patent infringement lawsuit, the objections were so forcefully presented that the Patent Office, on its own initiative, conducted a review of the grant. In an embarrassing but utterly necessary action, the technology-savvy agency reversed its ruling, pulling the patent from Tribune and dashing the company's plans for a major licensing fortune.

A much happier fate was in store for the patent holder of the telephone push-button menu. In the early 1980s, a prescient inventor registered a claim to the process of using the telephone keypad to create menu options. We all know the drill when calling the airlines; for example, press 1 for arrivals and departures, 2 for reservations, 3 for security information, and so forth. The process of moving into different menu options using a telephone keypad was this person's "invention." Irrespective of whether the patent holder actually exploited the grant, the patent enabled the owner to prevent others from using the technology without consent. Despite the outraged objections of many large companies, like airlines, hotel chains, and AT&T, the inventor was able to secure millions in license fees, for in the end, the users felt in this case that risking a patent infringement suit was simply was not worth it. The lesson is learned: Creative professionals should not ignore patent rights.

Trade Secret: A Patent Alternative

A trade secret may be a company or individual's most prized asset. Unlike patents, which require the filing of an application and, when granted, the disclosure of the patent for all the world to see, a trade secret is something that, first and foremost, is kept confidential. In fact, if one does not hold the details private, it may be lost forever.

How one goes about protecting the privacy of the information is essential to the nature of the protection that the law will afford it. A secret formula, a business plan and projections, or a treatment for a new movie are all things that are covered by copyright law. Yet, the way in which the work is handled can transform it and the protections the law can provide.

A company or individual must do two practical things to create and maintain a trade secret. First, it must make sure that only the people that need to know the secret are exposed to it. The more widely a secret is shared, the harder it is to maintain as a secret. Second, it must require that anyone who has access to the secret agree not to reveal it. This simple order is the one most often overlooked. A good practice is to have the recipient of the secret sign a nondisclosure agreement. An NDA, as it is commonly called, obligates the recipient to maintain responsible controls over the use of the secret, and, if the confidential information is maintained, the agreement is complete. If the recipient violates the NDA, severe penalties can attach.

Generally, trade secret law is governed by states. The Uniform Trade Secret Act (UTSA) serves as a model code for states, providing guidance for national uniformity to trade secret standards. Under the UTSA, the key elements for a trade secret include

1. *That it is not generally known or readily ascertainable through legal means.* This requires that one cannot go to public or commonly accessible information resources and discover the secret. It has to be truly private information.

2. *That the information has independent economic value based on its secrecy.* To be a trade secret protected by the UTSA, the secret has to be valuable in a way that can translate into something of real economic value.

3. *That the holder of the secret take reasonable steps under the circumstances to protect the secret.* If one fails to take such steps, including limiting who has access to the information and making sure that those who do have access respect its value and secrecy, then the protections afforded secret information can be lost.

Trade secrets are particularly important for software development, as engineering secrets can be embedded in computer codes. Many software developers keep the underlying code a secret even though it is also copyrighted. However, if a company tries to obtain a patent on its software, it loses trade secret status and protection, since patents, once granted, become public. Recognizing that the patent term lasts only for 20 years and the useful life of certain products never reaches two decades, software developers often eschew the patent track in favor of trade secret and copyright protection. Copyright applies as soon as the code is written. If one wants to register the copyrighted code with the Copyright Office (or must register as a necessary step in litigation), there is a special procedure for protecting software secrets. Rather than filing the entire work with the Copyright Office, as the law requires, in the case of confidential or secret information, the applicant is permitted to submit only the first 25 and last 25 pages of the code (which may consist of hundreds of pages of computer-readable text). Moreover, to add an extra layer of protection, the registration process allows the copyright owner to black out the majority of the information on the 50 attached pages, establishing only that there is a writing on the page, but making the content totally undecipherable. If this procedure is followed, not only can a copyrighted work be registered with the Copyright Office, the trade secret status can be maintained.

Chapter 19

The International View: It's a Small World After All

Creative works and the content rights associated with them do not rest at a nation's geographic borders. The power of thought expressed in books, film, music, graphics, paintings, sculpture, and photographs transcends space and boundaries. As a result, works are exchanged throughout the world in both the original format and language and in translated versions and revised formats.

In the digital era, where . . .

- A student in Athens, Greece, can enroll in a distance education course from the University of Georgia in Athens, Georgia;
- An author in London, England, can e-mail the draft of her book to an editor in New London, Connecticut;
- An Internet groupie from the Philippines can post a pirated version of *The Lord of the Rings* days after it is released to theaters in the United States;
- An auction website can offer for international sale memorabilia otherwise banned from sale under the laws of a foreign nation;
- A teenager in Bangkok can freely download and burn a CD of her favorite music from a file of someone she does not know in Budapest;
- A factory in China can turn out thousands of musical CDs that sound like the original;
- A printer in Peru can reproduce posters and photographs using scanners and inkjet printers;
- A baseball fan can log on to a renegade Italian site, www.yankees.it, and order World Series T-shirts at a fraction of the Major League Baseball price; . . .

one can appreciate that the commerce of copyrighted and trademarked works circles the globe.

A world in which rules of different countries apply unevenly is no longer fair for authors or users. The code word for creating international fairness is *harmonization*: If nations can harmonize their laws of copyright and trademark—establish shared, common principles that permit only a limited number of special exceptions in local environments—then an efficient expansion of commerce in works of intellectual property in a digital world can be achieved.

The Berne Convention: The International Copyright Standard

For centuries, nations organized compacts based on shared principles. In the area of copyrights and trademarks, such agreements have been around for more than 100 years. These agreements (treaties or conventions) and their organizing institutions serve as the basis on which most national laws are structured. The granddaddy of copyright treaties is the Berne Convention, on which we touched briefly in earlier chapters. The Berne Convention was inspired by Victor Hugo and the French intellectuals of the mid-19th century, who believed the individual author was being denied fair economic return on the fruits of his or her creativity. While it has been updated numerous times in the past 130 years, the Berne Convention has certain core principles, many of which sound familiar from our discussion of the U.S. Copyright Act:

- *A definition of specific rights.* Authors must be allowed to control certain key uses of their works. These include copying, public performance, public rental, public communication, and public distribution of their works.

- *A minimum term of protection.* The convention ensures that authors enjoy certain exclusive rights to their works for a minimum number of years, currently life of the author plus 50 years. All countries that belong to the Berne Convention may grant protection for a longer term; however, none can allow a shorter term. Today, the European and U.S. standard is life of the author plus 70 years.

- *No formalities.* An important principle of the Berne Convention is that no formalities should impede an author's entitlement to copyright protection. In particular, the former U.S. standards saying that each published work must have a proper copyright notice and be registered with the Copyright Office were contrary to this precept of the Berne Convention.

- *Limited exceptions to rights for public purposes.* As to limitations on rights, the Berne Convention recognizes free uses for education and news. The U.S. doctrine of fair use has been viewed as broader than the exceptions spelled out in the Berne Convention.

- *Fair treatment of foreigners.* Central to the Berne Convention and most international conventions is the principle that national laws should treat all persons equally, irrespective of where they live. Therefore, the Berne Convention requires all its signatory nations to treat the works of foreigners in the same manner as works of its own citizens. Put another way, a French citizen trying to protect his book from unauthorized copying in Spain should be treated no differently than a Spaniard would be treated.

- *National treatment.* An understanding of the Berne Convention is that nations are allowed reasonably to interpret or apply the obligations of the treaty in their own manner. This is not to say that signatories to a treaty can ignore their commitment to basic terms; rather, it means that precisely how the commitment is implemented may vary on a nation-by-nation basis. When the United States formally joined Berne, it required a ruling from the administrative agency for the treaty confirming that terms of U.S. law were consistent with the obligations of the Berne Convention. In recent and ongoing debates about digital copyright provisions, a common argument of representatives of owners against certain exceptions espoused by representatives of users (particularly those seeking new compulsory licenses, which are not formally recognized by the Berne Convention) is that any limitation on the broad grant of rights to owners is contrary to the Berne Convention and therefore not to be countenanced.

- *Droit de suite.* This right is the concept that an author's interest in a work remains even after the work has been sold. Under this principle, artists are entitled to share in the appreciated value of paintings and other artwork as a result of sales long after the creator sold his original work. This provision is one of the few Berne Convention sections that is optional, not mandated on all member states. Only if the nations where the artwork is bought and sold provide for such remuneration is the requirement enforced. If one of the two affected countries (assuming a sale across national boundaries) has not adopted a *droit de suite* provision, then the other nation need not enforce it in favor of the foreign national.

- *Droit moral.* Perhaps the signature principle of the Berne Convention is *droit moral,* or moral rights. Simply stated, the concept is that, aside from the economic interests an author has to exploit and benefit from a copyrighted work, there are noneconomic interests that should also be protected. Most particularly, an author's honor and reputation are deemed part of his or her creative endeavors, and the artist and his or her heirs should be entitled to protect that honor from the degradation that occurs when an original work is altered. We have more to say about moral rights in Chapter 25 in connection with the discussion of the prominent debate on the virtues and vices of colorizing black-and-white movies. Moral rights are implicated whenever digital alterations are made to copyrighted materials by someone other than the original author.

- *World International Property Organization (WIPO).* The Berne Convention is administered by WIPO. While not a judicial body governing copyright, WIPO provides practical and logistical support for the international harmonization of copyright rules. WIPO also is involved with most other intellectual property conventions, including trademarks and patents.

The United States Joins the Berne Convention after More Than a Half-Century of Debate

The headline in 1988 was that, after more than 50 years of sometimes polite, sometimes heated debate, the United States finally joined the Berne Convention. It had been ironic that the United States, the 20th century's leading exporter of copyrighted works, resisted joining the preeminent international convention. What was the problem, and how did things change?

The two biggest drawbacks of the Berne Convention were the absence of formalities and the presence of moral rights. The lack of prerequisites for obtaining a copyright was fundamentally at odds with the U.S. system, which relied on notice, registration, and renewal to organize its copyright system. Without a copyright notice, how would one know who held the right and for how long? Without registration and statutory renewal (which required the filing of a copy with the Library of Congress), how would one prove what the work was and what was the proper term of protection? Most nations of the world did not need these requirements, and they were able to enforce rights. So, starting with the major reform in the mid-1970s, the U.S. copyright law was amended to pave the way for the United States joining the convention.

Moral rights was a different story. The U.S. film production and software and print publishing industries, in particular, have relied on the concept of work for hire to maintain tight control over the public distribution of works. Their argument was that control was needed to recoup the financial investment in producing the work and make a profit. If an individual author could object to the way a film was released, a magazine edited, or a software program designed, not only could an investment be jeopardized, but profit could be lost. The solution for this concept came down to a sleight of hand; a legal analysis waved a wand and found that *U.S. law as a whole* (including copyright and the derivative right, trademark and Section 43(a), laws of defamation and slander, privacy, and publicity) *provided the equivalent of moral rights.* With a rationale embraced by Congress and WIPO, moral rights proved no longer an obstacle to U.S. passage of the Berne Convention.

On the other side of the ledger, the benefits of the United States joining Berne were substantial. The Berne Union was a ready-made institutional base for fighting piracy of film, software, and other digital content on a worldwide scale. Also, if the Berne Convention could be revised over time to harmonize with U.S. copyright principles (rather than the United States changing its core concepts), then the intellectual property of the United States could be transported to countries of the world, safe in the knowledge that the principles of protection embedded in American law were embraced elsewhere. With this goal in mind, in 1988 copyright owners broke with their past reluctance and pushed U.S. leaders in Congress and the government to accept the Berne Convention.

Eight years later, the United States led a WIPO-organized diplomatic conference to consider and ultimately adopt amendments to the Berne Treaty that became the basis for the DMCA and copyright reform in countries around the world (see Chapter 9).

While the influence of U.S. copyright principles within the Berne Union is substantial, there are other pressures for reform. For example, in 1999 a new treaty granting rights to performers (actors, musicians, and speakers) control over exploitation of their performances, much like composers and lyricists when their music is heard on radio stations. However, the Berne Union's adoption of a performer's right is optional for member states.

Also on the Berne agenda are matters of greater concern to less developed nations, like the proper treatment of folklore and aural works, but what is really important here is that the debate on copyright rights takes place on a world stage, and as the Berne Convention becomes universal, authors will be guaranteed control of their works and compensation for use of their creations no matter where it occurs.

Trademark Treaties: Paris, Nice, and Madrid

In trademark law, as in copyright, international treaties govern common standards. For trademark aficionados, the key conventions sound like cities in a sequel to Chevy Chase's movie *European Vacation*—Paris, Nice, and Madrid.

The Paris Convention dates back to 1883 and covers common standards for both trademark and patent laws. The principles in the Paris Convention are evident within the U.S. law, notably (1) a system of public registration, based on the principle of uniqueness and lack of confusion with other marks, which grants protection in classes of goods and services for a term of years, and (2) foreign nationals, whose mark is registered in one country, can apply for registration in a member state even without using the mark in that country.

In 1972, the United States took another important step in the internationalization of its trademark laws when it agreed to the Nice Convention Regarding Classification of Trademarks. The Nice Convention organizes and categorizes trademarks into 42 classes of goods and services. While the original U.S. classification scheme had over 100 different classifications, the Nice classification establishes broader categories with refinement within these categories. In a world made small by instant communications and economic treaties opening markets to trading of goods and services, the Nice system assures that the trademarks that apply cross-borders will have common definitions. Such uniformity supports efforts to clamp down on counterfeit goods and pirated services.

The dream of a single, international system for the protection of trademarks is embodied in the Madrid Agreement Concerning International Registration of Trademarks. Under the Madrid Convention, applying for registration in one country can result in the designation and protection of marks in other member countries. Often debated in U.S. Congress, the United States has thus far refused to join a unitary international system. The United States stands committed to a significant degree of international trademark standardization, but the ability to regulate trademarks on a national basis remains a core part of our intellectual property policy.

A single registration system was adopted by more than a dozen European countries in the mid-1990s, when the European Union implemented a Community Trademark Application (CTA) procedure. By filing a single application, the prospective registrant can obtain simultaneous protection in all 15 participating countries; another 12 candidate countries are in the process of negotiating to be included. (The 15 current participants are Austria, Belgium, Denmark, Finland, France, Germany, Greece, Ireland, Italy, Luxembourg, The Netherlands, Portugal, Spain, Sweden, and United Kingdom. The 12 candidate countries are Bulgaria, Cyprus, Czech Republic, Estonia, Hungary, Latvia, Lithuania, Malta, Poland, Romania, Slovakia, and Slovenia.) One filing for all these nations—quite a bargain. But the strategy of filing only one application is not always the best. It turns out that processing a CTA can take longer than the prosecution of an application in some of the participating countries. If one only needs protection in France, it may make sense simply to file for protection only in France. Further, because a registration review is conducted in the registries of all the nations, if only one country's registry poses a barrier to registration, the CTA will be denied, even though the trademark may be technically clear in all the remaining countries. If separate applications were filed, the protections would accrue in each of those cleared nations. In short, if one had a responsible search done in advance, the risks or benefits of a CTA could have been compared to the one-country-at-a-time approach, and the best result more effectively assessed.

Having covered the laws of copyright and trademark, as well as some of the collateral domestic and international concerns, we now turn in our next two parts to a focused discussion of content rights in established and new media. How do these rules work out in practice for the creative professional? Let's see.

Part Four

Content Rights:
The Media and Film

Chapter 20

News and Talk Programming: Competition for Content

Perhaps the most competitive arena in local television and the jewel in the crown of the national network organizations is their news, information, and talk programming. During the past decade, there has been a gradual movement of time allocation on local broadcasting stations from entertainment to news and talk. Comparing the daily schedules of stations from 1970 with those of 2000, one sees the entry of early evening local newscasts and late night competition. Independent and Fox Network affiliated stations claim a jump on late night information over their network affiliate competition with the 10:00 P.M. newscasts. National morning programs like *Today*, *Early Show*, and *Good Morning America*; news magazines such as *Dateline*, *60 Minutes*, *Prime Time Live*, *20/20*, and *48 Hours*; and Sunday morning interview shows, including *Meet the Press*, *Face the Nation*, *This Week*, and *Late Edition*, present up-to-the-minute information, contesting for viewership. Paralleling this trend is the evolution of all-news channels on cable television—CNN, MSNBC, Fox News, CNBC, and dozens of local-market 24-hour cable news channels.

Underpinning the development of news and talk programming is the critical issue of content. A blurry line marks what you can take from the competition in developing a story and who can claim ownership over the rights to information. Remember the copyright maxim: *Expression is protectable, ideas are not.* This is the single most important copyright precept in the development of news programming. Once a story is out, anyone can cover it. From a copyright law perspective, a broadcaster may quote portions of another news outlet's content, even without permission, provided it is within the limits of fair use. Since fair use is a fact-based analysis, caution must be exercised when using programming developed by the competition.

Moreover, a special provision of the Communications Act, the statute that governs the behavior of radio and television stations, interacts with copyright law and dictates what television and radio licensees can legally do. Under Section 325(a) of the Communications Act, a broadcaster cannot "rebroadcast" the programming of another station without the original station's permission. This means that, if a CBS station has videotape of a news story from an ABC competitor, even though the fair use doctrine of copyright law would justify limited use of the tape on air, the Communications Act requires that the CBS station obtain consent. In this respect, the Communications Act provision is in conflict with the fair use provision of the Copyright Act, because the copyright law would allow use without consent.

Recall the events in the example in Chapter 1 involving the gunman who marched into a television station, taking it over, only to kill himself on air. Reporting that compelling story involved use of off-air recordings of another station. Even if the local television competitors successfully developed a fair use claim under copyright law, the Communications Act has no equivalent exemption. Ironically, if the competing news organization using the TV footage was a *cable* news channel, the station using the footage would have been freer to grab the fair use portion and replay it on the air because the consent requirement only applies to "broadcast" facilities, which means radio and television stations. A television affiliate in the same market, creating the same story, could be violating a cardinal tenet of its broadcast license. This statutory conflict has never been resolved by the FCC or the courts. Therefore, broadcast affiliates need to seek permission if they intend to rebroadcast another station's programming. Fair use may be a defense to a copyright claim but not to a complaint filed with the FCC.

It is commonplace to have reporters from various media outlets set up outside a locale where news is breaking. Where each is writing his or her own story, filming events as they unfold, putting their own spins on developments, there is no problem. If one station's cameras capture an event unfolding before anyone else, it is a sure bet that, absent the most extraordinary circumstances, fair use will not justify another station's taking the video without permission. So competitive is the marketplace for news, so expensive the process of news gathering, that convincing an appellate court that use of another's work product was a fair use is difficult indeed.

Licensing news and information is an alternative. Because over 25% of a television station's budget can be allocated to news gathering, recouping some of that investment by licensing to third parties, especially those outside the market, is a practical necessity. Wholesaling video stories to organizations such as CNN allows stations to recover part of their investment when their news content airs in distant markets. Similarly, national news organizations can repackage programs with local emphasis and relicense their use.

Newscasts and Content Rights: Things to Consider

However, stations have to be careful that they hold the rights they grant to others. There are some misconceptions in this regard. Let us examine a few.

Interviews

Anyone who is interviewed owns his or her own words. While the station can claim copyright to the tape by virtue of direction, camera work, or editing, the subject of an interview holds rights to what he or she says. As a matter of good business practice, it makes sense to obtain releases from anyone who appears on camera. But that is not always practical, since interviews may be in response to fast-breaking events. The use and reuse of the interview can be justified on the basis of implicit consent and fair use. However, if challenged, a station could find that, after the initial broadcast, any use, including the licensing of a story to other news outlets, can create a legal exposure. The bottom line is this: Do not assume all interview footage shot by a station may be replayed without new permission.

Stringers

Many news stories are compiled by news-gathering specialists who are not regular employees. They may be hired to help produce a specific story or be in the business of selling stories they develop. In either case, very careful attention to their contractual relationships is necessary. Suppose, for example, a cameraman, who is not a regular employee but is paid to cover a story for an evening newscast, captures the video event of the year. What uses may the station make of that footage? One-time broadcast rights are clearly envisioned by the relationship, but how about resale of the footage to other stations or other news media, such as cable channels and foreign stations? How about clipping a photo out of the video and licensing rights to the photo to a newspaper or chain of newspapers or posting the image on a website? What about incorporating the footage into a videocassette on the "news stories of the year"? Absent an agreement, each of the uses constitutes a copyright exploitation that is not owned by the station. Unless a written agreement with the stringer transfers the work to the station, defines his or her contribution as a *work made for hire*, or specifically embraces reuses and resale to other media, those rights may not be held by the media. Only if the commonly accepted practices of the industries are very clearly known to cover these uses or the station's prior experiences with the stringer make it apparent that both parties anticipated such uses when the employment understanding was made and the fee paid, would the rights be held by the station.

The copyright rights of stringers, freelance authors, and photographers in a digital age are so important and complex that the U.S. Supreme Court was asked to resolve a dispute involving leading newspapers, magazines, online database services, and individual claimants. We discuss the 2001 decision in *The New York Times Company, Inc.* v. *Tasini* in detail in Chapter 30.

A variation of programming from stringers involves the corporate "whistle blower." To get the "inside story," some news media hire corporate employees to carry hidden cameras or tape recorders into business meetings. The tapes of confrontations may be telecast on news magazine programs such as *60 Minutes* and *20/20*. In one case, a network was caught in a novel copyright squeeze in its exposé of a grocery chain. The program included video footage taped surreptitiously by an employee. The store's attorneys raised the issue of copyright ownership of the videotape as well as fraud. While claims of libel are hard to sustain in light of the video proof, the grocery chain argued that, since the store's employee made the tape on the job, the store was the copyright owner under the work-for-hire rule and the network's broadcast was a copyright infringement. The novel argument, however, is burdened not only by a legitimate fair use defense but also by the argument that, unless the employee's job description covered taping meetings, it fell outside the scope of employment. The novelty of the claim, however, suggests that copyright infringement claims may become more common in an era of video reporting.

Viewer's Videotapes

With digital Minicams selling for under $1,000, the world of stringers expanded exponentially. When an amateur photographer captured on tape the police beating of Rodney King and the ensuing uproar after its disclosure, his video became the most celebrated amateur footage since Zapruder filmed the assassination of JFK.

George Holliday's tape of the beating of Rodney King was provided to a Los Angeles television station for local use. He reportedly received $150, not bad for a home movie. But no one could have predicted that the fuzzy shots would spark civil unrest, become a symbol for police brutality, and be seen around the world.

After the local airing, the television networks, local and national news magazines, and others clamored for copies, which were readily released by the LA television station. The tape achieved a level of notoriety rarely reached by home videos. However, while the station received on-air credit from other media, the LA broadcaster neglected to see if it had acquired the tape with an ironclad understanding of the station's rights. In fact, its contract acquiring the tape was loosely drafted and left a loophole that inspired a copyright infringement lawsuit by Holliday. The suit was ultimately dismissed because the judge interpreted the station's release of the tape to others within the understanding of the parties, an overly generous judicial interpretation of the deal between the station and Holliday. The station escaped liability, but it could have avoided the issue entirely with a simple but more thoughtfully prepared release.

As a word of advice to the creative professional workers at TV stations, any time a station obtains video footage from a viewer, get a release that allows the station to air the piece and disseminate it "in all mediums, now existing or hereafter created." Provide credit. Pay a reasonable license fee, but one based on the present value of the work, not the potential appreciated media value. Since most digital camera owners have no reasonable expectation that their home movies will make it big and the media outlet has the upper hand—it does not have to air the piece and most homemade videotapes are never seen on television—it is reasonable to obtain all useful rights for a modest sum. If the news department has the right nose for news, as our LA friends did with the Rodney King beating tape, it should pay for the tape. If the tape has commercial or hard news value, the money will be well spent.

There are firms in the business of tracking news events and licensing stations to use the videos they produce. One outfit in Los Angeles has a helicopter that trails traffic accidents on major thoroughfares and licenses footage that no other camera has caught. When LA broke out in riots after the Rodney King verdict, the helicopter crew caught the Reginald Denny beating on tape. That video also played nationally but for a fee. The local uses by LA stations were licensed; however, unlike the Rodney King footage, the helicopter entrepreneur and copyright owner captured the royalties from other media. The contrast of these stories underscores the evolving importance and exploitations that can be made of copyrighted videotapes. For the media professionals, it is urgent to appreciate that these works are not their own unless they are acquired outright. For the creative, professional videographer, the corollary is to retain what rights you may believe marketable in the future. At a minimum, a license should cover whatever needs are reasonably foreseen, which should include original and repeat telecasts. In cases of special footage, it should cover eventualities that might develop, such as licensing to a network or other news outlets as an integral part of a story. If the viewer knows the value of the tape or if another station in the market prizes it more, then bidding can go up. But in the marketplace, where fame is part of the coin of copyright and where use of a name in on-air credit can be worth a lot, stations should use that as part, perhaps a substantial part, of their consideration.

Rip and Read

It would be tempting for a radio station, eager to save a few bucks and still provide news and information, to deliver its hourly news headlines simply by reading the three-sentence news summaries that appear in the margins of many newspapers. This practice would push the envelope of what constitutes unprotectable facts as opposed to copyrighted expression. Taking more than 15 words of someone's news report is clearly dicey. Taking 15 words or more from 5–10 top stories of the day is even more problematic. With many news services, such as AP, Mutual, and

CNN providing news content for a price to any buyer, skimming stories off the top of a newspaper or magazine is a very questionable practice. Even though headlines are not copyrightable and quotation with attribution is appropriate in news reporting under the fair use doctrine, with the abundance of third-party licensed material, undisciplined use of third-party stories is legally suspect. To the extent that a station wants to save on news gathering while providing information to listeners and viewers, the strategy of "rip and read" other's works without payment should be flatly rejected.

Frame Grabbers

The digital photo analogy to rip and read is frame grabbing. With high tech equipment, publishable-quality stills can be made from videos. A digital machine that halts action with clarity and allows prints to be made enables the video media to make works available to print publishers. The photos derived from the video, which may require some cropping or touch-up, qualify as derivative copyrighted works. Stations should pay attention to this potential source of licensing. At the same time, they must also know the parentage of the video. If they grab frames from third-party videos or film and license or sell the stills, they may be violating someone else's copyright.

Bugs on Screen

In the past decade, the news media has sought more routine ways to make indelible identification of their work product. Hence, the birth of the bug. The current practice is to run on-screen, in the lower right or left corner, a logo for the news source. This trademark branding allows a copyright owner to ensure that, if video, which is relatively easy to copy and reuse, is appropriated by another, the source will be evident.

What is good for the national networks can be helpful for individuals, too. Digital cameras allow anyone to enter slugs, bugs, and other on-screen indications of source. If an amateur or professional is alert to what he or she is creating, then the idea of adding an identifier (name or logo) makes sense. While any digital markings can be undone, it takes effort and planning to do so. The markings can help in source identification if the question of authorship or authenticity arises. This is also true for all written work: place a copyright notice on the cover page and in footers of works distributed to third parties.

Titles of Newscasts

Action News and *Eyewitness News* are among the most common titles of newscasts. Yet, both phrases are registered trademarks, entitling the owners to assert rights against not only stations in their own markets but throughout the country. As a matter of practice, most stations that file federal trademark registrations do so to protect their status in their local areas. Nevertheless, the rights they secured through federal registrations are not so bounded.

The crucial point for federal trademark owners to appreciate is that, if their trademarks are registered and they learn of third-party use of the same mark, they must act promptly to demand that use cease or that it be licensed. Because broadcasting involves interstate commerce and commerce over technically wide geographic areas, the right to prevent use of the same program title in distant markets is well established. But sleeping on one's rights (in the legal term, *laches*) and allowing a third party to invest in building up a reputation transforms legal rights. Even if a broadcaster could have claimed exclusivity and stopped a use, that right could be lost if not enforced in a timely fashion.

The utility of enforcing federal trademark rights in the title of newscasts is made more urgent by the arrival of the Internet. Many stations have local Web pages under the ubiquitous www.(*station*).com. If a station has a registered trademark for the title of its newscast (*Action News*), not only can it claim www.actionnews.com but it can also prevent any other station in the country from using an identical name. (If you doubt it, review Chapter 15.)

Video Monitoring

In the 1980s, "video monitoring" became the new "clipping service" for the electronic media. A technological relative of the time-honored newspaper clipping service, video monitors set up shop by running a bank of VCRs, taping local and national newscasts, and selling clips to customers for a cool $125 per 5 minutes of tape. Starting out as a "mom and pop" business with a string of VCRs in the basement, the practice has grown into significant and sophisticated enterprises with national revenue in the tens of millions of dollars. Claiming that news is anyone's to take, these operations were challenged in a series of copyright lawsuits. The legal bottom line is this: Broadcast stations own their news programming, and the video monitors need a license to reuse the images. This is good news for broadcasters because it establishes that they can control an emerging market for focused information from their newscasts.

The principal difference between the video monitors and their newspaper clipping ancestors is that the newspaper services buy multiple copies of a newspaper and physically clip from the copies. Under the copyright *first sale doctrine*, the copies are owned by the purchaser and may be sold or given away, as long as no extra copies are made. By contrast, video monitors tape full newscasts off the air with commercial motivation (arguably a copyright infringement right there), then reproduce selected portions relevant to customers. Whether they are memory tapes (copies for people who forgot to turn on their home recorder when they or relatives were interviewed on camera or appeared in a "man in the street" shot) or more sophisticated telecast researching for a company concerned about newscasts on a particular topic (e.g., Philip Morris asking for all network and Top 10 market newscasts clips discussing tobacco issues), resale of the news is a new business opportunity for media outlets.

Sophisticated video monitors even fax summary reports for those who cannot wait for overnight delivery of the tapes. By grabbing a few frames and running edited transcripts, a quick report can be prepared on any newscast, and it can be faxed or e-mailed within minutes of airing. Unless licensed by the news media, all these uses—editing video clips and texts and frame grabbing—constitute multiple copyright infringements.

Unquestionably, video monitoring is a secondary use of the news content. While some stations fear it will increase the potential for lawsuits because it will be easier for third parties to spot libel or defamation when they can review tapes of live telecasts at their leisure and reflect on the content, video monitoring is here to stay. Broadcast stations and networks should assert their ownership of the content and either sell the clips themselves or license one of the willing video monitoring firms and recoup some of their costs.

Historical Writings and Plagiarism

There is a thin line between reporting historical facts and improperly claiming credit to the creation of works. Even Pulitzer Prize–winning authors can be ensnared in disputes. In January 2002, noted historian and author Steven Ambrose was forced to apologize for taking too much information from some of his source materials without adequate credit or quotation. The matter did not arise from a direct claim of copyright infringement, because the subject matter of the dispute—borrowing factual information from previously published works—is a gray area of copyright law. Rather, Ambrose was charged with plagiarizing published works, effectively weaving too much material from the work of others into his book and claiming personal credit and authorship. He is not the first, nor will he be the last, author trapped in such a web. Several decades earlier, Alex Haley, whose book *Roots* became one of the most acclaimed television series of all time, was accused of lifting the description of the voyage of slaves from Africa to the American colonies. Haley paid a significant sum to settle the claim.

In cases involving claims of plagiarism, the second author may not have copied passages from a previous work. Instead, the second author may be accused of taking the selection, organization, and arrangement of facts, and thereby short-circuiting his or her own research and writing requirements. A proper copyright analysis of this issue will take into consideration whether the selection, organization, and arrangement is dictated by the facts themselves (i.e., a natural order of things) or creative in choice and structure. Thus, a description of factual matters in chronological order or a recitation of the highlights of an event or career will receive little or no credit for copyright purposes. By contrast, the unusual juxtaposition of information or the insightful linking of events and analysis can create something copyright law will protect.

As noted in discussions throughout this book, a general statement of copyright law is that facts and ideas are not protected. A writer of history (or a newscaster) who borrows facts appearing in a published work is taking something that is not copyrighted. Nevertheless, copyright law grants protection to the words used to express the facts and the original selection, organization, and arrangement of facts. Even though the hard work needed to locate the facts, the so-called sweat of the brow embodied in individual research, is not a basis to grant copyright protection, originality of expression and creative composition are.

Despite the ambiguity under copyright law, scholarship and news reporting have higher demands. A serious author or newscaster who takes material from prior works or programs should adequately source the information, lest he or she be accused of plagiarism. Rigorous scholarship and news reporting can be more demanding than the law, and the damages are not monetary but scars to reputation or disgrace among respected colleagues.

News Management

Not too long ago, news specialists remarked about the way in which Soviet leaders doctored photographs to "eliminate" enemies of the state. Modern technology has only enhanced the capabilities of the media to manage news events. For example,

- During O. J. Simpson's trial, *Time* magazine was accused of darkening a photo of O. J., making him appear more sinister.

- The credibility of NBC's news magazine *Dateline* was brought into question when it was revealed that it had staged an explosion of an automobile to prove that the placement of gas tanks was a public hazard.

- The Russians were up to their old tricks, painstakingly editing and digitally mastering hours of tapes of a sick President Boris Yeltsin to produce a 3-minute telecast showing him in the best form possible on the eve of Russia's 1996 election.

While copyright law gives owners control over the content in their works and technology makes it difficult to spot alterations, the news media have a special obligation. Although entertainment and opinion-oriented articles permit exaggeration, video news must maintain a standard of honesty when it comes to reporting events. In a digital age, it may be only the public's trust of its news sources that separates fact from fiction. If facts are manipulated, even though copyright law may protect the product, society suffers. It is the obligation of the news operations to guarantee that the public trust is honored.

These are a few of the highlight issues in news programming. Next, we learn about another crucial aspect of programming, music.

Chapter 21

Content Rights: The Realm of Music

Music has been at the center of many important, hotly disputed copyright conflicts for the past 100 years. In the digital content revolution, music continues this time-honored role. From music's complex relationship with radio and television broadcasters, to the use of music in film and television production, to pirated music on tape and disk, to the Internet, MP3, and Napster, fair exploitation of music has been a burning question in the development of copyright rules respecting ownership and use. Beginning in the early part of the 20th century and growing more forceful during the ensuing decades, the debate over just compensation for use of music has been as contentious as it has been entertaining.

Core Licenses for Music

Flowing from these disputes, four crucial licenses took shape and are now an essential part of copyright law and the way in which musical creators are rewarded. The broadcast media—radio and television stations—offer a perfect place to start consideration of these licenses.

Performance License

Most fundamentally, broadcast media *perform* music. The radio industry is, by and large, the single largest performance outlet for music. As discussed earlier, the right to perform music on radio and television is licensed by ASCAP, BMI, and SESAC, as the three major performing rights societies, and by a host of smaller operations and individuals that grant rights in libraries of music or individual compositions.

Synchronization License

Synch rights involve copying music onto film or video and associating the words and songs with images. Most television programs and films merge musical components with photography. Advertising also makes significant use of music. Granting a synch license—in other words, clearing music works for that purpose—is legally distinct from granting a public performance license and generally handled by different music agents. The Harry Fox Agency is probably the best known of the group; however, many others also grant these rights.

Master Use License

Once a musical performance is recorded, there is often no need to rerecord the work using different musicians or orchestras. You can simply use the LP, tape, or CD. However, to exploit the original rendition requires copying the sound recording, which is the province of the record label that made the original. Recording companies license the copying, and deals must be made directly with them.

Compulsory (Mechanical) License

A special provision of copyright law allows that, once a musical work is published, anyone can create recordings of one's own adaptation of it for public distribution and play on mechanical devices. A procedure spelled out in the Copyright Act comes into play whenever a negotiated mechanical license is unavailable. Procedures must be followed and fees paid according to the rules set forth in the Copyright Act and accompanying regulations. The compulsory license may be an alternative to the mechanical license, but it requires that the media hire the artists to create the adaptation.

Let us take a closer look at these four crucial musical rights and licenses (Figure 21-1).

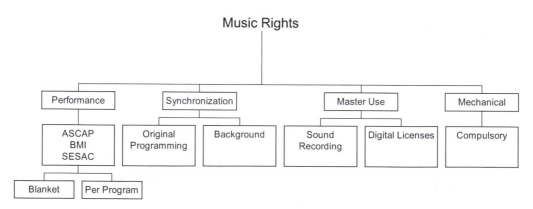

Figure 21-1   Music Rights

Performance Rights

Since the 1950s, ASCAP has labored, quite successfully, under a federal consent decree. The decree was issued because, as an association of competitors, ASCAP challenged federal antitrust laws. As noted in Chapter 17, these provisions hold that *conspiracies* (that is, more than two people) *in restraint of trade* (that is, setting prices or requiring customers to buy or license one product, such as an unpopular song, to obtain the rights to another product, say, a popular song) are illegal. ASCAP, as an association of thousands of songwriters, which licenses all the works in its repertoire on a total or blanket basis, technically fits that definition. However, the radio industry, and later the television and cable television industries, needed the economies of scale that derive from blanket licensing. What has evolved is a system of licensing reviewed by a federal magistrate, whose job it is to see that the music license fee structure is reasonably fair to the composers and the users.

For radio stations needing to perform hundreds of different popular or classic tunes on a 24-hour-a-day basis, blanket licensing of a whole repertoire is a bitter (expensive) pill that makes sense. Even though stations initially argue that radio play helps to sell recordings and therefore the stations should not have to pay for the privilege of promoting record sales, the truth is that the stations make a lot of money from the public performance of popular songs. So, licensing is a must, and blanket licensing is an efficient way to go. There is no need to identify and clear works one at a time. Hundreds of songs a day, thousands of songs a year, may be publicly performed without legal anxiety.

Of course, for some stations, such as all-news radio outlets, music is a minor part of programming, compared with the talk component. However, no station escapes the need to license the performance of music, if only to ensure that commercials with music can be aired. To fit all users, the performing rights societies have established special licensing fees for stations that have less than a full music repertoire.

For television stations, the use of music may also be sporadic. Typically, programming originating from the network comes with music performance rights attached. Local newscasts and public affairs shows, which can occupy up to 25% of a station's programming fare, contain some, but not a predominant amount of, music. Program theme music may be licensed at the source or composed by company employees.

In general, syndicated programming creates the greatest need for a television station to license music. By tradition, most syndicated shows are sold to local television stations without music performance rights. However, with the proliferation of daytime talk, game, and reality shows, which contain little music other than in a theme, the need for blanket licensing diminishes. More than 20 years ago, because it seemed to be paying very high music license fees, the broadcast industry challenged the prevailing blanket system in court. The television stations argued they were obligated to pay for music clearances they never used. The argument was positively received, and a decision resulted in the creation of the *per-program license*. The per-program license was developed as an alternative to blanket fees. We next contrast the two fee arrangements.

The Blanket License Allows Broadcasters to Pay a Set Fee and Use as Much Music as They Please

The blanket system allows a television station to use every song in the repertoire of the performance rights society, actually millions of songs, in exchange for a set monthly fee. The station can use as much or as little as it pleases. The fee itself is like a tax on revenue derived from programming, and the payments are collected much like the Internal Revenue Service collects taxes, with the completion of forms. Both advertising and program revenue, as well as on-air mentions where value is quantifiable (airline, hotel, or restaurant trades or credits; equipment leases; messenger services, etc.) is totaled and a percentage, averaging about 1.5% of income for radio to 1% of income for television, is assessed. Each station is allowed to take some deductibles off the top; the adjusted revenue is then calculated and the percentage applied. ASCAP and BMI routinely audit their licensees for accuracy in their reporting.

Per-Program License Offers a Break If Not as Much Music Is Used

By contrast, a per-program license measures actual use and charges fees accordingly. The per-program license involves a compromise and a complex formula. The rationale of the per-program formula is that stations should pay a licensing percentage according to how much money qualified music generates, and they should also be able to segregate programs that utilize ASCAP or BMI music but not both. A cost is paid for the privilege of opting out of the blanket fee in terms of keeping accurate records, but the effort can result in significant savings.

Briefly, the per-program license fee formula takes into consideration, on a market-by-market basis, (1) how much revenue ASCAP (or BMI) would be entitled to under the blanket approach, (2) each station's relative share of the total based on ratings, and (3) an X factor. The X factor is a 40% premium for calculation purposes. This station-by-station total is then multiplied by a fraction consisting of the revenue specifically generated from programs utilizing ASCAP (or BMI) music as a fraction of total station revenue from nonnetwork programs. An "incidental or ambient fee" of 15% of the blanket fee tops off the total. This charge covers most other uses of music, including music in commercials and news or public affairs programs.

The per-program license requires that stations keep good records of music performed and revenues with regular submissions of cue sheets (songs performed) and financial reports. On balance, if more than 40% of a station's weekly, nonnetwork programming revenue comes from programs that contain no ASCAP (or BMI) music, then the per-program formula saves the station money. When music license fees for big market stations can cost hundreds of thousands of dollars a year, the savings can add up fast.

Both the blanket and the per-program station licenses cover all nonnetwork programs; that is, programs licensed from syndicators and those produced locally. The performing rights societies negotiate separate contracts with the major networks for fees covering all network shows. Since the 1980s, the societies have negotiated directly with cable networks for performance licenses as well. Telecasts by affiliates of the network programming are therefore excluded from the blanket and per-program fee arrangements.

As noted, BMI adopted its own version of the blanket and per-program fees, which it offers all broadcast licensees. By comparison, SESAC, the much smaller European and classical music performing rights organization, typically licenses its repertoire on a fixed-market fee basis. Because it lacks the pop star recordings and performances, its charges are relatively modest. This society collects roughly 5% of the total musical fees paid. A few foreign performing rights organizations, including some in Europe, also license U.S. facilities. With licensing rights well exceeding half a billion dollars per year, performance revenues take a big bite out of the broadcast industry's wallet. Nevertheless, the entertainment value of music is undeniable. Try watching a movie with no music and see what you think.

The performance license for broadcast stations is only one kind of license offered by the performance rights societies. All other venues that offer music to the public are subject to licensing. This includes nightclubs and concert halls, restaurants that pipe in music or have a pianist playing during dinner, dance schools, and recital locations. One of the most hotly contested arenas is the Internet. We have more to say about the disputes that raged with respect to music on the Internet in Chapter 29.

Synchronization Rights

Producing original programming with music attached involves synchronization rights. Even if a station has a performance license, such permission does not cover copying the music to video or film. That merger of sound and images must be separately licensed. Let us take a closer look at how creative professionals who produce movies and videos clear music rights.

Original Programming

Most original programming contains music. Virtually all broadcast and cable television programs contain music. Even videos shown at conventions or professional meetings utilize music as a lure for attention. Theme or background music is an integral part of these programs. In movies, the soundtrack can be a big selling point for popular films. If musical recordings are being recorded onto the film or video, then a synchronization license must be secured for each song played. For programs that will be exhibited or televised, these rights are an essential part of production costs. Failure to clear these rights can render an expensive program unusable.

Background Music and Incidental Uses

How often does an on-the-scene telecast involve the incidental copying of music? A parade marches by and the performing band's rendition of a popular song is part of the video account. A sportscaster sums up the local team's weekly highlights by using background music to make a point. If the music is performed live and no independent copy made, there is no obligation to clear synch rights. The performance license permits the rendering of the music. However, if the station composes the video with music in anticipation of telecast or if it records the show as it is being televised live, then synch rights come into play. It is incumbent on the station to identify each composition to be used and obtain synch rights prior to telecast. Since it is often easier to replace a song with a comparable song before the telecast (e.g., one generic clarinet swing solo by an unknown artist in place of another performed by Benny Goodman), knowing at the outset whether a piece is going to be prohibitively expensive in relation to the program's overall costs is vital.

One special exemption under copyright can be effectively used to eliminate much of the synch headache. Under the *ephemeral copy exemption*, broadcast stations that hold performance licenses may use that right to justify making copies of music for limited purposes. Originally conceived as a way to allow radio stations to copy music from records to smooth the transition between songs, thereby allowing for playing many songs in a row with no need to cue the titles one at a time, the ephemeral copy license allows copying of music by "transmitting organizations." Those qualifying for the exemption are broadcasters licensed by music performance societies, under the blanket arrangements or any specific performing rights contract.

Under this exemption, stations can incorporate selections in any programming, provided that the use of the program is completed in 6 months and then either archived or destroyed. Since stations that warehouse programming for some time may replay pieces years later, technical violations of the exemption are common in the industry. To date, there has been no litigation against a station that held onto the work more than the 6-month retention period allowed under Section 112 of the Copyright Act; indeed, fair use may allow retention even beyond the period allowed by Section 112. However, if there is any expectation that the work will be reaired or marketed after the 6-month period, any exploitation could trigger a copyright infringement claim. Particularly as stations and networks dip into their archives to create new programs or rebroadcast old shows, determining whether all music is cleared may be the new game in town. Care should be taken with respect to any future use of these programs.

Master Use License

A commonly forgotten music clearance issue involves master use license rights. In part, this is because taking musical clips from CDs is extremely easy; if the synch rights have been attended to, why worry? Since 1972, however, the manufacturers of the sound recordings have been entitled to a limited number of copyright rights. Prior to 1972, the companies that made the records owned no independent copyright in their recordings. In 1972, Congress amended the Copyright Act and added sound recordings as a new category of protected works. This was done in response to rampant piracy of audiotapes. The rights granted to recording companies were limited, however, to reproduction, preparation of derivative works, and public distribution. Now, whenever music is taken directly from a post-1972 record, the manufacturer of the sound recording must be consulted and rights cleared.

With the arrival of the digital age, recording companies successfully established an additional copyright right, the right to control public performance of a sound recording by means of a digital audio transmission. For decades, during the era of traditional, analog transmissions, radio stations in particular had no obligation to compensate recording companies when music was performed. While the composers and publishers of original musical works were paid, the company that recorded the singers and musicians were not. This changed in 1995, when Congress yielded to the argument that some compensation should be made to recording companies when the audio transmission is digital, not analog. If listeners had sophisticated equipment and recorded a digital transmission, the near perfect copies could ruin the recording company's market. So, while nothing formal was done in copyright law to prevent the home recording, the recording companies were granted the right to receive payments via a compulsory license.

In 1995, with digital sound still in its infancy, the change in law went unnoticed by the public at large. However, as the 21st century began, digital was the medium of choice. The FCC has ordered television stations to switch to digital television services, satellite services offering hundreds of digital radio channels to home and automobiles are now available, and radio facilities are also changing over. The impact of the copyright law changes mean that how music is to be compensated when publicly performed will take on a different shape in the coming years. Combined with the anticircumvention rules of the DMCA, encrypted digital transmissions that require monthly access fees, pay-per-play, and anticopying codes make major changes to the practices of home recording and storage of popular music.

Mechanical License

The mechanical license is a long-established copyright principle, which permits anyone to create his or her own version of published music for play on mechanical devices, such as record, tape, and CD players, provided a statutory fee is paid. The compulsory license, which is used instead of a negotiated mechanical license, has three key parts.

First Performance by the Copyright Owner

The license affects only *published* music. In other words, the creator of a song is entitled to choose the first release of the work. Who sings a song and how it is marketed are within the absolute control of the copyright owner. This is a parallel of the copyright law's *first sale doctrine* that gives the copyright owner control over that initial public release.

New Arrangement Must Be Faithful to the Original

The license allows for artistic interpretation and variations, up to a point. There can be no significant change in the lyrics or melody under the compulsory license. Although parody—fair use—is another way to exploit a work without any clearance, if the compulsory license is employed, the new version must render the original in a faithful way, even if substantive changes are made for purposes of comment and criticism. The variation of style is key. In some instances, a song released by one artist can become a signature piece of another. For example, although Liza Minelli first sang "New York, New York" for the film of the same title, Frank Sinatra did his version as well. The publishers of the Sinatra recording were entitled to use the compulsory license to ensure that the rights were cleared for their production. Like "Chicago," "New York, New York" is closely associated with Ol' Blue Eyes.

Accounting and Paying the Fee

The license requires filing a notice with the Copyright Office and paying a fee of about a penny plus per minute of playing time or about 7 cents per song, whichever is greater. The fees relate only to publicly distributed copies. A report must be filed with the Copyright Office and the copyright owner. Regular follow-ups on sales figures must also be submitted. Rates can change periodically, so it is best to check on the most current rules.

Trademark also rears its head in music issues. While the easiest way to conceive of a trademark is a word or design, musical themes are also protectable as trademarks. The NBC chime is a perfect example of a musical signature that identifies the source of services. Similarly, television and radio introductory theme songs can constitute trademarks. But, remember that a trademark is a short phrase. Therefore, it is important to develop a cogent summary of a musical theme in a handful of notes to gain protection as a trademark. While the full song is copyrighted, the central lyric can be the signature sound. Programs such as *M*A*S*H* and *Seinfeld* are good examples of shows with thematic musical elements that may be protected as trademarks.

If a musical element is a trademark, an additional benefit is secured. Although copyrights last for limited times, trademarks are protectable in perpetuity, as long as they are in use and not abandoned. Themes can extend the licensing value of works well past the era when the copyrights would fall into the public domain. Since most television shows are under copyright protection, this is not an issue today. However, in the coming years, as shows enter the public domain, even as they have continued life on new media such as cable, Internet, and whatever the future brings, the trademark status of show themes will add to the value of the works.

Chapter 22

Advertising: Being Content with Commercial Content

Advertising is chock full of fascinating content rights issues. Ads often contain music (new and old), video and photos, jingles, trademarks of the advertiser and its competitors, digitally doctored images, claims, and come-ons. The commercial nature of advertising greatly circumscribes the scope of third-party content that can be used without permission; in short, what is fair use. While our focus is on copyright and trademark, advertising is closely scrutinized not just by competitors, but by public agencies and private watchdogs that want to make sure the advertising is accurate and not deceptive or misinforming.

Most obviously, commercials on television, radio, and cable generate the money to pay the bills at the facilities; however, the outlets cannot be insensitive to the copyright and trademark issues contained in advertising because they bear direct responsibility for errors. Sometimes, failure to attend to the logic of the law can result in heavy exposure for the stations in terms of lost revenue, monetary damages, and harm to reputation. Commercials produced for radio, television, and cable fall into three types: ads created by sponsors, ads they create for others, and ads they create themselves to promote their own operations.

Third-Party Spots

When selling commercial time to others, media outlets usually receive the finished spot from the advertiser and play it repeatedly. Since the content of these spots is given to the station by the ad agency or client, the outlet should require by a written agreement that the content of the spot already be cleared at the source. If music, photographs, trademarks—any third-party material—is used, a specific representation that the matter is either cleared or otherwise allowed for use must be provided, and the sponsor or agency must be prepared to stand by that warranty. Any spot from a third party that does not contain these representations or warranties should be not be aired, no matter how tempting the payment money. Only if a contract with the advertiser or the agency provides written assurance that the spot contains no infringement of copyrights, trademarks, or service marks as well as related rights of privacy and publicity can a station be assured that the advertiser will stand in front of the outlet in case of infringement. Not only is this good practice, most liability insurance policies for media outlets require such documentation.

Nevertheless, such contractual assurances may not be sufficient to shield the station from liability. The contracts between the station and the advertiser are not binding on the copyright owner or trademark proprietor. Therefore, station personnel experienced in looking for these issues should review all spots before they air and raise questions that come to mind. For example:

- *Music.* Is a theme used in the spot? Is it familiar? If so, has it been cleared?
- *Video.* Does the spot contain third-party video? Is there a known source for it, and has it been cleared?
- *Photos.* What pictures are used in the spot? Who took them? Are celebrities or trademarks of others prominent? Have the copyrights and images been authorized for this use?
- *Trademarks.* Are logos of anyone other than the advertiser used in the spot? If so, is the content of the spot designed as comparative advertising or is some exploitation of another's trademark designed to promote an association between sponsor and competitor? Is that association authorized?

The station's in-house reviewer should make certain that the spots have all vital material cleared. As publishers, stations can bear liability even if they innocently air the spot. Copyright law, for example, makes an innocent publisher liable for minimal damages of $200, even in the absence of any knowledge of wrongdoing. More critically, these disputes can tie up personnel and run up legal bills. Forethought in the handling of spots can eliminate the potential for these undesired expenses.

Spots Produced for Others

Many broadcast licensees are blessed with marvelous production facilities. For them, the ability to produce spots for advertisers can be a significant source of extra revenue. But if a station composes the spot for a client, great care must be exercised to ensure that no copyright or trademark infringements are embedded in the commercial. Not only would the station have violated a duty to the client, it would also bear direct liability to the owner of the works or the marks. Moreover, the opportunity for foul-up is high because (1) the desire to please the client is great, (2) recall of third-party material from available sources or archives is easy, (3) spots are often produced quickly, and (4) cutting corners helps maximize revenue return.

Every element of a spot should be analyzed as to proper use in commercials. In-house materials available from the station's archives, like photos or video clips, may be the property of the station, but it is a separate question whether they can be used in advertising. For example, photographs taken by station personnel, which are clearly the copyrighted property of the station, may include individuals whose right of publicity could be violated if included in a commercial. A spot for a local shoe store could not use a station's photo of Ken Griffey sliding into home, without clearing the right with Griffey's agent. If Griffey is shown wearing Nike shoes and they are prominent in the spot, the ad may suggest that Griffey is a spokesman for the company. If that is not true, Nike may object, forcing the station to pull the ads and compensate Nike and Griffey, even perhaps the shoe store. Video obtained from a viewer who responded to a hotline request for breaking news stories should not be included in a spot without consent, even though the station purported to obtain "all rights" to the tape.

As discussed in the preceding chapter, music should be scrutinized for its source and cleared. The use of common musical notations in commercials is a recipe for an infringement claim. A local department store thought its Christmas spot that contained five bars from "Rudolph, the Red Nosed Reindeer" was perfectly acceptable. After all, the song was as old as the hills. It turned out that Rudolph is still under copyright. The grandson of the composer learned about this spot and was on the telephone, threatening an infringement case. The settlement cost the station and the advertiser far more dearly than if the music had been cleared in advance (or an alternative song selected).

Station Promos

Even if the station is not in the business of producing spots for advertisers, every station creates and airs its fair share of station promos. These spots contain clips of upcoming news stories (motorist distracted while eating a McDonald's Happy Meal crashes a Ford automobile into local Wal-Mart), use familiar logos in contests (guess where the DJ Donnie will appear and win a GE microwave oven), or associate the station personnel with events of the day (sports anchor witnesses local football players in fistfight at training camp). As with spots for clients, someone needs to scrutinize the content of these ads and make sure that all the elements are appropriate for inclusion. While greater latitude is allowed when presenting spots for upcoming evening newscasts, because the advertisements themselves are creatures of the news programming, there is no absolute safe harbor in using third-party content in advertising.

Generally, the fair use doctrine is not available for commercial content. While not an absolute rule, it is a good standard to live by, because commercials can be easily shown to lie on the negative side of several of the fair use formula criteria:

- *Commercial use.* The spots start out as commercial content. Although public service announcements (PSAs) are an exception, the vast majority of aired commercials are designed to generate profits for someone.

- *Substantiality.* Because spots are short, most often ranging 10–60 seconds, use of third-party materials will be for only a fraction of the total and, therefore, will encompass a relatively modest amount of time. However, since the sponsor has a message to present, taking the original work of others is probably done because of the fame of the original work. Therefore, even though only a small percentage of a copyrighted work is involved, the taking is often the "heart of the original" and hence substantial.

- *Economic impact.* Many copyrighted works are or could be sold for use in commercials. A thriving business licenses the use of copyrighted material, including videos, photos, and music, for commercial use. Think of the widely telecast spots for U.S. Healthcare, incorporating old film footage from Laurel and Hardy, Buster Keaton, Charlie Chaplin, and others. Or the Alcatel spots featuring Martin Luther King on the steps of the Lincoln Memorial, delivering his "I Have A Dream" speech to no one. Each video clip from a classic film or from the archives of Dr. King must be cleared.

  By contrast, some copyright owners actively forswear any interest in allowing their work to appear in commercials. The composer of an inspirational theme, such as "Chariots of Fire," may simply refuse to allow the work to be licensed for commercial purposes or certain types of products or services. Therefore, the impact on the marketplace value for the works, a key copyright test, is usually a heavy negative for the infringer.

Treatment of trademarks poses an interesting contrast in advertising. During the 1950s, the standard television spot compared the advertiser's products to the infamous Brand X. Wisk got out stains better than Brand X. Not surprisingly, so did Tide. No mention was made of a competitor's product name for fear that casting negative aspersions would result in a lawsuit. Then, in the early 1970s, the Federal Trade Commission clarified public policy: By all means, use a competitor's trademark in the ad to generate useful marketplace comparisons for the consumer. The key, of course, is that all claims must be truthful. Paint a competitor in a false light and one faces assertions of trademark misuse and deceptive advertising.

This policy shift has not guaranteed that all spots are true; however, it permits Ford to say that Taurus outsells Toyota Camry and Honda Acura by two to one; it allows Safeway to say its prices are lower than Ralph's or D'Agostinos'; it ensures that Channel 4 can say its newscasts are watched in twice the number of homes as Channel 7's, as long as the statements are based in truth. While some puffery creeps into advertising, the stations bear the burden of challenging claims made by advertisers that are questionable, lest they be liable for contributing to patently false claims and trademark misuse.

While we focus on the media side of the ledger in noting commercial rules, the rules for ad agencies and PR firms also deserve mention. Often, they need to be as attentive as the media to the copyright and trademark issues of their work. When dealing with sponsors, advertising agencies are independent contractors. If the arrangement between the sponsor and the ad agency is not in writing or if, as is often the case, it lacks a clear *work for hire* copyright clause, then copyright law holds that the agency owns the copyright to the spot, even though the advertiser has the right to use it in its market. How far an agency can go in redirecting advertising for different clients is a delicate matter, but if there is no understanding to the contrary, the option at least exists for the agency to reuse the ideas and images in the created spots.

Chapter 23

Sports Content: The Olympic Law of the Rings and Other Games

The quadrennial quest for the gold has turned into alternating hot and cold biannual events. With the split of the Olympics into winter and summer games that are now held 2 years apart, viewers are surfeited with information and advertising associated with the golden rings. Among the trademarks in the United States, the Olympic symbols have a rarefied status—they are the subject of their own special trademark statute.

The Amateur Sports Act and the Olympic Symbols

Passed in 1978, the Amateur Sports Act is a special warning to the world that the Olympic symbols are trademarks not to be falsely used. The statute protects the words *Olympic*, *Olympiad*, *Citius Altius Fortius*, and the five interlocutory rings, and it prohibits any mark that falsely represents a connection to the U.S. Olympic Committee or the International Olympic Committee. Any unauthorized use of the marks in trade or advertising or that promotes programming or athletic events can be challenged by the U.S. Olympic Committee. The statute is so broad as to grant an absolute property right to the words. The U.S. Supreme Court held that the U.S. Olympic Committee's control over *Olympic* is unlimited, even by the Lanham Act defenses to a claim of trademark infringement. The rule does not infringe the First Amendment.

While phrases like *Atlanta '96* or *Lillehammer Games* test the limits of the statute but do not violate it, it has been held that the "Gay Olympic Games" is a violation. For the Winter Games at Salt Lake City, Utah, in 2002, a host of new trademarks were registered well in advance of the start of the Olympics. The phrases, like *Salt Lake 2002* and *SLC 2002*, are not covered by the Amateur Sports Act but are fully protected by the trademark laws of the United States and other nations.

The elements of the statute are as follows:

- *Protected trademarks.* Olympic, Olympiad, Citius Altius Fortius, and the five interlocutory rings.
- *Prohibition.* Any unauthorized use of the marks for purposes of trade, inducing the sale of goods or services or promoting any theatrical exhibition, athletic performance, or competition.
- *Penalties.* The statute authorizes as much as $250,000 for penalties, injunctive relief, and destruction of offending material.
- *Protected parties.* The International Olympic Committee and the U.S. Olympic Committee and their licensees have standing to bring an action.

For the media, the test of the statute comes in two key ways. First, advertising that contains Olympic symbols must be screened and aired only with confidence that the users of the Olympic trademarks hold rights. Contracts with advertisers should contain guarantees that the use is authorized.

Second, programming must be monitored. There is no prohibition on news reporting of events or scores relating to the Olympics. It is touchier when stations not affiliated with the network licensed to broadcast the Olympic games try counterprogramming to attract an audience interested in the Olympics. The programming is protected by the First Amendment or may be copyright fair use; however, the use must be truthful and the promos for the programming must not suggest a false association with the games and a station or sponsor.

Olympic Controversies

During the 1996 Summer Games, there was much grousing by non-NBC affiliates as to how the network, which had paid billions to televise the Summer Games for many years, controlled access to events. While it is common for sports telecasts to be blacked out on nonaffiliated stations, in 1996 NBC took this practice one step further by restricting access to press briefings of Olympic news-related stories. Tightly controlling media access to news developments within the Olympic Village, NBC was able to prevent the other networks from televising news stories within the confines of the Olympics.

This control sparked controversy among the networks and brought charges of news management. While, under copyright law and the contracts that enforce the acquisition of those rights, NBC had the legal ability to control media access to the venue and the content that emanated from it, whether it be sports or news reporting, the degree to which it limited access to public statements by Olympic officials was unprecedented. NBC learned its lesson and did not repeat this news management practice when a judging scandal became hot news at the Salt Lake City 2002 Games. Other news media had full access to the news conferences and athletes.

Although doctoring photographs or staging events to re-create actual events are unacceptable media practices that have overt copyright implications, the 1996 isolation of news media from ongoing events raises novel concerns that may be more ethical than legal. Except for the DMCA's provisions regarding technological protection measures, copyright law facilitates control of content use rather than regulation of access to content. The degree to which other media should be restricted from unfolding events of public importance poses an important content dilemma. Does the policy supporting copyright law, which permits exclusivity in ownership of works tempered by fair use, need further recalibration? Will the legal tools at the command of the media now work against society's interests in a vigorous and competitive press? These issues will undoubtedly test the resolve of policy makers.

Copyright and access to content were not the only issues highlighted at the Olympics. Trademark questions also abound. The Atlanta Games were, by all accounts, the most commercialized Olympics ever, but the Salt Lake City Winter Games of 2002 gave their summer brethren a run for the money. Licensing rights to Olympic symbols are carried to an art form by the U.S. Olympic Committee. Dozens of product categories have been carved out, and many companies pay handsomely for the privilege of calling themselves an "Official Sponsor of the Olympic Games."

However, that did not stop some creative professionals from pushing the Amateur Sports Act to its limit. For example, during the Atlanta Games, Nike—not an "official" sponsor—took over a warehouse just outside the Olympic Village and emblazoned it with the Nike "swoosh." Visitors and passing camera crews would have been surprised to learn that Nike was not an authorized sponsor.

Counterfeit merchandise also generates much attention, because unofficially logoed merchandise can sell for a fraction of the cost of the real thing. Before official Olympic merchandise appeared in Salt Lake, 75% of all hats, T-shirts, and knickknacks were bootleg copies. Trademark police cleaned out the "bad stuff" to help ensure that tens of millions of local sales went to providers of the "right stuff." This experience was consistent with every other recent Olympics. Private and public police now scrutinize the local venue outlets very carefully, and thanks to international treaties and federal legislation that specifically targets counterfeit goods designed to deliberately mislead consumers and misrepresent the source of branded goods, domestic and international purveyors of unauthorized

Olympic and trademark goods can anticipate huge fines, damages, and even jail time, if caught.

Then, too, NBC's advertising practices played a role. While Olympic sponsors had first crack at network commercial availabilities, if any category for commercials did not sell out, they were offered to others. When product categories failed to sell out to official sponsors, spots were made available to competitors, who gleefully rushed in. As a result, in 1996, MCI spots aired in time slots that the official sponsor, AT&T, vacated. To the national audience, the placement of MCI spots within Olympic telecasts provided the same effect as if the upstart carrier paid for the privilege of being an Olympic sponsor.

The moral of the Olympic story is pay heed to intellectual property. The "road to the gold" is paved with copyrights and trademarks.

Digital technology has made major inroads in Olympic events, coverage, and merchandise. For the 2002 coverage, NBC featured digitally imposed flags on ice lanes to identify the home nation of speed skaters. "Simulcom" technology, pioneered by a small European firm, enabled NBC to superimpose two downhill skiers on the same path to show differences in form and speed on the same course. *The Today Show* revealed that one of the most popular Olympic gifts was a face photo superimposed on pictures of Olympians in action. Youngsters dreaming of Olympic gold could see their faces on the bodies of Sarah Hughes and Michelle Kwan in mid-air. Alert to copyright implications, *The Today Show* host, Matt Lauer, checked with the company making the digital pictures about copyright permissions for photographs. Yes, they pay photographers for rights. But what about the athletes? Matt did not inquire, but the rights of publicity and privacy require their approval, too.

Major Sports Means Major Content Rights

From collegiate campuses to professional arenas, the merchandising of sports teams grows annually and dramatically. Many teams squeeze every dollar they can from the value of trademarks and copyrights. Leading the pack is the New York Yankees, which formed sports cable and satellite networks (YES, Yankee Entertainment and Sports Network), announcing it wants $2 per month per subscriber. This fee is more than fivefold what other entertainment channels ask. The team gets it, because the Yankee brand is synonymous with legendary sports accomplishments.

For many professional teams, building new stadiums is the necessary ingredient for profitability. The gigantic costs of building new exhibition fields is passed down by naming rights, licensing to the highest bidder the right to put one's name on a stadium. The practice, which can generate millions of dollars annually, has a potential dark side: the link between a successful sports franchise with an ignoble commercial enterprise.

Perhaps the signature example involved the Houston Astros, whose home park was called Enron Field until Enron's 2001 bankruptcy made its mark synonymous with nefarious business practices and disgrace. It cost the Astros over $2 million for the right to remove Enron's name from its field. A similar price was paid by 2000 Super Bowl champs, the Baltimore Ravens, to delete bankrupt PSINet from its stadium walls. The lesson for all clever sports franchises in an era of high-flying business crazes is hold onto quality control and termination rights. Keeping an eye out for escape clauses can save a lot of embarrassment.

Chapter 24

Call Signs, Slogans, Jingles, and Characters: The Bits and Pieces of Broadcasting

For broadcasters, disputes over call signs, slogans, jingles, and characters can be the most intense and important encounters with copyright or trademark law. They mark the media outlet's public persona and reputation. Since imitation of the leader is not only great flattery but also an effective way to compete, a competitor's taking of key trademarks usually signals a strike at the heart of a broadcaster's base.

Call Sign Disputes

The FCC is the agency that grants call letter assignments. With tens of thousands of broadcast facilities, finding a combination of letters that also creates an acceptable image or theme is not always an easy task. While the FCC assigns letters to stations for new facilities on a random and arbitrary basis, stations can request preferred allocations. The key obligation is to limit call letters beginning with W to stations east of the Mississippi and K to stations west. The three remaining choices among the 26 letters of the alphabet permit a wide variety. Many stations try to link their call sign to some theme or format; so an oldies station might go for WSGH—Solid Gold Hits or a regional channel might apply for KGLB, Great Lakes Broadcasting.

Touchy subjects arise when two competitors in the same market, whether in the same city or in an urban-suburban relationship, have call signs with similar visual, rhythmic, or phonetic elements; for example, WSGH and WSGA or KGLB and KGLP. Until the mid-1980s, the FCC handled these disputes. Then, in a policy statement, it indicated that it would allow the disputes to be treated like all trademark conflicts, by resort to negotiations between interested parties and, if necessary, filings in court. Stations have taken up the challenge, and a number of call sign disputes have ended up in the courts. As a result, trademark rules apply to call letter disputes.

A spin-off issue involving call letters is the impact of relinquishing call signs when format or management changes. Call signs of long standing in a community may be relinquished for FCC purposes, but the issue is, who is free to pick them up? Since call signs can be registered with the PTO as trademarks, does a change in call letters constitute abandonment for trademark purposes, allowing anyone to use the letters? This issue has never been resolved in court, but creative broadcast managers can do a few things to protect themselves against an archrival taking released call letters and trying to get a competitive lift.

First of all, register the call letters with the PTO. Federally registered trademarks stay on the books for up to 10 years. Abandonment of trademarks requires active intent. If a station can demonstrate that, even though the call sign has been released, there is still a long-standing local recollection of the phrase and a plan to use it, then it would be confusing in the community to allow an unrelated station to grab the call sign. Indeed, this time-honored trademark trick can be used by nonbroadcasters as well. For example, Exxon used this ploy to protect the mark *Humble*, seemingly abandoning the word following consolidation of all its trademarks.

Second, maintain some actual use after the change, including such helpful notice as "WGLB, formerly WSGH." Surveys have shown that the public remembers call signs long after they cease to be used in the market. Maintaining awareness could also help the people who keep diaries for rating services to locate the right station, even as the image of the facility is changing.

Third, sell the right to some other distant facility, or at least encourage a nonmarket station to take it over. Sometimes, call letters have a real market value for another and can be sold for a decent price. When Ted Turner converted Channel 17 into a cable superstation, he hunted around for another station with the initials of his company, TBS, and paid a handsome sum for the call sign WTBS. Moreover, with the elimination of rules prohibiting ownership of more than one television station in a given market (so-called duopoly rules) and the consolidation of station ownership, station owners may control dozens of radio properties, some in the same broadcast market. Swapping call signs within group owned stations can prevent call signs from being gobbled up by local competitors.

Slogans and Jingles

Slogans for media outlets are their key identification to the public. "News 4 You" or jingles such as "Are You Ready for This? It's the Sports Blitz!" are prime examples of stations selling an image to their viewers or listeners. In some cases, firms in the business of developing station image packages license subscribers the right to a slogan and related material, such as bumper stickers, video spots, jingles, on-air personalities or voices, and the like in a specific market. This means that, as one travels around the country, other stations may have the same package. To the traveling public, there may seem to be a connection between the stations; however, the only link would be a common licensing source.

For stations, this permits an efficient way of capitalizing on a proven commodity. However, there are some things to keep in mind:

1. *Contracts.* As a licensee, if a station varies the slogan package it might run afoul of the contract requirements. Since a licensor of slogans, or any trademark owner for that matter, needs to maintain *quality control*, stations are not free to modify the package without prior approval. Most often, artwork, use of the marks, and other key elements may not be changed without licensor approval. Read the license contract carefully before considering modifying the package.

2. *Ownership of changes.* If a station develops a unique and successful edge to the licensed slogan, does it own the change? The answer to that question may not be as simple as one might expect. Look at the license agreement for starters. Even assuming a special stamp could be placed on the way the facilities use the slogan and other elements, the licensor may claim ownership of any changes under a variation of *work made for hire.* Before signing on, the station may wish to modify the license agreement to ensure ownership of the elements it develops.

3. *Facilities covered.* Often, license agreements have strict limits covering the precise facilities to which they apply and the market within which they may be used. Especially for owners of several media properties, there is no guarantee that a successful slogan can be transported to another market. Read the agreement carefully, and, if plans call for using station 1 as a tester for sister facilities, make sure the agreement permits extension into other markets.

Characters

Especially in the radio business, on-air personalities create their own persona. Whether it is a cute name, an identifiable voice, or a musical interlude, there is a need for tangible identifiers with which the public can associate. Often, the people who let the rating services know what programs they are listening to or watching do not remember station call letters or precise time periods when they watch or listen, but they do remember a key character by name. Radio listeners may not know the station's frequency but remember they listened to Rush Limbaugh at 2 P.M.

In some cases, popular personalities are wooed to competitive stations. The issue that personality mobility raises is who owns the character. If we are dealing with someone's real name, absent extraordinary circumstances, the station to which the personality defects can refer to the individual and, if desired, call the show by his or her name. In some limited situations, a name may be so prominent that the original station might contract for its exclusive use in the market for a period of time. These agreements are disfavored because people should be free to use their own names in their chosen occupation. However, there may be a reason, such as a big up-front fee that the personality received from the original station, to justify setting a limit on what happens when he or she leaves.

In the case of fictitious names, the rules are more restrictive. Was the character or routine developed by the person under a work-for-hire arrangement? If so, the *employer* owns the work product of its employees and has a right, not only to prevent a defecting employee from using the fictitious name at the new station, but also to allow a replacement employee to use it at the home station. When an on-air personality known as Mr. Frank O. Pinion left one St. Louis radio facility for another, the tussle over rights to the names hit the front pages of the local newspapers. The originating station retained its rights by early contract protection. As we saw in Chapter 10, when David Letterman jumped from NBC to CBS, the fight over his Top 10 segment also made headlines. It behooves all media outlets that encourage the development of themes and characters to look closely at the ownership of these properties. Particularly in an industry where people move around frequently, not just from stations within a town but across states and the nation, defining who owns what can be difficult. If an on-air personality (DJ Donnie from Denver) adapts a routine made successful by another DJ (DJ Derbie from Dallas, Donnie's former city of employment), who owns what? Does DJ Derbie and his employer have a claim? You bet they do.

However, unless the preliminary work in protecting the copyright and trademark elements has been done, the rights entitlement becomes murky. DJ Derbie and the employer need to have adequate proof of first use, and these records may be hard to construct. Rarely is action taken when imitations are performed in a geographically distant market. However, if the second user (DJ Donnie) achieves regional or national prominence, the originator (DJ Derbie) may gnash his teeth because he failed to act. If Donnie reemerges in Derbie's market, the stakes automatically become higher, and the likelihood that the dispute will intensify increases.

Here are a few handy hints for the creative media team that can be applied to many other situations and help prepare for these inevitable conflicts:

- Keep a checklist of the key on-air elements of the facility and rank them in order of importance.

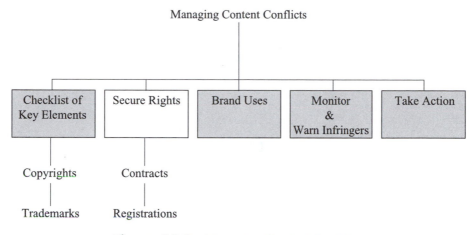

Figure 24-1 Managing Content Conflicts

- Determine what rights need to be secured and how: first by contract with all the participating parties, then by filing registration claims with the Copyright Office or the PTO.
- Brand intellectual property as copyrighted works or trademarks.
- For the valuable material, monitor the marketplace and warn would-be infringers, no matter where they are, that you will not permit theft of this property.
- Take action. Serve notice on the infringers and, if necessary, seek injunctive relief and damages under copyright, trademark, or unfair competition.

To repeat: you don't have to be in the media to follow these handy hints (Figure 24-1).

These elements are the bits and pieces of broadcasting. They are also the personality of the stations and the heart and soul of the media operation. They should not be taken for granted; if they are, sooner or later, they will simply be taken.

Chapter 25

Colorization and Artists' Rights: Whose Work Is It?

In the mid-1980s, technology brought a marvelous capacity to moviemaking. With the ability to convert film stock to digital format, changes to content could be made that appear seamless to the naked eye. Filmmaking techniques pioneered in *Who Shot Roger Rabbit?* were made dramatic in *Rising Sun*, Oscar-winning in *Forrest Gump*, prehistoric in *Jurassic Park*, and totally animated in *Toy Story*. Placed in the hands of directorial masters, the technology can revolutionize programs shown on television and in movie theaters.

"They're My Movies, and I'll Do Anything I Want to Them!"

But the precursor—or, in the view of many legendary directors, the curse—of the technology is its ability to change old films to please modern tastes. The most dramatic example of this development is the colorization of old black-and-white movies. The purpose, to make classic films palatable to the MTV generation, requires color tinting so that kids will keep the set on when classic films are shown. After Turner Entertainment bought the old MGM film library, consisting of 3,600 movies, about half of which were black and white, colorization had its P. T. Barnum in the person of Ted Turner.

Determined to turn his newly acquired library into a stable of films for new movie channels on cable, thereby increasing the product at a fraction of the cost of making new films, Ted Turner announced that the MGM classic film library was fair game for digital modification. "They're my movies, and I'll do anything I want to them!" declared the owner of the film library. His decision was greeted by expressions of outrage from many of the great names in moviemaking, such as Frank Capra, Jimmy Stewart, Woody Allen, and Steven Spielberg.

When first confronted with the challenge of raising their protests, the talented core of filmmakers had to understand the rules of copyright law, which the owners of movies had mastered over the years. The core of their problem was that virtually every classic film was not the solitary work of a lone individual but the collaborative effort of scores of people—performers, writers, directors, cinematographers, producers, film editors, set designers, composers, and on and on. Take a few minutes to read the credits at the end of a movie, and you will see how many folks it takes to create a film. Also with the credits is a notation, usually at the very end, that the producing company is the "author of the motion picture for copyright purposes."

Under the work-for-hire system, all the employees involved in making a movie, even those whose inspiration, writing, and direction created it, are contractually employed. Most often, ownership of the work belongs to the company that pays the bills to make it. Unless the employment agreement provides otherwise, the copyright owner is allowed to change a work without regard to the interests of those whose names are attached to it. It is the rare filmmaker who has insisted or can insist on retaining postrelease control over the final product.

Mr. Stewart Goes to Washington: Debating the Berne Convention and Classic Movies

When the Directors Guild of America (DGA) determined to raise public consciousness about the changes being made to classic films, which they characterized as a native American art form, the U.S. Congress was debating joining the Berne Convention. As noted in Chapter 19, the Berne Convention is the preeminent international copyright treaty, a compact that dates back to the days of Victor Hugo and the French refinement of human rights principles. Central to the heart of the Berne Convention is Article 6*bis* and the principle of *droit moral*. *Moral rights*, as it is known, is the legal notion that an individual artist has the *right* to have his or her name associated with any artistic work he or she creates and to prevent alterations that harm the individual's honor or reputation.

For decades, key copyright interests, such as motion picture producers, had opposed the United States joining the Berne Convention solely because of the moral rights clause. Its impact on their ability to exploit films was very worrisome. However, to stem the tide of international copyright piracy, which was costing producers over $1 billion a year, and gain legal protections in key piracy strongholds such as Thailand and Egypt, accession to the Berne Convention became financially compelling to film producers and other copyright owners, especially software companies.

For the directors, who, along with screenwriters and cinematographers, are internationally recognized as the artistic "authors" of motion pictures, the Berne

Convention debate afforded an opportunity to put the colorization issue center stage. By going to Washington, D.C. in the late 1980s, actors Jimmy Stewart and Ginger Rogers and directors Woody Allen, Sidney Pollack, Milos Forman, Steven Spielberg, George Lucas, and Elliot Silverstein forced the issue into the spotlight. Altering classic films without the permission or involvement of the artistic authors, just to fit the perceived interests of viewers, was, they declared, wrong. On the other side, producer interests feared success of the protest would diminish their ability to tailor films to key markets, such as television, cable, video, and airlines, as well as newly developing digital environments. Full moral rights for artists could substantially cut the value of their film library.

When the legislative dust had settled, the United States decided to join the Berne Convention, but Congress chose not to enshrine Article 6*bis* into U.S. law. Rather, it concluded that *moral rights* were already adequately recognized in a potpourri of American laws, including the derivative copyright right, Section 43(a) of the Lanham Act, and the laws of libel, slander, privacy, and publicity as well as state statutes. As an additional element of the Berne Convention compromise, Congress created the National Film Preservation Board, whose function is to identify and honor original versions of classic American films. Classic works, selected at the pace of 25 films per year by the Librarian of Congress, are duly praised, but only in their original versions.

The tension that surfaced during the colorization debate between artists, whose goal is to preserve their original works, and producers, whose goal is to gain maximum economic benefit from the art, endures. Proposals to force producers to tell the public how movies have been changed when they air on television or in video formats and whether the original artists object to the changes have been offered in Congress over the last few years.

Digital Changes Alter Movies

Most fundamentally, the issue bears on the relationship of the medium and the faithfulness of the message to the original *artistic* concept. While colorization is probably the most dramatic example, the relationship of technology and alteration of copyrighted film works is also spotlighted by

- *Panning and scanning:* the reduction of the aspect ratio (screen image) from the rectangular, wide screen to the square, television format.
- *Time compression/time expansion:* the practice of speeding up or slowing down frame speed.
- *Lexiconning:* the ability to alter pitch while changing film speed to keep the sound level constant and mask the speed changes.

- *Morphing:* the technique of digitally altering video.
- *Editing:* the decision to delete content for a variety of reasons, including fitting films into time slots and removing offensive words or nudity.

Informing Consumers: An Alternative Approach

Recognizing that engrafting full artists rights into the U.S. copyright system is an epochal challenge, film artists have proposed a half-step of informing the public about changes made to films by a label that would precede the telecast and explain how many minutes were edited out; whether the work was colorized, time compressed, morphed, or lexiconned; and whether the artistic authors (the director, cinematographer, and screenwriter) object to the changes. In response to the pressure, the studios and broadcast networks (ABC, CBS, NBC, and Fox) agreed to experiment with a modest notice to air before a televised version of a theatrically released movie. The studio's notice, which is voluntary and applies only to network telecasts of recently released films, informs the public that films were "edited to fit a time slot," "formatted to fit a viewer's screen," or "colorized," without further details or artistic objection.

Although the producers believe this approach fulfills their obligations, a 1995 arbitration involving a Fox Network telecast of a movie raised questions about the approach. When Columbia TriStar licensed the Fox Network to telecast *Thunderheart*, a film about life and death on an Indian reservation, it allowed Fox to cut 22 minutes off the running time and speed up the movie by 6 minutes. All this was necessary to eliminate 25% of the film so it could run in a 2-hour movie block of time, permitting 30 minutes of commercials.

The film's director, Michael Apted, a noted British documentarian, saw tapes of the show and concluded the changes gravely mutilated the work. In making the movie, Apted and the screenwriter, John Fusco, had promised Native American participants that their story would be sensitively told and that their current life on the reservation would be related. Among the scenes cut for time were those that told that vital part of the story. Apted brought an arbitration complaint against the producer and won an order that required the distributor either to carry the full notice of changes and his objection or to replace the director's name in the credits with the pseudonym Alan Smithee. This name is a director's code to let critics and the public know that the director objected to the final cut. The studios chose to use the pseudonym and filed an appeal, which they lost.

Michael Apted was not the first to legally challenge alterations to his work. In the 1970s, ABC was sued by the creators of the *Monty Python* television program, who objected when the show was severely edited for a network telecast. In a decision based on Section 43(a) of the Lanham Act, the producers prevailed in convincing the court that the altered show misrepresented their work (*Gilliam* v.

American Broadcasting Companies). One of the judges even suggested that the Berne Convention's moral rights could be found embedded in Section 43(a).

As the *Monty Python* and *Thunderheart* cases demonstrate, the issue of moral rights reaches deeply into the conscience of the filmmaking, film distributing, and film watching communities. It foreshadows additional battles in this area. Every time a movie is panned and scanned, a photo cropped, a story edited, or a tape sped up, the issues of misrepresentation of the work and of discrediting the original artists are raised. Phrased another way: Who should the law recognize as the author of a work, and who should be entitled to control its fate in the marketplace? With digital technology now so refined, alterations are hard to recognize. The screen does not light up with the warning phrase: "Here's something that has been changed." If anything, the alterations are seamlessly integrated into the original work, and the viewer is left with no appreciation of what has been done.

Copyright is essentially an economic interest in works. Moral rights are the noneconomic interests that involve individual artists and their reputations. While motion pictures and television shows are collaborative works, involving the active participation of many people, they represent a body of work honored in our time as art. To modify these creations without regard for the artistic elements violates the interest of artists. Alteration of art may also be decried as an alteration of history. *I Love Lucy*, *The Honeymooners*, and *The Ed Sullivan Show* were made in black and white. That is part of their public reality. Should they be colorized because more TV sets are in color? Doing so would certainly deny their originality.

One idea floated during the colorization debate may deserve to be revisited in the future, if the practice of materially altering works of film art persist. The idea, endorsed by one congressional committee, was to require that, if a new owner wants to change a work, then it should be prevented from calling the revised work by the same title. In this way, trademark law principles of properly identifying the source of a product counter the suggestion that the two works are identical. If *Casablanca* were colorized, then it simply should not be called *Casablanca*. To keep the original title while changing the underlying work, often against the expressed wishes of the artistic creators, reveals a lack of respect for the Berne Convention principle that an author's work embodies his or her reputation and that honor should be respected.

What is equally true is that the Berne Convention plays an increasingly important role in U.S. copyright policy. Because trade in copyrighted works constitutes one of the leading export commodities of the United States and is vital to the national economy, protecting works and halting piracy through the auspices of the Berne Convention is vital to maintaining the economics of the movie and television industries. Expanding copyright protection through changes in the treaty is a major policy goal of U.S. trade negotiators in the era of digital transmission.

Finding the right balance between the economic concerns of the Berne Convention and the respect for the human element in the creation of art works will be the delicate balancing act of the coming years.

Visual Artists Rights Act

A footnote to the filmmaker's story involves a different group of artists—painters, printmakers, sculptors, and photographers. In response to more than 10 years of persistent effort, primarily by Senator Ted Kennedy, Congress amended the Copyright Act in 1990 to give visual artists a limited version of moral rights. An artist, during his or her life, whether the copyright owner or not, can control the use of his or her name with respect to works created and can prevent mutilation or distortion of the work that prejudices that artist's honor or reputation. The rights cannot be transferred, but they can be waived. The Visual Artists Rights Act (VARA) permits an artist whose outdoor sculpture or public mural falls out of contemporary favor to prevent the work from being removed or defaced. It can ensure that a photographer's picture is properly credited. VARA is a limited but nevertheless significant bow of U.S. copyright law to the Berne Convention obligations. Whether it will stand as the first interpretation of Article 6*bis*—or the only one—in the United States remains to be seen.

Chapter 26

Licensing and Distributing: The Business of Programming

The production and distribution of television shows and movies are stories of the business side of copyrights and trademarks. You cannot create these works, bring them to outlets, or show them to the public without appreciating how much these legal issues are embedded in the system. This chapter offers a short tutorial on the system.

Start with an Idea

Every program and movie ever launched started with an idea. As you know, ideas are not protectable. A sitcom about a lower-class couple that lives in the suburbs, fights a lot, has three kids, and loves pizza or a movie about aliens racing through space to recapture a comrade and destroy the world of their enemies is not a substantial enough expression to claim copyright. But take the kernel of the idea and give it more complexity, more detailed expression, and you move into the layer of protectability.

Flesh Out the Idea

For a movie or a TV series, "detailed expression" usually takes the form of a treatment or proposal. Fleshing out ideas into a story is the work of a lonely screenwriter or the effort of a small, collaborative team. Creators are often leery of showing ideas to others for fear they may be stolen. The basic intellectual property advice is always the same: Flesh out your ideas first, expand the notions, and *write them down*. Once written, copyright law comes into play. The more refined is the storyline and the characters, the more protectable they become.

Give Access to the Story to Others So It Can Happen

Access is another key issue. In most cases, creators need to take a risk: They need to tell others about the story. Many people believe their ideas are so precious that, if they tell anyone else, they will be stolen. However, if a creator wants to give that idea the chance to move from one person's private mind to the world at large, he or she must take the chance. Nevertheless, there are ways to protect one's creations. The simplest is to have the recipient of the treatment sign the "nondisclosure agreement" discussed in Chapter 18. An NDA is a short legal agreement that provides that the creator will tell the recipient about an idea or plan provided the recipient agrees not to use it without permission, usually for a limited time. The standard NDA usually has some saving clauses that indicate that, if an idea is public knowledge, already in development by someone else in the recipient's company or presented to the recipient by some independent party, then there is a presumption that the idea is not protectable. Not every recipient is willing to sign such a document, but if one does, the NDA offers a creator some legal protections.

If a recipient refuses to sign an NDA, a creator may have to decide whether to disclose an idea without a formal legal agreement. Even in such cases, if the recipient receives the idea, dismisses the creator without so much as a "thank you," and later uses it without consent, there still may be a basis for the creator to cry foul and prevail. Copyright law is replete with tales of recipients who learned the hard way when they were sued for taking a character or idea developed in an unsolicited movie script.

Protect against Unfounded Claims

For the producer or media manager, protection against such events is essential to smooth business operations. Generally, this means not taking work on an unsolicited basis. Return unsolicited scripts *unopened*. Do not get fooled into accepting a work without a contract or at least a short document that acknowledges that the producer owes no duty to the person disclosing the story or idea if

- The producer has a similar idea in development independent of the submission.
- The idea or story is already in the public domain.
- The idea or story comes to the producer from another legitimate and unrelated source.

Of course, if material is useful, be prepared to pay for the rights. Paying early is key, because early is when the producer has the most bargaining flexibility.

Who Is Involved?

Sometimes an idea is pegged to a particular person's involvement. A story may come attached to a writer, director, or actor. In such a case, if the idea is a winner, the best course is to allow the principal a role but leave open the option of replacement, if necessary. Frequently, successful concepts fall victim to egos and unworkable bargains. So anticipate the need to bring on qualified replacements for the original creators. This is a touchy topic, but one that needs to be negotiated early in the process so that the work does not fall victim to the players.

The Funnel

The process of developing television programs or movies can best be visualized as a large funnel. At the wide-open mouth, thousands, even tens of thousands, of ideas float around. As the funnel narrows, so do the number of ideas that get converted to treatments. As you might expect, few treatments make it to the script stage (Figure 26-1). While a theatrical script can be sold for $100,000 or more and a television script for $25,000 and up, when interest is established in a script, you are at about the halfway mark in the program or filmmaking process. Getting to that point is so competitive that most folks have long since retreated and returned to their day jobs.

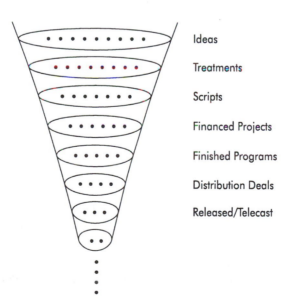

Figure 26-1   The Content Funnel

Once a script is finished, financing for the project must be arranged. The studio system, which bankrolls projects, is the most visible and reliable source for big projects. However, independent producers are also key players in the process. Many films and pilots are developed and paid for by someone with cash and a dream or companies with resources and a plan. Even then, only a handful of finished programs actually get distributed and publicly released.

Among the things the creators of works, as well as the producers and the managers of the media outlets, must think about are these:

- *Production costs.* What are the likely costs of making the work? This includes everything from hiring the creative team and performers to having the sound stage, microphones, camera equipment, lights, location fees, sound and visual effects, legal and insurance, accounting, food for all, and clean-up crews.

- *Clearance of rights.* What is needed to make the work, such as underlying storylines, privacy rights of individuals, music (original and cleared), clips, third-party content? *Document everything* with signed releases, consents, and permissions.

- *Ownership.* Who owns what? Copyrights are divisible, which means that the law will separate into parts all the possible rights associated with a work. When acquiring rights, producers usually demand, "All right, title, and interest in and to the work in any medium now existing or hereafter created." It is vital that the rights are spelled out clearly in the beginning, lest there be confusion as new use is found for the works, new technology develops, or new media evolve. It is easy to make a mistake, and even the big boys slip up occasionally. A few years ago, when Paramount Pictures converted many of its old films to video, a song from the movie *Medium Cool*, "Merry-Go-Round," became the object of litigation because the composer claimed Paramount had failed to acquire the video rights to his music and the use of the music in the video was a violation of his copyrights. The court agreed, and Paramount had to dip into its bank account to square things up. You can be certain that many older films that were poorly documented have not been cleared for Internet-broadband digital uses. This failing requires distributors to identify those who hold rights to the work or elements within the film and reclear them for 21st century purposes. This can be a Herculean task.

- *Ancillary rights.* What are the related uses or spin-off properties? Nary a major movie or television series gets produced today without a number of spin-off properties, including clothing (T-shirts, hats), music (CDs, cassettes), cross-promotions (McDonald's or Pizza Hut giveaways), kiddy goods (lunch boxes, action figures, notebooks), videos ("The Making of . . .")—you get the idea.

Every one of these can be viewed in relation to the copyrights and trademarks. Ownership of those two key rights is vital to market the ancillary aspects of the works.

- *International rules.* Who controls foreign markets? As recently as the 1980s, an American film made the vast majority of its revenue in the United States. For television series, the percentage was even higher. Today, for many films, less than half the revenue comes from the domestic marketplace. It is a *global content environment*, and media works are among the most important and valuable of our international trade commodities. Planning for international distribution and licensing overseas is a vital part of the business. For example, clearing rights to music requires knowledge of the distribution plan. It may be cheaper in the short run to buy rights for the United States and Canada only instead of worldwide, but if the distribution plan calls for an international release, it could be a rude shock to learn how much more expensive it will be to add worldwide rights after initial release. In short, few works can be developed without a keen sense of the impact of international sales on the product. In some cases, international sales help define the internal content; that is, producers make the work compatible with international needs from conception. Big budget movies that do not keep this global opportunity in mind are unlikely to realize the full returns of the investment.

One international battle that has materialized involves the effort of France and other European nations to limit the percentage of a broadcast day (for example, no more than 40% of time) that can be devoted to exhibition of programming originating from the United States. Motion picture distributors protested this development, and the subject has become part of international trade treaty discussions. Content xenophobia is clearly economically inspired. American films already dominate European theaters, and the keepers of the cultural keys want to preserve broadcast time for local products. Like most attempts at censorship, the exclusion of content based on arbitrary criteria is destined to fail; however, in the meantime, the struggle to ensure fair access to the European marketplace will remain a hot-button issue for years to come.

The Movie Distribution System

Producing works is only part of the equation. What separates the studios from the rest of the world is that they not only produce movies and television shows, they distribute them. The major revenue is realized in distribution. While producers look to recoup their investment and make a profit, distributors take a somewhat reduced risk, hoping to hop on the joy ride when a movie breaks out of the pack.

Just one or two unexpected blockbuster films can make a company a giant in the field. That is what happened to Miramax when *The Crying Game* grossed over $60 million at the box office or New Line Cinema, whose *Teenage Mutant Ninja Turtles* surprised the field with over $125 million in revenue. With Miramax and New Line taking in a hefty share of those figures, they were able to break out of the pack and establish themselves in the independent film distribution marketplace. Their successes led Miramax and New Line to be acquired by two major studios, Disney and Warner Bros. (AOL Time Warner). Of course, these numbers pale in comparison with the high stakes in moviemaking and distribution as played by the studios. These companies not only pay for making films but the costs of distribution, and they control all revenues. The average production cost of movies released by the studios ranges from $35–50 million, and distribution fees can be as much as $20–25 million. Big budget films range from $80–130 million in production costs, with distribution fees also rising.

One of the most fascinating stories of securing distribution for a film project was told by Peter Jackson (director of *The Lord of the Rings: The Fellowship of the Ring*, a massive 2001 Oscar-nominated epic) to TV talk show host, Charlie Rose. The New Zealand director, having acquired rights to create the Tolkien trilogy on film, convinced Miramax to develop the project in exchange for distribution rights. But when preproduction costs soared to $20 million, and the price tag on the epic (which was planned in two parts, original and sequel) neared $140 million, Miramax balked. Its parent company, Disney, set a $75 million limit on its projects and would not gamble $140 million on the two films. Refusing an offer to tell the trilogy in one 2-hour movie, the moviemakers were faced with a Hobson's choice—lose rights to the film or find a substitute distributor who would not only bankroll the production but reimburse Miramax $20 million.

The filmmakers had 30 days to complete the distribution deal. They gambled on a unique selling device. They spent their first week making a 36-minute documentary on the "making of the movie." With this in hand, they went to LA to pitch their tale to the big hitters on Hollywood Boulevard. After being turned down even for pitch appointments, they reached their "last opportunity" listeners, New Line Cinema.

Playing it cool by suggesting their appointment book was overflowing when they had nary an entry, they presented New Line with their video. New Line executives instantly understood what they had—a great story of magic and mystery told by brilliant filmmakers. The only problem New Line saw was, since the Tolkien work was a trilogy, how could the film be only two episodes? To do justice to the work, it had to come in three parts. The creators were flabbergasted, and they achieved a movie miracle, a deal that reimbursed Miramax and guaranteed a three-part epic. With the first film achieving boffo box office receipts and nominated for dozens of film awards, New Line was handsomely repaid.

Another insider look at the way money runs in the studio distribution system was revealed in litigation initiated by Art Buchwald, a syndicated columnist, who claimed to have developed the idea for an enormously popular film, *Coming to America*, starring Eddie Murphy. The headline was that the film managed to gross $325 million but not make a profit.

How is that possible? The secret lies in the way money is raised to make movies, the hidden costs, and ultimately the accounting system of Hollywood and the definition of *net profits*. Here is a capsule look at the money side of making and selling movies.

Once a filmmaking idea takes shape, a production company (other than a studio that usually bankrolls an entire production) either covers all the costs of making a movie or obtains gap financing—the amount it needs to close the gap between raised funds and actual production costs. Sometimes distributors make up that gap by advancing funds in exchange for distribution rights; sometimes the money comes from other borrowed sources. Among the sources that are available is the "presale" market: Producers presell rights to certain venues or media, such as foreign, video, or television, licensing those rights and the rewards to those marketplaces to raise money to make the film. Those who guess right in securing the presold markets can strike it rich when the film becomes a hit. Witness Miramax's pickup of *The Crying Game* and the tens of millions of dollars it derived.

Paying the costs of production, which include acquisition of rights and paying all the personnel who work on the film (take a peek as the credits roll at the end of the movie to see all who must be paid), is the biggest need of the money chase. Finding a distributor for the film is the next key. Since many more films are produced than released, engaging the right distributor is a highly competitive and critical task.

The distributor chooses how to tell the public about a film, including

- Making a trailer (an art form in itself).
- Determining where the film will open and on how many screens.
- Promoting the film in newspaper ads, television spots, placing actors on the talk show circuit, and creating news stories about the film.

For these efforts, the distributor usually takes several chunks of the first money to come in. In the case of theatrical releases, the box office revenue is split with the theater venues. On average, the division is 55% (distributor)/45% (theaters), but in practice it can vary widely, from 90% for the distributor during the opening week, which is usually the biggest revenue-generating time, down to 20% in later weeks. The theaters, of course, have concession sales to compensate during the opening weeks, especially if the movie is a hit and brings in popcorn-munching, soda-drinking, candy-eating patrons. Out of that 55% of gross revenue, the distributor recoups many line item costs, which are factors in defining *net profits*. A close look at the recoupments reveals the keys to the distributor's financial success. The biggest items are these:

- Distribution fee (usually 25–35%).
- Recoupment of all payments to production (gap financing).
- Recoupment of all distribution expenses.
- Interest on all money advanced.
- Collateralization (recoupment) of costs from other markets, such as foreign, video, and television.

When one tabulates these costs and reduces the gross, the discovery is that little is left. When Paramount did its accounting on *Coming to America*, it kept coming up with new costs against which to play off the increasing revenue. That is how the $325 million movie *lost money*.

The Television Distribution System

Television distribution has some important differences from theatrical film distribution. First of all, the venues are different. Television has no box office, so all its funds must be made from licensing fees. Second, television programming fits into two key markets: network and syndication. For *network* productions, the costs of production can run as high as $1.5 million per hour. To raise money to cover the huge cost of creating a program for network television, producers license the show to a network, which in turn pays a license fee. On a per-hour basis, the network fee rarely equals the actual cost of production. Typically, ABC, CBS, NBC, and Fox pay producers 70–85% of the budget for the right to air the show on its affiliated stations during a selected time slot. Doing the math, that leaves a significant deficit. This shortfall is financed during a network run, and the producers hope to make up the shortfall with huge premiums in *syndication*. As we note later, for the successful shows, this formula works; for the network busts, the deficit may never be paid off. The escalating costs of network programming has created a backlash, where the networks work to reduce their outlays. One effect has been the rash of lower-budget reality and game shows (like *Who Wants to Be a Millionaire*, *The Weakest Link*, *America's Most Wanted*, and *Survivor*). These programs occupy key time slots and cost a fraction of a dramatic series.

Traditionally, the networks pay their affiliates a fee for the right to program each hour of prime time and other times during the day. In exchange, the networks make their money by selling national advertising time, while allowing affiliates to keep a few minutes of network broadcast periods for local sale. The sale of the time, based on the ratings of the programs, allows the networks to recoup their out-of-pocket costs.

Recently, some of the networks, notably NBC, have suggested that the network fee to stations might become a thing of the past. With national ad sales fluctuating and the local spot time holding its own, the networks think the time may be ripe to eliminate certain fees paid to stations for the privilege of carrying network programming. This change is sparking huge debate with the television community, and we will simply have to see what develops.

If the deficit is the bane of producers, syndication is their hope. Syndication involves selling episodes of programs, one station at a time, for rebroadcast over a number of years. The rule of thumb has been that a network telecast needs about 80 episodes to make it to syndication. With an average network run of 15–20 episodes a year, that means that a show needs a multiyear run on a network to have a decent chance to break out in the syndication marketplace. Some shows, like *Friends*, launched original episodes into syndication while the network run was still ongoing. Others had to wait for the network run to end. To every rule, there are exceptions. Jackie Gleason's *The Honeymooners* is a perennial with less than half the average number of needed episodes.

In the 1980s, prices for syndicated product went into the stratosphere, as stations vied for a handful of popular off-network television series. Topping the list was *The Cosby Show*, which collected hundreds of millions of dollars in syndication fees for its first 5- to 7-year run. With numbers like that, program producers saw green, and station affiliates were in a tough battle to guess what shows could help carry them in ratings battles during key off-network time slots, when stations keep most, if not all, the advertising revenue. Some shrewd station managers guessed gold when they planned their schedules. Early buyers of *M*A*S*H* paid a relatively small sum and made millions as the show's rerun popularity soared. Others guessed wrong on different shows and had a hard time recouping.

While the off-network syndication marketplace grew, so too did "first-run syndication." Sparked by game (*Wheel of Fortune* and *Jeopardy*) and talk (*Oprah*, *Donahue*, *Jerry*, *Sally*, and *Rosie*) shows, this venue went from nowhere in the 1970s to the big time in the 1980s and 1990s. The key difference between network and first-run syndication is that producers must make all their money from the original sale of shows, many of which have little or no rerun potential. As a result, producers of these shows keep costs down and are creative in selling their product to the marketplace.

One creative selling mechanism that developed in the 1980s was *barter syndication*. In barter syndication, the producer fronts the costs of the production, while the station pays no any cash for the program; rather, the station gives the syndicator a certain number of minutes of air time. Then, the syndicator, patching together minutes from a hundred or more affiliates, creates a quasi-network of markets and sells time to advertisers for all the stations combined. In such an environment, having clearances in time periods that are attractive, as well as major markets that generate large viewerships, is vital to the revenue chase. Unless the first-run syndicator can stitch together about 70% of U.S. households, the chances of successfully selling barter time to meet expenses is difficult.

Strategic marketing can be all important. A first-run syndicator may choose to roll out programs slowly to build a national audience. The highly successful *Sally Jesse Raphael* talk show was distributed by Multimedia Entertainment in that fashion. Developed originally as a local show on a Multimedia-owned television station in St. Louis, *Sally* was gradually released in more markets, until it built a loyal following and had affiliates in over 95% of U.S. households viewing in that time slot. It lasted almost 20 years in syndication.

Some successful first run syndication programs produce a "leveraging effect." One TV distributor, King World, which reinvented the game show with programs such as *Wheel of Fortune* and *Jeopardy*, introduced *The Oprah Winfrey Show* on the basis of its success with these shows. *Oprah*, which quickly rose to the top of the talk show format, has generated hundreds of millions of dollars in profits for the producers. The success of King World led to its acquisition by CBS/Viacom as a wave of media consolidations played out in the late 1990s.

Of course, with every success come many false starts. At the annual NATPE Convention, dozens of promising pilots and first-run programs are peddled, but the marketplace has little room for weakly achieving programs. As the movie funnel has a very narrow spout at the bottom of the chain, so too does the television syndication marketplace. The number of independently produced and distributed television shows that can make it is quite limited, even as the number of media outlets themselves have recently increased. This is because, with the movement of independent television stations to new network affiliations, such as Fox, UPN, and WB, fewer hours of the broadcast day are available for independent programs. Moreover, stations find that the competition for local viewership has shifted to news in recent years, so stations are reluctant to release time periods to syndicators when they can program local news instead.

The one bright spot in this picture has been the advent of cable channels. They have taken up some of the slack by offering new telecast opportunities for specialized programming. But cable itself is a unique marketplace, which strives to cater to niche audiences. Cable channels, such as Discovery, Home & Garden, A&E, and Bravo, set tight budgets and acquire programs for 10–20% of what the major networks pay. Therefore, dealing with the cablenets comes at a price. We discuss cable in more detail in the next chapter. What is important to keep in mind is that each venue—network, off-network, first-run syndication, reruns—requires rights clearances. The savvy programmer knows that maintaining control over the properties in the expanding but highly competitive marketplace is the key to success.

Chapter 27

Cable TV: A Pipe Dream

A pipe dream is a dream about transmitting programming through pipes of all sorts—cable, beams from outer space, even the electrical company's line into the home. The specter of new delivery mechanisms has been an enticing image for all programmers. Originally, there was fear that the new mediums would so destroy old habits that they could bring down an industry. Did not film producers of the 1940s and 1950s worry that television would be the end of their business? Even more recently, the studios fought the advent of videocassette recorders, which posed a threat to the box office. But today, revenue from videocassette sales dwarfs the take at the box office. While movies continue to draw $5 billion or so, video sales are close to $15 billion and Blockbuster and other video stores are neighborhood fixtures.

Among cable networks, dozens cater to specialized interests in new movies, old movies, sports, nature, children's programs, sitcom reruns, music videos, country and western, art and history, Spanish language, golf, garden, courtroom hearings—the list continues. What has developed is a fragmentation of the marketplace and, at the same time, an expansion. Whereas a dozen years ago, the big three networks combined to rule 80 percent of the ratings, that percentage has shrunk to below 60 percent. What makes up the difference is a new national network—FOX, some wanna-bes—Warner Bros. (WB) and Universal (UPN)—and the host of cable networks. Folks still watch television, they just have many more choices.

Establishing a Cable Presence

In this complex offering environment, a few principles stand out.

Trademarks and Brand Names Count More Than Ever

To discriminate in a multichannel environment, people make choices, most often based on familiarity. When NBC launched its first cable channel, it was coined

CNBC. A later channel offering, which was formed in a venture with Microsoft, was called MSNBC. Maintaining the brand is part of the business strategy. ESPN started ESPN-2, ESPN Classic, and ESPN News; C-SPAN has C-SPAN2; Fox has FX and Fox News; and A&E's popular program *Biography* launched an entire channel. HBO has a half-dozen channel offerings on digital cable. MTV begot MTV2 and VH1. Sundance Film Festival inspired its own programming network.

Copyright Rights Define Market Entitlements

All too soon, some folks who believe they have rights to programs in all media in all markets learn that that may not be the case. It has already been mentioned that the composer of the song "Merry-Go-Round" thwarted Paramount's effort to convert the film *Medium Cool* to videocassette without the studio checking on rights. In the media of cable, satellite, and cyberspace, similar questions can be asked. Since rights are divisible into infinitesimal parts, without ownership of rights "in all mediums now existing and hereafter created," questions can materialize as to who can exploit a work in the emerging markets.

Spin-offs and Sequels Are Part of the Game

For television series, it is the spin-off. Establishing a popular program, endearing characters, or social themes can result in spin-off shows. *Mary Tyler Moore* begot *Rhoda*, and *The Cosby Show* led to *A Different World*. In films, it is the sequel: *Terminator*, *Terminator 2*; *Alien*, *Alien 2*, and *Alien 3*. Seinfeld's costars, Elaine, George, and Kramer have been granted series deals, playing different characters. While Jason Alexander's and Michael Richards's shows qualify as busts and Julia Louis-Dreyfus's a possible keeper, none of these star vehicles is likely to match the success of the original. If the original producers do not sanction the move, the new shows cannot use the names or persona of the original characters. So *The Michael Richards Show*, which bombed, was not about Kosmo Kramer.

To capitalize on success requires planning. It is not enough to hold the rights to the idea and its initial work. Derivative works, which may evolve from plot, characters, or theme, are part of the mosaic. To maintain a hold on the work and all the fruits of its labor requires knowledge of copyrights and trademarks.

Establishing cable channels, one of the new games in town, means starting with an idea, refining it into a viable niche, tying down programming, and selling, selling, selling. The creators of the Sci-Fi Channel needed more than 3 years to put together such a plan. One essential ingredient was claiming trademark rights to the title. With the establishment of *intent to use* rules, it is possible to apply for a name of a channel years before a launch. (To review the ITU rules, go back to Chapter 11.) A key problem cable channel originators face is that a descriptive title will not be allowed as an ITU. Since many new networks have very descriptive titles (e.g., The Golf Channel or The Game Show Channel), applying for a trademark on an ITU basis may be foiled by the trademark examiner.

It is useful to bear in mind that it takes roughly a year to process a trademark filing, and with good counsel on your side, the time can be strung out even longer if necessary. In the meantime, if some use can be made of the title, then a "use-based claim" may be substituted. But, since highly descriptive marks require secondary meaning, which is acquired after a campaign targeting public awareness and expending a healthy advertising budget, it remains a roll of the dice to secure protection for the descriptive title of a niche channel. This also explains why some channel ideas face stiff competition and similar-sounding names, such as the independent but concurrent development a few years ago of Talk TV, The Talk Channel, and America's Talking.

To cover one's bets, it may be desirable to link a channel to an established market participant. Successful magazines are viewed as a top source for new channel titles. The House & Garden Channel is a prototype of taking a magazine and extending the line to cable programming. CNN's sport channel, CNNSi, was a co-venture with *Sports Illustrated*. CNNSi was eventually dumped in favor of AOL Sports, which provides significant linkage to the 2001 merger of AOL and Time Warner (the parent company of CNN).

Aside from a logo, lining up programming rights is critical. A cable channel may begin as a 2-hour segment on another facility or an independent operation with about 6 hours a day of original programming. By *original* we do not mean brand new, because the staple of many channels is reruns, reruns, and more reruns. But with 6 hours of programs a day, repeated three to four times, a full channel can be born.

In most cases, programming costs must be pegged pretty low, lest the channel consume itself before establishing a loyal audience. It takes 3–5 years and some breaks to lock a channel into a large enough public awareness to make a go of it. With about 70 million plus cable homes, two thirds of the off-the-air marketplace, survival means being able to charge for subscriptions or have enough eyeballs for advertisers. This translates into reaching no less than 15 million households and getting 5–10% to actually watch.

Another route is to exploit content in different ways. We already mentioned that NBC created CNBC and MSNBC (merging two powerhouse marks in Microsoft and NBC). Part of NBC business strategy is to use content developed by NBC in varied forms on MSNBC and CNBC. It can carry news stories with different depth and focus and relate them to other programs such as talk shows. It is not uncommon to see NBC news footage used not only on *The Nightly News* and *Meet the Press* but also on *America Now*, evening news with Brian Williams, and *Hardball* with Chris Matthews.

Cutting Deals and Building an Audience

In the tough world of cable access, cutting deals with the leaders of the cable marketplace (companies such as Comcast, Time-Warner, Cox, and Charter) is a fact of life. Being available on their systems is the answer to the cable channel creator's dream. But the price of access can be high. Often, the originator of an idea sells large chunks of it to those who can help advance the ball. That happened to the Discovery Channel, when virtually 99% of its stock ended up being owned by the cable companies that carried it. One of these companies, TCI, also secured a big stake in Turner Entertainment (WTBS, CNN, CNN Headline News, TMC, and the Cartoon Channel) during a period of Turner's vulnerability in the 1980s, which was spurred by the company's rapid expansion, expensive acquisitions, high startup costs, and cash shortages. Later Turner was bought by Time Warner (now AOL Time Warner, after their latest merger). TCI was in turn acquired by AT&T, whose broadband/cable operations were purchased by Comcast. That is how a big share of the two largest cable companies (Comcast and AOL Time Warner) came under common ownership. As a condition of obtaining Department of Justice and FTC approval of the AT&T/Comcast merger, spinoff of the interests in AOL Time Warner systems should be a must.

Even being on systems serving 15 million homes or more is not a guarantee. It has been suggested that, while the public watches more television today, an individual viewer's loyalty is limited to about 8–10 channels. Tops in the group are the networks, and usually a leading independent signal and public television station. That accounts for more than half the public's viewing. Most of the balance comes from a handful of other specialized program categories: movies, sports, news, sitcom reruns, children's programming, and arts or nature. This leaves very little room to attract a large enough loyal following.

To move past competitors in the race for public attention requires more than clever marketing. Events or circumstances may catapult a channel into public awareness. For CNN, it was the Gulf War and O. J.'s trial. O. J. also put Court TV on the map. The War on Terror and some spicy talk show programming catapulted Fox News into prominence.

In its early development, Discovery's business plan had a crucial programming feature, cheap programs. It was able to acquire rights to hours and hours of science programming for a very low price. The content owners parted with their property, which was otherwise gathering dust, for a bargain price. This enabled the channel to offer a varied schedule, as well as a clear market identity. But as a fully matured network, Discovery cannot rest on running cheap science shows. It needs to feed the appetite for new content and has become one of the important sources for original—and expensive—programming.

Building the different ingredients of his cable network was also expensive for Ted Turner. One of the visionaries of the medium, Turner invented the cable super-station by taking a downtrodden UHF station based in Atlanta, changing its call letters, and making it available to cable systems around the United States. At the time, cable served the primary purpose of making fuzzy pictures clear. When FCC rule changes in 1972 opened up the possibility of extending cable, it was not until Turner offered WTBS to systems nationwide (soon followed by WGN, Chicago, and WOR-TV, New York) that the relatively small cable industry (serving 20% of television households) got a big boost. Turner's acquisition of the Atlanta Braves baseball team and his movie packages converted his sleepy UHF station into an attractive programming alternative.

The satellite delivery of the three superstations provided the first new national offerings directly for cable. The arrival of Home Box Office (HBO) in the latter part of the 1970s, and ESPN in the early 1980s, gave cable a marketing advantage compared with traditional broadcast stations. Access to first-run movies, live sporting events, and the superstations provided the public with a reason to subscribe—programming alternatives to the networks. By the end of the 1980s, dozens of cable channels were established, and cable subscriptions exceeded 50% of all television households. For some, channel overload was taking hold, but, thanks to the remote control device, speedy access to the myriad of choices was easy.

Yet, as cable gained in popularity, the marketplace changed. The costs of developing new channels skyrocketed to tens of millions of dollars. Copyright and FCC rule changes destabilized cable's financial picture, and new competitors emerged from satellites in outer space and telephone wires from the home. Fast on the heels of cable's development, the satellite resale industry established itself as a real competitor to cable. With the advent of micro-sized home dishes, receiving units that could take signals directly off the air and bring them into the home, bypassing the need for cable hookup, the number of players in the marketplace expanded. As digital technology advanced, in many homes satellite services replaced cable and served the home viewer directly.

Common to the early days of all new media, many players emerged, but after time two were deemed the most potent—EchoStar and DirecTV. The latter was created by Hughes Electronics, which in turn was bought by General Motors. GMHughes's satellite business helped boost the company's stock value dramatically during the late 1990s. With hundreds of channels of programming floating around space, gaining access to as many of them as possible became the obsession of many dish owners. By 2002, GM grew weary of the satellite business, and it put its operations up for sale. Bids by Fox and others were overmatched by EchoStar, which hoped that the unification of the two largest satellite operations would make the combination a real competitor to cable television. As anticipated,

this proposed merger sparked an important antitrust debate: whether the consolidation of the two largest companies in the satellite industry was good or
bad for competition (see Chapter 17).

As the telecom industry boomed in the 1990s, thanks in part to legislative
deregulation in 1996, the newest players in the programming puzzle were the telephone companies. With digital and fiber optic lines brought into the home, thereby
increasing the technical capacity to deliver video as well as voice communication,
telephone companies (the Baby Bells and their cohorts) were perceived as the next
big player in the video marketplace. FCC rule changes allowed a video dial tone,
making it legally feasible for the phone companies' wires to serve as program
pipes. However, by the time the Internet bubble burst in 2001, so did the telecom
explosion. Talk of telephone services fully competing with cable in the near term
disappeared overnight. While a handful of upstart operations like StarPower
offered local and long distance phone service, DSL (Internet) access, and cable programming, most put video on a back burner. Creating relationships that encourage consumers to obtain television programs from these traditional common
carriers will require marketing skills and a wealth of content, both new and old,
in digital format. In the next decade, we will learn whether the video delivery
systems will consolidate into a limited number of national firms or be open to
many more players.

Chapter 28

Media Consolidation: Content Synergy

Mergers and alliances have been the code words for the relationship between content providers and the companies controlling the means of distribution for the past 15 years. Foremost, the cost of content drives parties together. It is so expensive to fill up a broadcast day with attractive content that unaffiliated players can rarely accomplish the feat. Furthermore, there is a desire to leverage the goodwill that comes from public associations in one market with another. For that matter, trademarks, which brand content or pipelines, provide an important lever in the swing to secure the loyalty of viewers.

Turner and MGM

In the 1980s, borrowing money was easy, whether in the form of direct loans from banking sources or public financing through junk bonds. Some entrepreneurs, chief among them Ted Turner, expanded their base accordingly. By the mid-1980s, Turner's cable strategy was paying off. WTBS was established in over 90% of the cable homes, and cable was reaching half of all U.S. households. This meant that his local station in Atlanta had access to 45% of U.S. homes, over six times the number of homes reached by stations in New York City, the largest broadcast market in the United States with more than 7 million homes. WTBS was spending over $25 million a year in license fees for telecast rights. Turner needed more programs, because he was competing not just against Atlanta stations but against the national networks and local independent stations throughout the country. To attract enough viewers to be able to increase his advertising rates, Turner needed content.

His approach was focused and designed to attract mass audiences. Turner sized up the two big content markets—sports and movies. He acquired sports franchises in baseball and basketball, the Atlanta Braves and the Atlanta Hawks. These acquisitions gave him year-round sports coverage of two of the top national games. Then, he bought a movie library, and not just any library. Turner made a bold decision to buy the MGM Studio and Film Library. It represented the richest lode of moviemaking, over 3,600 films, including classic works like *Gone with the Wind* and *Casablanca*, and the greatest American movie, *Citizen Kane*. The net cost was $1 billion, after selling off the MGM studio and lot. To fund this programming appetite, Turner sold junk bonds on Wall Street. He became so indebted that he was forced to turn part control of his business over to the cable companies that carried his channels, including the largest cable operator at the time, TCI.

The purchase of the library, later complemented by acquisition of the RKO library, turned Turner Entertainment into one of the great treasuries of film, which it used to expand its place in the cable marketplace. Turner launched new movie channels, Turner Network Television (TNT) and Turner Classic Movies (TCM). He became a catalyst of controversy by colorizing many of the premier 1,800 classic black-and-white films in the MGM library, remaking them in his vision, so they would be palatable to the MTV generation. (Remember the discussion of colorization in Chapter 25.)

Time Warner Takes Turner and Gets Taken By AOL

Ironically, Turner's success brought him into the target range of other bigger players in the media marketplace. While he lusted after CBS (making an offer for the company in the 1980s), Turner built CNN and Headline News. In 1995, Turner agreed to merge with Time Warner. Time Warner itself was a company formed by the merger of two great companies, the Time publishing house and Warner Bros. film studio.

It took the merged Time Warner company almost a decade to blend its disparate corporate cultures and resources into a unified whole. The planned union with Turner was the next ultimate merger of content-based industries. Because the concentration of content was so substantial, the FTC and the Department of Justice very carefully reviewed the impact of the merger on the information and media marketplace. (See Chapter 17 for the discussion of antitrust issues.) In the end, those agencies signed off on the deal, which placed more content-based properties under one roof than has ever been owned by a single source.

Less than 5 years later, Time Warner agreed to yet another megamerger, this time with America Online (AOL), the most conspicuously successful Internet service provider in the world. Conceived at the height of the Internet boom, this merger was the fulfillment of the next stage of visionary imagination, joining old media (print publications) with new media (cable, satellite, and film/TV/video production) and new, new media (Internet/broadband). AOL Time Warner stands today as the symbol of the source of all media content our nation has known, a remarkable accomplishment.

Consolidations and Alliances

These acquisitions, however, are in keeping with two trends. One is the rapid consolidation of media entities during the last 5 years: Westinghouse taking over CBS; Viacom buying Paramount Studios, Blockbuster, and then Westinghouse (CBS); Disney acquiring ABC-CapCities and Miramax; AT&T buying TCI Cable; Comcast buying AT&T Broadband. The other is the movement toward alliances, such as Microsoft and NBC, various Baby Bells, Fox and TCI, and all kinds of software firms with programmers and distributors.

In the late 1990s, at the moment when telephone was thought to be the next media distribution system, AT&T announced a bold plan. Recall, AT&T was the mother of all local telephone companies, which were forcibly separated from their parent by strict application of antitrust principles in 1984. Following divestiture, AT&T became strictly a long distance service, with local telephone service provided by seven newly created regional phone companies. As they grew in strength and long-distance telephone service competition materialized in the form of MCI and Sprint, AT&T looked for a new strategy. It saw cable television as a logical direction. Led by an aggressive new chairman, Michael Armstrong, AT&T went on a bidding spree for large cable operations. It did not start small but bid for and won Media One, the successor of TCI, the nation's largest cable company.

For several years, AT&T tried to meld its telephone-cable strategy, which envisioned consumers using a single company for both services. But the burden of rebuilding the antiquated Media One infrastructure, coupled with the reluctance of the market to accept the telephone company as the provider of video services, proved devastating, even for a company as large as AT&T. Initially splitting itself into separate companies for wireless, long distance, and broadband, AT&T set off a bidding frenzy for its broadband division in late 2001. Those vying for the division include the largest cable operators (Comcast, AOL Time Warner, and Cox). Spicing up the hunt was Microsoft. Several years earlier, Microsoft had made a strategic investment in Comcast, and it looked at both Comcast and Cox as preferred alternatives to AOL Time Warner, with which Microsoft was engaged in several high profile business and legal battles. In the end, Comcast prevailed, promising to create the newest, largest cable operation, reaching over 22 million homes. Henceforth, any serious content provider would have to walk through the doors of Comcast if it hoped to have sufficient access to the cable subscriber universe.

While we have already discussed the plan of GMHughes, owner of DirecTV, to merge with EchoStar, another reality is international consolidation. The world, not just the United States, is the media marketplace. Vivendi of France, led by its own visionary, Jean-Marie Messier, foresaw the need to acquire U.S. content as part of a global plan. Vivendi first acquired Universal Studios, with its vast film library and film production and distribution operations, from the Bronfman family. Then, it added USA Studios, with a stable of cable networks, including the Sci-Fi Channel, USA Network, and television production operations. It also purchased Napster.com during its legal challenge and added other dot.com ventures. To compete on the world stage, Messier believed the chief players need to assemble world-class resources. But Vivendi paid a huge price for those assets, buying at the zenith of the stock boom. When world entertainment and Internet markets dropped dramatically in 2001–2002, Vivendi shareholders rebelled. Messier was forced out in the summer 2002, replaced by a less flamboyant and more traditional executive. An era of international retrenchment may be initiated. Nevertheless, the trend toward globalization of content will continue, because sales of content are worldwide in all media, especially entertainment.

There is no question that the leadership of American companies has created a new look in the international content marketplace. With new technologies and modes of communication opening up, most notably the Internet and satellite, it is urgent that major players have a global strategy for developing content and marketing it. This does not mean there is no room for individuals. In fact, it remains a truism that the individuals who create visionary businesses or content can succeed and, indeed, succeed on an international scale. The creators of the Home Shopping Channel, for example, defined a popular programming niche with international appeal. They walked away from their creation with great wealth.

Yet, the most impressive combination remains strong content linked to international and multidimensional means of distribution, in short, the studio system grown up: The moviemakers and movie distributors, the broadcast programmers and broadcast networks, and the cable and satellite systems were interconnected and ready to exploit new markets. In the 1970s, the broadcast program and network combination created by CBS, NBC, and ABC was so powerful and such a barrier to entry that the big three broadcast networks were ultimately prohibited from syndicating programming that originally aired on their facilities. Viacom, a media powerhouse, was born from the rib of CBS when the FCC's financial syndication (FinSyn) rules required CBS to divest itself of CBS-produced programming.

As the 1990s drew to a close, the networks were allowed back into the business of syndication by an FCC that concluded that the programming industry no longer needs regulatory protection. The FinSyn rules, which restricted the networks for almost 30 years, were inspired by the concern that off-network programming tends to dominate the syndication marketplace and the broadcasting networks could, by controlling original network release, artificially preclude third parties from marketing syndicated programming. The elimination of the FinSyn rules led to the mergers of Disney and ABC and CBS, first with Westinghouse, then with Viacom. Combinations of program producers and distribution networks, which always make sense, now dominate network broadcasting.

To bring the movement full circle, we now turn to the newest media, the world of the Internet. In this interactive marketplace, old content issues are being challenged by the very force of technology.

Part Five

Content and New Media: The Internet Has Arrived

Chapter 29

Cyberspace: Napster and the Code of the Wild West Revisited

For a time during the past few years, it seemed as though technology was changing so fast that it was hard to imagine a set of rules that could bind the marketplace. Indeed, the Internet, discovered as a friendly environment by scientists and hackers, was transformed into the newest mass media. Tens of millions of people learned the ease of turning on and tuning in to the information explosion at their desktops. Even some politicians have been known to sing its praises. To comprehend where we are, we need to understand where we have come from. To do that, we scroll back a few years.

The Promise of the Internet

The promise of the Internet—the code word for interconnected networks, including the special one run by complex rules established by the U.S. government—could be summarized very briefly: It enabled anyone to be a publisher. Unlike every other mass medium, for which a hefty investment in infrastructure was required and for which only the investor was able to control content, the Internet and its related online service companions demand only minimal commitment of resources. For a modest sum, anyone could acquire a serviceable computer, a modem, and a service connection, permitting interaction with others. With software that enabled e-mail or by establishing an Internet address (domain name) communication with a broad universe became possible. As participants in a new democratic means of communications that required little financial stake in its publishing infrastructure, users did not absorb or feel committed to the legal principles that guided traditional media (print publishing) and new media (cable and satellite). As the Internet grew in commercial popularity, it was being compared to the prospector days of the Wild West: No rules applied. Anything goes.

Then, some people and businesses started to get burned. Famous trademarks were being taken by upstarts and used as domain names without clearance. Content was being shared without regard to traditional publishing procedures and pricing. Digital files containing music and films were being silently, swiftly, and electronically transmitted across international data highways. With the explosive growth of the Internet came a backlash. The essence of the legal debate—predominantly a copyright debate but with important echoes of trademark, privacy, and trade secrets—is that many users of cyberspace can too easily publish materials or information belonging to others without restraint. Popular software programs, famous pictures, stories or articles, entire books, the latest CDs by popular musical groups, even first-run movies—all could be transferred without the owner's knowledge and with no compensation to the creator. Not only do such practices fly in the face of traditional legal standards, they also could wreck the economic base on which the very essence of creativity is built.

Culture Clash: Copyright Owners and I-Gen

A culture clash occurred between the copyright-owning community, some creators, and the Internet generation, or the *I-Gen*. The I-Gen believes that access should be universal and sharing should be free. The copyright-owning community believes access should be controlled and copying paid for. Some creators who challenge traditional means of distribution (e.g., the established record labels), side with the I-Gen. For these creators, the opportunity to have one's work and ideas freely circulate is more important than initial compensation. If one gains in popularity by such exposure, then financial rewards will follow, these creators believe. Thus, the battle lines were drawn. At the core of the legislative debate over passage of the DMCA was essentially the issue of access. As discussed in Chapter 9, controlling access to digital works is the significant contribution of the DMCA. By allowing owners to restrict access, even in the face of long-respected limitations on rights of copyright owners to prevent certain uses of works, the DMCA carved out new and contentious ground that will be tested by the I-Gen view of the world. For the present time, access controls are at the heart of the new copyright regime.

Among the clashes that have marked the early days of the DMCA are these:

- *IcraveTV.com.* This website in Canada streamed video of U.S. television stations without permission. Under one interpretation of Canadian law, the practice was permitted. But U.S. broadcasters and programming and sports interests challenged the site, claiming that their copyrighted programs were being recycled without consent. Because the site secured a domain name from a U.S.-based registry, they were able to bring a lawsuit in the United States and won an injunction against the retransmissions.

- *Napster.com.* This site became a synonym for the Internet debate. At its peak, more than 40 million subscribers worldwide logged on to Napster and, utilizing the searching facilities of the website, identified computers around the globe that contained files of published songs and effected a file transfer. The file of music was copied and sent from one computer to others without clearance or compensation to the owners. The largest recording companies launched a coordinated legal attack against Napster and prevailed in a copyright infringement case that effectively shut down the site.

- *Scour.com et al.* Other websites, utilizing the principle that people should be allowed to share files of information, just as individuals trade books and magazines, made music and movies available. One at a time, the recording and motion picture industry has identified them in cyberspace and filed legal actions to shut them down as well.

- *Reimerdes* (CSS/DeCSS). Content scramble system (CSS) is a code phrase for a system that encrypts data on CDs and DVDs and prevents users from copying the content (e.g., music or movies) or playing them on nonauthorized DVD machines. An enterprising young Norwegian figured out how to crack the CSS code, so that DVDs could play on DVD machines run by an operating system popular with techies, which would otherwise not be useable for most DVDs. Dubbed *DeCSS*, his code-cracking program traded throughout the universe of computer hackers. The movie and recording industry launched challenges to the DeCSS program, successfully prevailing against defendants, including Reimerdes, to convince the courts that that the renegade program violated the new anticircumvention provisions of the DMCA.

- *Professor Felton.* Shortly before Princeton University professor Edward Felton planned to speak about the DeCSS program at a conference, he received a letter from a recording industry representative, threatening reprisals under the DMCA. It was posited that the speech explaining DeCSS could violate Section 1201(a)(2) by offering the public "a service primarily designed for the purpose of circumventing protection afforded by a technological measure that effectively protects a right of a copyright owner." Foolish as it may sound, the notion was that merely talking about DeCSS was a threat equivalent to an access-cracking technology. Even though it was later clarified that such a result was not intended and the threat effectively retracted, Felton sought a declaratory court order that the DMCA was unconstitutional because the threat permitted improper interference with Felton's free speech. In light of the retraction, the court refused to consider the case a live dispute and simply dismissed his complaint.

Controlling Access to Content

The various disputes involve competing claims regarding access to and use of information and works in a digital world. Matters are made more crucial because the technology of the computer, the digital transformation of words and images to zeros and ones that can be read and understood by machines, enables copying with amazing success and clarity. Unlike the wizardry of video and audiocassette recordings or the trusty photocopy machine, digital copies *perfectly* reproduce the original. When CDs are replicated by computers, they sound as true as the ones you buy in the store. This means that copying becomes more reliable and precise. And it is also easy.

Pushing one letter on the keypad, a user can download and store all the data at one's command. In copyright parlance, we have

- A *transmission* from the host server or computer, via telephone lines or other transmission circuits, to the receiving unit.
- *Copying* when the work is stored on the receiving computer and printed out.
- A *display* when it is visually seen on the monitor.
- A *performance* if speakers translate the sounds.

The reality of these activities constitutes one of the greatest challenges to effective policing of copyrights (Figure 29-1). The content industry was very concerned that the attitude of users of the Internet, bolstered by an early image of "anything and everything goes" and sharing information for free, renders their published works unmarketable. After all, if you can locate the text online for free, why buy it?

But buried in the technology itself are some solutions. Prime among them is *encryption*. The content owners are moving quickly to establish parameters by which content can be coded so that access to it is denied unless the user's activity has been approved. In other words, encryption makes pay per use possible. In addition to encryption, high-tech solutions are being developed, such as *digital signature*, a sign-in authentication process that would have to be displayed before one could access data, or *anticopying codes*, computer programs that would prohibit downloading before it starts.

The battle over cyberspace content is playing out in several venues, primarily in the courts, but also in Congress. A handful of lawsuits mark some of the important principles of ownership of works. In general, the courts have been willing to apply copyright law directly to the Internet. Therefore, a hacker who uploaded software so that thousands of his nearest and dearest could benefit from the works is held to be an infringer. Even more compelling, the online service that promoted the transactions as a way of popularizing its services also is held accountable. That

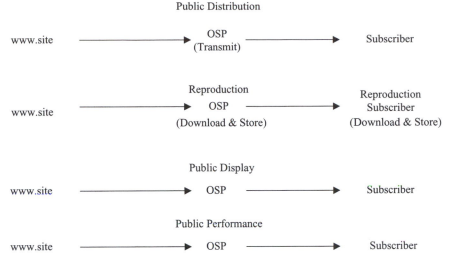

Figure 29-1 OSP Activities That Have Copyright Significance

ruling sent shivers down many online service providers' spines, because the ability to permit access to the many and varied Internet sites was now in question. When a different court held that the service provider was not responsible for every text transmitted by it, a sigh of relief was heard throughout the industry.

The posting of copyrighted works of the Church of Scientology gave birth to a couple of lawsuits testing whether it was fair use for a disgruntled disciple to allow the public access to the closely guarded texts and for the *Washington Post* to print portions of the texts from the website. In two equally defensible, but seemingly inconsistent, rulings, the same court held first that the disciple was liable for copyright infringement and second that the newspaper qualified as a fair user.

It is important to note that these seminal decisions in the law of cyberspace apply only in the jurisdictions where they operate. Unless Congress revises copyright law or the U.S. Supreme Court issues an opinion, many of these issues may not be definitively resolved. Especially in light of the international nature of the transmissions, no single lower court can be said to offer the authoritative order for the treatment of works in the new media.

Chapter 30

Digital Doctrines: Defining Rights in an Electronic World

Congress's consideration of the DMCA was the setting for many digital debates. However, passage of the law did not resolve all the issues that digital technology raised. Defining rights in an electronic world is an ongoing policy debate that will rage into the foreseeable future. Some of the battles will be in legislative arenas, as special interests press for reforms to counteract weaknesses in the legal structure at the federal and state levels. Some of the battles will be in the courts, spearheaded by those who want to enforce or challenge newly defined rights. Among the skirmishes already under way are these: database protection, rules for electronic commerce, and digital first sale. How these matters are resolved will tell us a lot about how content rights will be defined in the digital decades to come.

Digital Debate: Dueling Database Proposals

One of the most contentious discussions during the DMCA debate was over *database protection*. *Database* is a code word for the digital compilation of facts and information. While the content of a database can be anything from news articles on Afghanistan, to real estate listings in Milwaukee, to scientific tabulations of cancer research results, the copyright issue posed by databases is simply stated. As explained by the Supreme Court in 1991 in *Feist Publications, Inc. v. Rural Telephone Service Co.*, copyright law does not provide protection for facts, no matter how much effort it took to assemble or maintain them. Therefore, databases that consist primarily of factual information are not protected by copyright law. Equally unprotected are databases composed of U.S. government works, like federal agency reports, listings of merchandise seized during FBI drug raids, and court decisions.

The *Feist* case caused consternation among many publishers almost as soon as the ink was dry on the opinion. The stress was particularly high among those who compiled databases of government reports, judicial opinions, and factual information, like real estate listings, stock ticker information, and sports scores. Indeed, the Yellow Pages and the Almanac lost their unique franchises as a result of that ruling, as did the compilers of many court decisions. Since data is the stuff of e-commerce, publishers whose business is to create and maintain databases have been living in uncertain times since 1991. No longer does the effort to compile data, so-called sweat of the brow activity, justify copyright protection for the works of the creators. They may have valid and binding contracts that control the uses that an authorized user can make of their data or technological protection measures that control access, but if they have no contractual control over the user or do not use TPMs, they have no legal hook on which to hang a lawsuit if they feel someone is taking their data without consent.

To remedy the problem, the advocates for database protection created a proposal that was attached to the DMCA. The idea was to bypass the constitutional copyright problem of "no protection for facts" by creating a legal right in the *investment* it takes to make and maintain a database. Under the database protection proposal, "information" collected and organized to bring discrete bits of data together in one convenient place for users to access could be protected. "Information" would include facts, data, works of authorship, or any other intangible material capable of being organized in a systematic way. The information can be stock quotes, real estate listings, weather information, or sports scores. It can also include court opinions, poems, or recipes.

Under the proposal, extracting all or a substantial part of a collection of information and causing harm to the primary or related market of the creator of the collection is prohibited. While individual items of information or insubstantial portions of a compilation could be taken, the broader concern is that one could quickly amass a "substantial part" of a collection by adding together small parts. Amassing such material amounts would be prohibited. Certain exceptions would apply, including collecting information for (1) news reporting; (2) nonprofit educational, scientific, and research purposes that have no impact on the database owner's primary market; (3) reasonable uses for comment, criticism, teaching, research, or analysis; and (4) extraction of genealogical information for nonprofit religious purposes. Also, the Securities and Exchange Commission and other agencies regulating markets could regulate the exploitation of real-time stock market data. Databases would be protected for 15 years, and civil penalties and injunctions could be ordered by a court. Even criminal sanctions (fines and jail time) could apply to willful violations. Moreover, databases created up to 15 years before enactment could be protected. In other words, the bill would apply retroactively to existing databases.

To counter the push for database protection, a group of interested entities assembled with a common purpose to support an alternative to locking up bits of data. These entities include educators and librarians concerned about the impact of this bill on research and scholarship, telephone companies and other service providers who use data and enable subscribers to use data, companies in the business of marketing their own version of databases that use public information, and equipment manufacturers whose devices facilitate easy sorting of information. The concept of this competing group is that, rather than prohibiting the extraction and use of parts of a database, the real problem is the misappropriation of databases for the purpose of competing with the original source. Their proposal is grounded in the notion that use of the information for traditional educational purposes is not the problem; rather, piracy of databases that shatter the established marketplace for the original database creators needs to be prevented. In short, to establish a claim, competition between the original database and the second comer's compilation is a must. Misappropriation and dissemination of real-time market information obtained directly or indirectly from a market information processor would be prohibited. A private lawsuit against such violations would be allowed, and a court could issue appropriate injunctions and order the payment of monetary damages. A host of exceptions also apply to this alternative, which is intended to ensure that fair use, allowed under copyright law, would not be diminished. Aside from real-time information claims, violators would be subject to the jurisdiction of the FTC, much as that agency handles disputes involving unfair competition. Importantly, the alternative bill would not apply retroactively to existing databases. It would affect only newly constructed databases.

With much at stake for each proposition, the dueling sides have stalemated each other, but intense interest in the concept of database protection remains. Before too long, one side or the other may blink, and the concept of database protection will be added to the realm of legal protections for content.

Supreme Court Issues a Landmark Copyright Ruling for Freelance Writers

Another marker in the digital debate involved the claim of freelance writers that the reuse of their articles and photographs that once appeared in newspapers and magazines could not be sold to online databases or used in CD-ROMs, without renewed consent. *The New York Times Company, Inc.* v. *Tasini* was decided by the U.S. Supreme Court in summer 2001. After almost 5 years of legal debate, the Supreme Court's interpretation of an arcane provision of copyright law settled a dispute that has important ramifications for authors, publishers, and the content that is available in electronic formats.

Under Section 201(c) of the Copyright Act, a daily newspaper or periodical magazine (which are called *collective copyrighted works* because they combine independent works—news articles, opinion pieces, and photographs in particular—into a single edition) could republish material from one edition in a revision of the collective work or in a later collective work in the same series. Therefore, when the *New York Times* publishes an Op Ed article written by an independent writer (not a member of the staff or editorial board) in its early morning newspaper and then reprints that same article in the day's final edition, there is no need to clear the article for multiple publications. However, when the *New York Times* licenses Lexis/Nexis to republish the articles that appear in its daily edition as part of the online service's total database, must the *New York Times* get permission of the freelance author? For years, the newspaper that prided itself on "all the news that's fit to print" followed a common practice of providing Lexis/Nexis all the stories and articles from its print edition. At the same time, the *New York Times* and other publications were creating CD-ROM versions of their daily or periodic publications. Both digital versions were created without renewed clearance from independent authors.

When Jonathan Tasini, a freelance writer, complained on behalf of himself and a handful of other writers that the publishers were reaping a secondary stream of income from the electronic texts without sharing some of the money with the writers, the publishers rebuffed the overtures. The publishers claimed to be exempt under the established copyright principle that this was merely a revision of the original newspaper or magazine or a later collective work in the same series.

However, the Supreme Court did not see it that way. The online services were able to reformat the digital data, eliminate advertising and the continuity in the appearances of the pages, and apply sophisticated searching software that allowed a user to create new compilations of articles (such as all the Op Ed articles written by Jonathan Tasini that appeared in the *New York Times* and other newspapers within the Lexis-Nexis catalogue). To the Supreme Court, there was a material change in the work. The standard of an early and late edition of a daily newspaper hardly applied. Therefore, the copyright law did not grant unfettered use of the material. If the freelance author held the copyright to the article, then the *New York Times* had to obtain a license for electronic use of the work.

This decision was the first authoritative interpretation of copyright in a digital age. However, once the decision was made, the publishers took aggressive action to undermine a key conclusion of the ruling, that authors should share some of the revenue generated by the digital conversion and use of their works. Shortly after the ruling became effective, the *New York Times* and other publishers sent notices to freelancers advising that if they did not grant the publishers gratis permission to digitize their articles, the publishers would delete their works from the online and CD-ROM versions. Rather than paying for the privilege of keeping the content of the daily edition intact, the publishers wanted to eliminate any future obligation to authors.

Independent authors face a difficult choice, either relinquish the right to share in the financial benefit derived from having their works maintained in a collective database or face the prospect that their works will not be as readily accessible to a wider audience. That choice is certainly not what the Supreme Court intended. For the Supreme Court, the obligation of the publishers to clear the digital use of the works was evident. Sharing some portion of the money secured from the digital publishing seemed fair. There are models, the Supreme Court noted, for handling the complex problems of clearance, including the mechanism adopted by the music performing rights societies, ASCAP and BMI. It behooves representatives of publishers and authors to reach an accommodation that ensures not only respect for the principle of authorship within copyright law but also that guarantees that "all the news that was fit to be printed" is preserved for future readers in digital formats.

Finally, it should be noted that, even after *Tasini*, not every reference to a prior work of a freelance author requires new consent. Publishers may maintain index-type databases, abstracts of longer works, and image-based databases (PDF files) that show the freelancer's article in full context of the original publication. These are clearly viable ways to republish or reference portions of collective works. However, if a database organizes information differently from the original or adds software in a way that permits restructuring of original works into new collective works, then the exemption in Section 201(c) will not apply.

UCITA: Electronic Commerce and Copyright

One of the more practical but densely technical areas of law is commercial transactions. This body of law guides the ways in which people buy and sell things, use credit cards, and cash checks. Since these activities typically extend across state boundaries, the legal profession has turned to experts to develop a uniform code that all state legislatures may use as a standard in setting local rules. If their representatives want, states can simply formally adopt the sections of the Uniform Code of Commercial Transactions as their local laws, and by and large, most governments do just that. In the world of legal jargon, the Uniform Commercial Code of Commercial Transactions is a prize winner.

As e-commerce in information—the sale or licensing of software and online, electronic-based works—grew in the 1990s, the legal experts who keep track of the uniform code determined it was time to adopt a specialized set of rules for this newly defined area of commerce. Since the information was subject to unauthorized copying, software publishers wanted a strict set of rules to govern e-commerce. When the initial proposal for the new uniform code, known as the

Uniform Computer Information Transactions Act (UCITA) was published, important legal associations urged its speedy adoption. At the height of the Internet craze, many states were intent on adopting the code as a way of proving their leadership in electronic commerce.

Primarily, the authors of the new code decided that the contractual arrangements set out in electronic licenses, known by the phrases *shrink-wrapped licenses* for software packaging purchased in stores and *click licenses* for the online versions that require a user to move his cursor to the "I ACCEPT" box and click Okay, should be allowed to control all uses of content. After all, it is a time-honored tradition that, while copyright law regulates the ownership and use of expressive content, two parties can agree to any variation of the legal relationship by a simple contract.

Although the principle that parties may agree to terms and conditions that trump copyright law is well respected, when applied to the devices of shrink-wrapped and click licenses, a serious problem emerges. Most often, the user of the electronic content is not able to negotiate the terms of this license. Rather, in the case of online services, the user is presented with all the terms and conditions and required to say "I ACCEPT" or be denied access. In the case of store-bought or boxed electronic works, the contract is deemed accepted by removing the packaging. In legal terms, this is known as a "contract of adhesion," an imposed, not negotiated, deal.

Under UCITA, a fine-print contract could legitimately provide not only that no fair use can be made of the content but also that software has to be used on a specific machine or in a specific location and that one can be prevented from giving software or a DVD to a friend or relative. What is more, software publishers could prohibit public criticism of their products and avoid liability for damage caused by defects in their software, even if those defects were known by the seller and not disclosed to the buyer. Further, as is common, an agreement could decide where legal disputes must be heard. One company's software agreement required that all disputes be settled in Ireland.

While the principles that govern e-commerce in information may need certain uniformity, the more UCITA became the focus of attention it became evident that proponents of the toughest portions of UCITA had stepped outside the bounds of fair dealing. By mixing concepts associated with the purchase of goods and the licensing of access to information, the provisions severely curtailed the interests of users of content to the detriment of other legal principles, notably consumer rights protections and copyright law. Although legal scholars were involved in the drafting of the code, as criticisms were piled on UCITA, the American Bar Association and the Association of State Attorneys General asked the drafters to go back to the writing table and urged states not to act until the bill's defects were rectified.

Although bills to adopt UCITA were introduced in states across the nation, only two (Virginia and Maryland) have passed it. For the present time, the movement to adopt UCITA in all 50 states appears stymied. It will take many redrafting sessions before it overcomes the objections of its many opponents.

Digital First Sale: A Doctrine Whose Time Has Come?

During the debate on the DMCA, certain parties argued that the combination of anticircumvention rules and licensing restrictions makes it impossible for many people to enjoy the privilege normally associated with the acquisition of works, the ability to freely transfer control over one's copy. As noted, copyright law and policy long ago recognized the difference between owning a copyright and owning a copy. The author of a work, as we know, holds the copyright for life plus 70 years (or 95 years in the case of an entity), even if he or she does not retain a physical copy of the work. By contrast, someone who buys a book or video acquires ownership of the copy. In the copyright equation, the first sale doctrine allows the author to choose the medium for first sale and the buyer to receive a copy to keep or pass on to others. This does not mean that one can pop over to a neighborhood Kinkos and order three dozen copies of the manuscript for distribution to friends, colleagues, or students. It also does not mean that one can publicly perform the video even if not charging an admission fee. But it has always meant that one could pass the book or tape on to a friend so the friend could enjoy it, show it to relatives in one's living room, or even donate it to a public school's annual fund-raising flea market.

However, if the copyrighted work is not purchased outright but acquired through a "click license," the equation changes. One is not strictly within the copyright law domain and has to determine what impact the licensing terms have on the sharing of the work with others.

As learned in Chapter 2, under pressure to conclude the DMCA debate, Congress added a provision that required the Copyright Office to take a close look at digital first sale. Congress sought an analysis of the relationship in a digital world between the new anticircumvention provisions and related requirements, on the one hand, and Sections 109 (which grants the copyright owner the right to choose the first forum for release of the work) and 117 (which provides that it is not an infringement to make a copy of a computer program as an essential step in using that program), on the other.

In typical fashion, the Copyright Office launched a broad public inquiry, soliciting comments far and wide. As is common in these proceedings, the hot issue of the day tends to dominate the debate, but there was also opportunity for a more general expression of views. The hot topic when the DMCA digital first sale study was under way was CSS/DeCSS, the scrambling and descrambling technology associated with DVDs and their players.

Fundamentally, the Copyright Office framed its analysis by focusing on the purpose and operation of the first sale doctrine. From the Copyright Office's perspective, the doctrine is a limitation on the copyright owner's public distribution right and should not be expanded to embrace the reproduction right. Paralleling this viewpoint is the recognition that copyright law has historically respected the role of contract in complementing statutory entitlements. With respect for contracts embedded in the Constitution, just like the rights of authorship, it is understood that what parties freely agree to in a binding contract has to be respected. Hence, the licensing term sheets that are part and parcel of digital works have as much legal force as the copyright law itself. What is more, parties to a contract can agree to abide by principles that limit the legal privileges spelled out in the Copyright Act. In other words, a license can strip someone of the claim to fair use, the right to use a work for free in a classroom setting, or just about any other limitation on copyright. A properly worded agreement can result in someone agreeing for all time, not just 95 years, never to copy a work.

From this perspective, the Copyright Office report concluded that the first sale doctrine was not jeopardized by the impact of the DMCA. Since the real issue in the public debate was whether one who holds a digital file can copy and then transfer that file to another, the first sale doctrine (or the distribution right) was not decisive. The digital first sale debate was really about the ability of users to make copies of digital files and send them to friends and others. To the extent that TPMs embedded in digital works prevented that unauthorized sharing, there was no wrong that required a remedy and nothing that the first sale doctrine had to say about it.

On the day the Copyright Office report on first sale was published, news reports spoke in detail about the soon-to-be-released Windows XP operating system from Microsoft. Heralded as the most secure and important advance in computer operation, Windows XP promised to usher in a new era for the first sale doctrine. Buried in the Windows XP license was a provision that Microsoft had included in prior license agreements but never enforced. Now, with the wonders of more modern technology, Microsoft announced it would require every user of Windows XP to activate the software by dialing into a central processing center. That center would register the copy of the software with the user and with the user's machine. In short, the software is tethered to a specific machine. A consumer who spends the $200 to acquire the Windows XP software, places the CD-ROM into the computer's drive, and activates the software is prevented from using that software on any other machine he or she owns. The activation process reads the unique CPU information from the computer's motherboard and, through TPMs embedded in the software, prevents the software from working on any other computer. So, a user who has a desktop and a laptop must purchase two copies of Windows XP if both machines are to have the same operating system. Tethering the software to a specific machine, coupled with the DMCA civil and criminal prohibitions on bypassing TPMs that control access to a work, means that a user who is talented enough to determine how to make the software work on both machines has committed a felony.

In its report, the Copyright Office acknowledged that, should the practice of tethering software to specific machines become a common practice—it did not believe it to be common yet—there could be serious consequences for the first sale doctrine. That issue is riper than the Copyright Office understood, and the time will come in the near future when the matter of digital first sale will receive new attention.

Digital Rights Management: Content Control

Digital rights management (DRM) is the new code phrase for technical systems that control access to and use of digital files. Born out of content owners' concerns that files pass too freely between someone with access and those without, DRM identifies systems that can regulate access, copying, saving, and altering digital texts, images, sounds, and graphics. By technologically instructing operating systems, software, and hardware, DRM systems can control who can open a file, how long digital material can be viewed and how frequently, and whether a copy can be made or stored. DRM systems employ devices such as passcodes and encryption to establish limitations on opening files. They also incorporate methods for watermarking data to identify the source and ownership of a work and to instruct a computer or other device how the work may be utilized.

When Congress adopted the DMCA, it foresaw the potential for technological measures that control access to works, and DRM systems are just that technology. For content owners, fearful that releasing digital files means unbridled access to works and illegal copying, DRM systems are a crucial part of the technological solution. The penalties, both civil and criminal, included in the DMCA are the legal component of that solution.

Despite the real and legitimate concerns of owners and the benefits that DRM systems offer, there are costs as well. Among the key concerns are that DRM systems raise extreme copyright control and privacy issues. If DRM systems are effective in their processes, they can prevent fair use copies from being made of portions of works and they can negate other limitations that provide balance to the copyright law. Further, by specifically identifying the recipient or user of a work, such systems have the capability of converting digital content into a pay-as-you-read format. If user information is retained, it can lead to creations of databases of information about people's digital habits. For some, this scenario resembles an updated version of Orwell's "Big Brother Is Watching" from *1984*.

It is equally true that, for every digital barrier confronted, talented I-Gen hackers consider bypassing the barricade a challenge. With the DMCA offering powerful legal tools for owners, such an approach could have sad consequences. In 2001, a Russian programmer, Dmitry Sklyarov, became the subject of a criminal action after he published a software program that can defeat a DRM technology used to secure Adobe eBooks. The U.S. Justice Department (with the active encouragement of Adobe) arrested Sklyarov while he was delivering an academic paper on cracking the Adobe ROT-13 copy protection system and indicted him for trafficking in a device or program designed to circumvent a technological measure. He was jailed for several weeks and released after posting $50,000 bond. With the help of the Electronic Frontier Foundation, charges were subsequently dismissed. But a crucial lesson was learned: The DMCA has real teeth. Nevertheless, some DRM proponents are not leaving anything to chance. Working with Senator Fritz Hollings, chairman of the Senate Commerce Committee, they pushed two new bills designed to require equipment manufacturers to embed government-approved copy protection systems into all computer equipment and other devices that can receive digital media, such as high-definition television sets, DVD players, and digital audio receivers. The Security Systems Standards and Certification Act and the Consumer Broadband and Digital Television Promotion Act are mouthfuls of complex requirements intended to curb any unauthorized access to or use of digital content.

DRM systems are clearly a wave of the future. If content owners decide to make their most valuable digital works more widely available, DRM systems will be the reason they move with confidence.

Chapter 31

Teachers and a Digital World: How the Classroom Has Changed

The Copyright Act Shows Its Age

By 1990, the Copyright Act of 1976 was showing its age. In a number of critical respects, the statute had fallen behind developments, but nowhere more clearly than in the case of distant education at the undergraduate and graduate level. Although the Internet had not reached the masses, it was a medium commonly used by higher education. Electronic courses were being offered by many institutions to link faculty and students in the United States and overseas. However, to the extent that course content and electronic transmissions incorporated third-party copyrighted works, Section 110(2) of the Copyright Act, the existing statutory exemption permitting transmission of public performances or displays of certain works to remote locations in connection with instruction, was inapplicable.

Section 110(2) was written for the children of the 1950s' Sunrise Semester. It did not address the use of computers in the classroom; rather, its focus was on closed-circuit television or the dedicated delivery of a live classroom to remotely located classrooms or similar places of education. While the exemption facilitated the common practice by institutions, such as state universities, of beaming courses taught by faculty in one branch of the system to receiving sets viewed by students located in other cities within the state system, it did nothing for those who employed computers to reach distant students.

During the congressional debate on the DMCA, representatives of educational interests, particularly universities and libraries, sought to add the issue of updating copyright law to address the evolution of distance education. From those discussions came a provision in the DMCA that authorized the Register of

Copyrights to conduct a study of digital distance educational issues. Based on the Register's report, a bipartisan bill implementing copyright reform, affectionately dubbed The TEACH Act, was introduced by the key legislators controlling copyright law in the U.S. Senate, Senators Orrin Hatch (R-UT) and Patrick Leahy (D-VT).

For our purposes, *distance education* refers to any instruction that reaches students outside a physical classroom, and *digital distance education* is a version that involves the use of digitally networked computers to reach those students. In digital distance education, the students can be enrolled in a course at their school and use computers from their dorms or elsewhere on campus or they may be located in different cities.

Review of Distance Education in the 1976 Copyright Act

Four statutory limitations in the Copyright Act are the crucial legal foundation for current uses of copyrighted materials in the distance learning context. These provisions are Sections 110(1), 110(2), 112(b), and 107.

Section 110(1) is a limitation on the exclusive rights of owners covering the performance or display of a copyrighted work in connection with "face-to-face" classroom teaching. Under this limitation, any work that is the subject of copyright may be performed or displayed in class by an instructor or student during face-to-face teaching activities.

The only real qualification on the use of works inside a classroom is that, in the case of motion pictures, the work must be "lawfully acquired" to qualify for the face-to-face exemption. It is important to note that Section 110 deals only with "public performance" and "public display." It does not address questions of "reproduction" or "public distribution."

Section 110(2) is a further educational limitation on the public performance and public display rights of copyright owners. This provision permits the performance of a "nondramatic literary or musical work" or the display of a work in the course of a "transmission" if

- The performance or display is a regular part of the systematic instructional activities of a government body or nonprofit education institution.
- The performance or display is directly related and of material assistance to the teaching content of the transmission.
- The transmission is made primarily for
  1. Reception in classrooms or similar places normally devoted to instruction.
  2. Reception by persons to whom the transmission is directed because their disabilities or other special circumstances prevent their attendance in classrooms or similar places devoted to instruction.

3. Reception by officers or employees of government bodies as part of their official duties or employment.

In brief, Section 110(2) is the 1976 Act's "distance education" exception. While the requirements of Section 110(2) are subject to interpretation, the exemption by its terms does not expressly authorize the use of certain types of copyrighted works (such as motion pictures and other audiovisual works) and it does not exempt the reproduction or public distribution of works. Therefore, it fails to exempt the use of particular works and certain activities necessary for effective digital distance education in a computer-networked world.

Section 112(b) establishes the parameters for a limitation on the exclusive right of owners to control copying. The "ephemeral recording" exception permits educators to make a few copies of the classroom performance (e.g., videotapes of distant learning sessions) at a remote location for a limited time. The provision, which is expressly tied to Section 110(2), allows eligible institutions to make up to 30 copies of the transmission embodying the exempt performance or display and to keep those copies not more than 7 years (although an archival copy may be retained indefinitely). This allows students who missed the class to catch the video.

Fair Use Defense in the Educational Setting

To the extent that a performance, display, or other use of a copyrighted work is not covered by Section 110(2), an educational institution must fall back on the fair use provision to justify its use of works in a distant learning context. Recall that Section 107 is a broad and effective defense to many claims of copyright infringement. Fair use allows one who has exploited copyrighted works without consent of the owner to justify that use by resorting to a claim under recognized public purposes. Since these purposes include scholarship and research, digital distance education is a natural fit. Indeed, when Congress adopted the current copyright law, the committee reports explaining the bill specifically anticipated Section 107 would fill in the gaps covered by Sections 110(1) and 110(2). Among factors Congress expected to be considered in the fair use analysis are these:

- Whether the producers of the broadcast were paid.
- The size of the audience.
- The size and nature of the excerpts taken.
- The number of copies made and how they would be used and reused.

But fair use is not a "bright line" test. Therefore, unlike Section 110(2), which is an express exemption with specific requirements, fair use is a defense based on criteria that must be evaluated and judged according to the facts presented in each case. Nevertheless, since the 1976 Act's distance education exemption does not cover copying and public distribution, essential activities for use of the Internet in education, and does not cover many classes of works (e.g., audiovisual materials), most digital distant educational uses of copyrighted works must be evaluated under the fair use doctrine. This reality places a qualifying educational institution at risk, because certain uses may exceed the parameters of the fair use exception.

While it is rare for educational uses to inspire copyright litigation, a few cases of note involve analysis of the fair use defense in an educational setting. In one instance, Encyclopedia Britannica challenged a consortium of public school districts for recording motion picture works and providing copies to member schools. The schools lost the case, and their fair use defense was rejected.

Based on case law in other fair use cases, it is reasonable to conclude that educational uses made by nonprofit institutions that "transform" the work used (add meaning, context, explanation, or criticism) as opposed to merely reproduce the work (distributing a complete copy with no commentary) do better when the purpose and character of the use factor is evaluated. Courts also consider whether the work exploited is factual or creative, published or unpublished. The more factual and more widely released the work, the easier it is to justify fair use. Similarly, the intended market for the work and its ready availability are important facts. In the case of distant educational uses of textbooks produced for and accessible to the teaching marketplace, the doctrine may be severely limited or even unusable. "How much of the original work is used?" and "What impact could the use could have on the market for the original?" are vitally important questions in all fair use analyses. Thus, in a digital environment, the ability of students to receive and pass on perfect copies of an original text is a legitimate concern. The controls on access and further use imposed by the institution on students are highly relevant considerations.

If the user, who has the burden of justifying the fairness of the use, fails to persuade a court that the provision applies, then liability can attach. As we saw in Chapter 6, the damages and injunctive relief provisions of the Copyright Act include the potential recovery of actual damages and an accounting of profits. In the alternative, copyright law permits the owner to claim "statutory damages," defined as $750–30,000 per work infringed, if infringement occurs after federal registration. Further, the statute allows for recovery of attorney's fees by the prevailing party. Since a typical distance education course could utilize many individual works, the exposure to many infringement damage claims is significant. One important protection for educational institutions is the qualification in the Copyright Act that instructs a court to not to assess statutory damages for educational uses if the institutional employees reasonably rely on the fair use defense.

As with all fair use defenses, schools may find such protection unavailable, based on particular facts. In sum, while fair use always is a relevant defense to any educational institution's use of third-party materials, most educators would prefer to know that a particular use is specifically exempt from liability and not subject to critical review based on the fair use criteria.

DMCA and the Copyright Office Study

In 1998, when educators were negotiating the terms of the DMCA, they seized the opportunity to place Section 110(2) on the agenda in hope of securing clearer protection for digital distant educational uses of copyrighted materials. As the DMCA negotiations moved forward, several digital distance education issues came into clearer focus, but complex questions remained; for example,

- Which institutions should receive the exemption?
- Who is a qualified student?
- What "works" are covered?
- How should the new provisions dealing with "technological protection measures" be treated?

With time drawing short on developing statutory language and pressure to pass the DMCA increasing, a compromise was struck at the urging of Senators Hatch, Leahy, and Ashbrook. The Copyright Office would be empowered to study digital distance education issues with the goal of proposing changes to copyright law. The three senators gave their commitment to follow through on legislative recommendations. Therefore, the DMCA contained a provision requiring the Register of Copyrights to provide Congress with its recommendations on "how to promote distance education through digital technologies, including interactive digital networks, while maintaining an appropriate balance between the rights of copyright owners and the needs of users of copyrighted works."

Soon after implementation of the DMCA, the Register of Copyrights announced a proceeding to consult with representatives of copyright owners, nonprofit educational institutions, libraries, and archives, focusing on many factors, including

1. The need for an exemption from exclusive rights of copyright owners for distance education through digital networks.
2. The categories of works to be included in any exemption.
3. The extent of appropriate quantitative limitations on the portions of works that may be used under any distance education exemption.

4. The parties who should be entitled to the benefits of any exemption.

5. The parties who should be eligible to receive distance education materials under the exemption.

6. Whether and what types of technological measures can or should be employed to safeguard against unauthorized access to and use or retention of copyrighted materials as a condition of eligibility.

7. The extent to which the availability of licenses should be considered.

At public hearings, commercial publishers argued that they saw little if any reason to update the rules. They suggested that the marketplace for digital distant educational content will evolve and works will be made as readily available as other courseware. They expressed concern about individual and institutional misuse of copyrighted works and feared that an expansion of the statutory limitations would erode fledging enterprises. Libraries and educational institutions responded that, not only was the marketplace not functioning effectively, but also, and more important, the law should be updated to embrace current and projected digital distance educational uses.

The Copyright Office's report, released in May 1999, urged that the law be updated. The Copyright Office made the following key recommendations:

- *Clarify the meaning of transmission.* The term should cover digital as well as analog transmissions.

- *Expand the coverage of rights to the extent technologically necessary.* Since Section 110(2) covers only performance and display, it is necessary to add reproduction and distribution rights, but only to the extent technologically required to transmit the performance or display authorized by the exemption.

- *Emphasize the concept of mediated instruction.* A responsible member of the faculty needs to guide students working at their own place and time.

- *Eliminate requirement of physical classroom.* Since digital distance education does not require a classroom, elimination of a classroom as a statutory requirement is necessary. However, to prevent inappropriate availability to a larger audience, transmissions should be limited to students officially enrolled in a course.

- *Add new safeguards to counteract new risks:*
  1. Transient copies should be retained only so long as reasonably necessary.
  2. Copyright policies should be instituted and information on copyright compliance should be disseminated to faculty and students, together with notice that works used may be subject to copyright protection.
  3. Technological measures associated with works should be included.

- *Maintain the existing standards of eligibility.* The exception should be limited to qualified educational institutions, nonprofit institutions, and government bodies.

- *Expand the categories of works covered.* The limited categories in current law should be expanded to include audiovisual works, sound recordings, and dramatic literary and musical works.

- *Require the use of lawful copies.* The requirement in Section 110(1) that applies to motion pictures should be expanded to all works.

- *Add a new ephemeral recording exemption.* To permit asynchronous use of works (use anytime a student wishes to log on, not at a specific hour of the day when the class meets in a room), Section 112(b) should be expanded to permit uploading copies of works onto a server for subsequent retransmissions to students.

Often, passing a legislative issue off to a study is the kiss of death. In the case of digital distance education, the recommendations were taken seriously by the legislators and action initiated in spring 2001.

The TEACH Act to Transform Digital Distance Education

With the encouragement of educational and library interests, Senators Hatch and Leahy prepared legislation to implement the Copyright Register's report. The TEACH Act (short for Technology, Education, and Copyright Harmonization Act) was introduced in spring 2001. The bill was designed to fully implement the recommendations of the Register of Copyrights.

After several days of hearings, the senators brought representatives of the educational and content communities together in a windowless room inside the Library of Congress. The parties were told to take the Copyright Office framework and work through relevant issues until a compromise was reached. After several weeks of intense negotiations supervised by the Copyright Office staff and periodically reviewed by Senate staff—negotiations that often lasted well past government office closing hours—the TEACH Act was finalized. The highlights of the bill are these:

- *Expansion of covered works.* All copyright works are covered within the digital distance education exception, except (1) those produced or marketed primarily for performance or display as part of mediated instructional activities transmitted by digital networks and (2) those not lawfully made and acquired when the qualified institution knew or had reason to know that fact.

- *Rights affected.* As with current law, performance and display rights are directly involved, but the manner of use of particular works is explained. With respect to performance, all nondramatic literary or musical works may be used, but only reasonable and limited portions of other works, such as movies and multimedia works may be exploited. Display of any work in an amount comparable to that typically displayed in a course during a live class session would be permitted.

- *Eligible parties.* The exemption applies to (1) government bodies and (2) accredited nonprofit educational institutions. Accreditation would be a new requirement and could eliminate some nonprofit institutions. The exemption would not be available for use by any for-profit institution. Recipients of the transmissions must be students officially enrolled in the course or qualified officers or employees of government bodies.

- *Mediated instructional activities.* A key concept that must underlie digital distance education is "mediated instructional activities." These activities have several common characteristics: (1) the qualified works must be used as an integral part of the class experience and (2) an instructor must control or actually supervise the use, which is to be analogous to that in a live class. Activities that use in one or more class sessions works such as textbooks or course packs typically purchased by students for their use and retention (or at K–12 for student possession and independent use) are not covered.

- *Copyright policies.* Eligible institutions must institute copyright policies and apply reasonably effective technological measures to prevent retention beyond the allowable periods and unauthorized further dissemination. In addition, the institutions must not engage in activities that could reasonably be expected to interfere with technological measures used by copyright owners to prevent retention or further unauthorized distribution.

- *Transient storage.* Transient or temporary storage of materials is expressly allowed as part of the automatic, technical transmission process.

- *Ephemeral copies.* Copying necessary to effectuate the exemption is covered by the amendment to the ephemeral recording exception in Section 112(f). Eligible institutions are allowed to make copies or phonorecords of works that are needed in the transmissions.

- *Digital versions.* In addition, the institution can convert works in analog form to digital, if no digital version of a work is available or if the only digital version available is subject to technological measures that prevent permitted uses.

As the compromise was being finalized, the parties clarified a few additional points. First, legislative history refined certain elements of the agreement. For example, one agreed point is the understanding that not all educational materials or materials having educational value are works produced or marketed primarily for "mediated instructional activities." Second, accredited educational institutions that are "for profit" are not included in the exception; however, the Register of Copyrights may conduct a study regarding their activities and could make recommendations in the future about their role in the exception.

The TEACH Act passed the Senate promptly in summer 2001 and was referred to and passed through the Copyright Subcommittee in the House. Then, the bill hit a brick wall. With the chairman of the House Judiciary Committee looking for action on another pet copyright proposal (database protection), the TEACH Act was put on a seat in the principal's office and told to "wait." Throughout 2001, despite all the efforts of educators and legislators, action on the bill was stalled. Suddenly, in summer 2002, the logjam broke and the bill was voted out of the Judiciary Committee without any change. Final Congressional action occurred in October 2002.

The current distance education law is outdated. The new legislation serves an important public purpose, helping digital distance learning become a full-fledged participant in the educational process without unreasonable legal restraints on the use of materials online.

Chapter 32

Webcasting: A Primer for Digital Communication

The promise of the Internet is that anyone can be a publisher. The ease of communication offers revolutionary facility in sharing one's thoughts and expressions, art and images, and sounds and speech. But with that promise comes the obligation to understand content rules.

Traditional publishers, from trade book distributors to movie studios, spend a significant portion of their assets to ensure that they comply with the legal requirements of copyright and trademark law, not to mention rights of publicity and privacy, trade secrets, and unfair competition. They have lawyers and business people who are savvy as to content rules and scrupulously follow these requirements, lest they become subject to a third-party claim of infringement. While errors occur in the content review process or someone makes the deliberate decision to take a chance, the formality of review is part of their publishing routine.

The same is not true for many of the Internet's untraditional publishers. In the early days of the Internet, those inexperienced in content rights and wrongs were blissfully (or naively) ignorant of what it means to violate someone's copyright or trademark. While the privacy of e-mail offers the illusion that no one other than a solo recipient is paying attention, the ability to forward or share a digital file can shatter that sense of intimacy. And when one sends e-mail to a seemingly limitless crowd of contemporaries or creates a website for anyone to access, then the webcaster knowingly is engaging in a broad distribution of material. Has the webcaster reviewed a proper checklist of content rules before engaging in that ultimate Internet experience, sharing works with the world? What follows is a webcasting primer for the content savvy and a virtual review of subjects covered in this book (Figure 32-1).

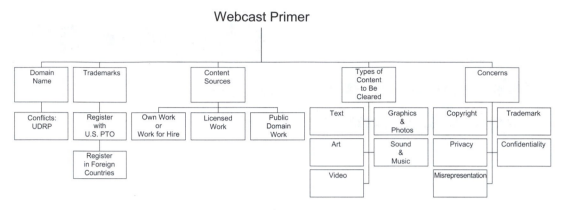

Figure 32-1   Webcast Primer

Domain Name

To establish yourself online, you need a domain name. The process has been greatly simplified in the past number of years. Just log on to www.register.com or a similar domain name registration site. You will be escorted through a process that can assure that the name you want is available in some form, whether it is www.NAME.com or .org, .net, .biz, .info, or whatever.

Trademark Check

The availability of the name is not the end of the story but just the beginning. Clearly, if you want to post family photographs on a website you wish to call www.kodak.info, you cannot assume that, because the site is available, you can lock it up without a second thought. A webcaster should do a trademark analysis of the availability of a domain name to ensure that it does not infringe another's trademark rights. Even someone without serious money to spend can take a few minutes and head to the PTO's official website, www.uspto.gov. Click through to the Trademark Office portion and go to a New User Search. Pop in the word or phrase and determine if anyone has already registered it with the PTO. If someone has, even if it is in a different line of commerce, that person or company may have a claim against your proposed use.

More formal legal searching is appropriate if the webcaster intends to invest significant money in the development of the site or if the site is related to a planned or existing business venture. In such cases, one needs a complete trademark analysis, covering federal and state registrations as well as common law uses. Then, too, for a website designed for serious business activities, a webcaster needs to take a close look at foreign markets. Trademark rights are geographically based, and, since the Web is an international medium of expression, a domain name based in the United States may run afoul of rights of someone elsewhere in the world.

Protect That Title with Federal Registration at the PTO

It bears repeating that, if the name selected is important to any long-range plan, consider registration of the trademark or service mark. This means filing an application with the PTO for exclusive rights to the phrase in connection with Internet services and any related business activities. The need for foreign registrations should also be evaluated.

Think about Other Trademark Uses

The domain name is only one of many trademarks a website owner typically uses. Scroll down through website pages and you will encounter many different words, phrases, images, and designs that bear trademark significance. Like sections of a newspaper or magazine, different identifiers can constitute trademarks if they are capable of signifying a source. Headings, subheadings, words, and phrases—each element should be assessed for trademark value and for potential trademark problems. Designs, art and shapes, even colors should also be scrutinized. It may not be feasible to assess the trademark status of every one of these; however, the most important and visible ones should not escape a thoughtful analysis.

Do a Content Audit

Of course, the inquiry does not stop there. Once you have a web address and some structure to the pages, think about the content you are placing on the Web. Initially, carefully determine what is being placed on the pages—text, graphics, photographs, charts, maps, clip art, sounds, videos, and links. Then, assess the use of the content by answering the relevant questions. Here is a handy sampling of the some of the more important issues to think about:

- Did you create the content or rely on someone else to make it?
- If it comes from someone else, is that person an employee or an independent contractor? Is there a written agreement covering the work created, and do the work-for-hire rules apply?
- Is the content taken directly from a third-party source? If so, does the content need to be cleared?

- If the content needs to be cleared, have sufficient permissions been obtained?
- Are any of the content uses covered by a limitation in copyright law? If so, which one, and have all the necessary conditions been met?
- Are any issues of publicity or privacy associated with the use? Is there a person whose name or image is being exploited? Is he or she a private person or someone famous?
- If a private person, is there any potential for placing the person in a false or embarrassing light?
- If a famous person, does the use exploit that fame without permission and for profit?
- Does the use affect any confidential information? Does someone's permission have to be obtained to disclose the information?
- Is there a potential misrepresentation in any statements made, particularly about another person?

Special Content Issues for Webcasting

After thinking about these various questions, certain special content issues should be considered.

Text

Assume that most of the text matter on the website is original. Still, some material may come from somewhere else. If the webcaster quotes or paraphrases another's work, the use of that material may be fair, but one cannot just assume that to be the case. A fair use analysis should be undertaken to ensure that the borrowed text is not so substantial that permission is needed. It helps if the borrowed text was created by someone working within the federal government, is a string of facts, or is so old as to qualify for the public domain. While those exceptions cover a large amount of source material, they still represent a very small fraction of potential text.

Graphics, Photographs, Charts, and Maps

What has made the World Wide Web the publishing center for digital works is the ease with which images can be transmitted. Every graphic, photograph, chart, or map adds color, texture, and interest to Internet communications. But the rules for using this material must be scrupulously adhered to, lest the user be exposed to potentially gigantic damage claims.

Remember, if a registered copyrighted work is infringed, statutory damages of $750–30,000 per work may be assessed, plus the legal costs of the prevailing party. If dozens of images are used, the claims multiply for each copyright.

Photographs have become a particular point of contention on the Internet because near perfect duplicates can be made from digital files. Unless the webcaster or an employee snapped the image, the photo should be considered covered by someone else's copyright and cleared accordingly. Unlike books or magazine articles, it is hard to take a "fair use" portion of a photograph. The entire work is usually published. Therefore, if the photo has not been cleared, a more complex fair use analysis must be relied on to justify the posting. Avoid the photo briar patch: Clear the images before you use them.

Clip Art

Clip art is deserving of a special word. Many software packages come with images for use on computers. Simply cut and paste the image into a text. It is fun and simple to do. However, use of most software packages is regulated by a detail license which the user agrees to by opening the software package ("shrink wrap license") or checking "ACCEPT" if it is obtained directly online ("click license"). We talked about these licenses in Chapter 30. Most typically, clip art is packaged for private, noncommercial use. The terms of an individual license can vary, but it is necessary to read the license if you intend to post an image on the Internet. While an individual may use the clip art to make private calendars or school reports, when one publishes on the Web, a different audience is reached and different permissions may be required. The license may inform you how to secure the necessary permission to make broader public use of the works. Even so, many licenses, including some offered by Microsoft, simply warn you that additional clearance may be required but do not tell you where to get the consent quickly and easily.

Sounds and Music

Aside from graphics, the Web has popularized the use of digital sounds, voice, and music. The conversion of signals to streams of bits of data that a computer can interpret and communicate is a technological miracle of our age. To use sounds and music on a website is an ultimate Internet experience and a core benefit offered by the medium. However, if the sounds and music were uttered, composed, and recorded by someone else, then permission is needed to disseminate them from websites.

Of course, even before the transmission, this content must be preserved in a digital file on a server. This means it must be copied. That very act requires consent if the sounds and images are not original to the webcaster. The permission may be inherent in a limitation on copyright, but checking that out first is a necessity.

Digital conflicts already have many victims in the Internet webcasting battles. Prime among these is Napster, which offered a website to facilitate file sharing. Wildly popular but disdainful of copyright rules, Napster learned that even merely facilitating the transfer of music files on the Internet can violate content rights.

Since webcasting is a form of public performance, licenses must be obtained from the performing rights societies (ASCAP, BMI, and SESAC) if any of the songs in their repertoire is transmitted. All three societies have developed webcasting licenses, which can be downloaded and obtained from their websites. Any webcaster who uses music must obtain one or all of these licenses.

Equally necessary for use of digital sounds is a license from the recording company that pressed the original sound recording. Because finding the proper source of such a license and negotiating its terms can be a daunting task, Congress added a provision to the DMCA that establishes a compulsory license for sound recordings on the Internet.

In 2001, the fee for the compulsory license was the subject of an arbitration proceeding managed by the Copyright Office. In spring 2002, a CARP ruling proposed set fees for radio stations and other (nonbroadcaster) users of music. The CARP panel determined that a reasonable fee, on a per song per recipient basis, is 0.07¢ (for broadcasters) and 0.14¢ (for nonbroadcasters). After mandatory review by the Librarian of Congress, the nonbroadcast rate was reduced to 0.07¢ as well. This translates into 7 cents for every webstreamed recording that reaches 100 people. For entities that hope to make their web fortune by playing music, these compulsory license fees add an expense—potentially a large expense—that affects the bottom line.

Videos

The ultimate application of the Internet is delivery of video content. Whether by download (transmitting movie files for storage on a recipient's home computer) or streaming (transmitting small portions of video files on a flowing basis, so that the entire video file is not available at any one time), having access to video content via the Internet makes the medium directly parallel to television (and perhaps directly competitive with it). With broadcast stations costing millions of dollars to build and license from the FCC, the potential for video transfer via the Internet is a unique, economical way for creative professionals to reach out to a broad audience.

Because the medium is so powerful and videos and film so valuable to traditional content owners, a webcaster needs to be particularly scrupulous in attending to content rights for video. The fights over music files already have video parallels in websites known by the phrases *icravetv.com* and *scour.com*. Webcasters that use video clips, not to mention full-length works, must carefully follow the content rules of the road.

There you have it: a webcasting primer designed to guide uses online. Webcasters must now think carefully about the content rights the law grants creators and the obligations it imposes on content users.

Chapter 33

Afterword: A Closing Thought

We crossed a divide, from an era of media that directed content at the public into the era of interactive communication in which the public participation in the reshaping of content, from broadcasting to interactive digital communication. In an age marked by new means of transmitting data and information, the definition of legal rights to content will be tested as never before. Content will be exploited without consent in ways that traditionalists will abhor and new school creators applaud. An effort to bring order and reason to the new medium is being met with a countervailing cry: Copyright is dead. Internet guru Esther Dyson surmised that content cannot be protected, so there is really no reason to try. Turn it over to the wolves and earn your living selling ancillary goods and services—this is a bleak specter for those who believe in the regime of content developed over our history and whose livelihood is based on that system remaining in place a few more years.

The chances of copyright law, or trademark law, for that matter, dying in the new millennium is apocryphal. True, there is concern about how to protect rights, how to stop unauthorized copying in an age of wonderfully easy copy machinery. But that does not mean the system does not have technical and legal solutions. Rather, as the 21st century moves forward, we face the challenge of instilling in a literate electorate a new appreciation for the values that underlie the faith—a belief that the fruits of intellect deserve society's respect, praise, and protection.

Appendix: Useful Websites

Official Government Sites

Copyright Office: www.loc.gov/copyright
Patent and Trademark Office: www.uspto.gov
Federal Communications Commission: www.fcc.gov
Federal Trade Commission: www.ftc.gov
Congress: thomas.loc.gov

International Sites

WIPO: www.wipo.org
European Union: www.europa.eu.int

Domain Names

ICANN: www.icann.org
Registrations: www.netsol.com, www.register.com

Educational Associations Sites

American Library Association: www.ala.org
Association of Research Libraries: www.arl.org
Digital Futures Coalition: www.dfc.org
Electronic Frontier Foundation: www.eff.org
Electronic Privacy Information Center: www.epic.org

Educational Sites for Intellectual Property

Berkman Internet Center at Harvard: www.cyber.law.harvard.edu
Cornell University: www.law.cornell.edu/topics/trademark

Stanford University: www.fairuse.stanford.edu
University of Texas: www.utsystem.edu/ogc/intellectualproperty

Publishing Sites

Focal Press: www.bh.com/fp
Copyright Clearance Center: www.copyright.com
Music Licensing Societies:
  ASCAP: www.ascap.com
  BMI: www.bmi.com
  SESAC: www.sesac.com
  Music Publishers/Harry Fox Agency: www.nmpa.org

Trade Association Sites

Broadcasters: www.nab.org
Cable systems: www.ncta.com
International Trademark Association: www.inta.org
Motion pictures: www.mpaa.org
Publishers: www.publishers.org
Recording companies: www.riaa.org

Glossary

Access In the copyright context, availability of copyrighted content to users. Controlling access to content in a technological era is at the heart of digital copyright debate and has spawned technological protection measures, devices to circumvent those measures, and devices to circumvent the circumvention devices.

Action letter A letter from the PTO, prior to denial of a trademark application, to which a response is required.

Amateur Sports Act A law passed in 1978 that grants broad trademark protection to the words *Olympic, Olympiad, Citius Altius Fortius*, and the five interlocutory rings and prohibits any mark that falsely represents a connection to the U.S. Olympic Committee or the International Olympic Committee.

American Society of Composers, Authors and Publishers (ASCAP) One of the three major performing rights societies (along with BMI and SESAC), which licenses the rights to perform songs on behalf of the songwriters and lyricists they represent.

Anticircumvention Methods developed to render circumvention devices ineffective.

Anticopying codes Method of controlling access to digital data by preventing downloading to a printer.

Anticybersquatting Consumer Protection Act (ACPA) A law adopted in 1999 to address the unfair taking of domain names by amending the Lanham Act to prohibit cybersquatting.

Arbitrary marks Common words applied with a novel meaning to products or services. These marks are awarded a good deal of trademark protection due to the complex task of creating a new meaning for a known word.

Author(s) The person or team of people responsible for the creation of a copyrighted work and thus the owners of that work's copyright.

Barter syndication Licensing television programs by trading the right to televise a show in exchange for advertising time. Barter syndication allows the program distributor to earn money by selling time for commercials and contrasts with a cash deal; that is, licensing rights for direct money payment from the licensee station.

Berne Convention for the Protection of Literary and Artistic Property The leading international copyright treaty, which the U.S. joined in 1988. To conform to the Berne Convention, the United States completed a process, begun in 1976, of stripping copyright law of required formalities.

Blanket license A license to use all works in a collection as opposed to a separate license for each work; for example, the major performing rights societies (ASCAP, BMI, and SESAC) offer blanket licenses for all works in their repertoires.

Brand extension Leveraging of a trademark into a new and different market.

The Bridgeman Art Library, Ltd. v. Corel Corp., 25 F. Supp. 2d 421 (S.D.N.Y. 1998), on reconsideration, 36 F. Supp. 2d 191 (S.D.N.Y. 1999) A New York court decision that held that transparencies and digital images of works of art were mere "slavish copies" (similar to photocopies) and therefore not entitled to copyright protection.

Broadcast Music, Inc. (BMI) One of the three major performing rights societies (along with ASCAP and SESAC), which licenses the rights to perform songs on behalf of the songwriters and lyricists they represent.

Call signs Identifiers assigned by the FCC to radio and television stations.

Children's Online Privacy Protection Act (COPPA) A law passed in 1998 to regulate the online collection of personal information from children under age 13.

Circumvention The methods of rendering ineffective technological measures designed to control access to works. *See* Anticircumvention.

Colorization The practice of computer-coloring old black-and-white movies and television programs.

Comedy Three Productions, Inc. v. *Gary Saderup, Inc.,* 25 Cal. 4th 387 (2001), cert. denied, 151 L. Ed. 2d 692 (2002) The case in which the heirs of the Three Stooges successfully stopped an artist from using their images on T-shirts and lithographs.

Common law The body of law composed of the legal decisions of judges based on equity or simple fairness.

Community Trademark Application (CTA) A single trademark application implemented by the European Union to allow the prospective registrant to obtain simultaneous protection in all participating countries.

Common law copyright Prior to the 1976 Copyright Act, the prepublication copyright that made a work the exclusive property of its owner and his or her heirs forever.

Compulsory license A government-mandated use of copyrighted material in exchange for a fee set by the government. The license relies on the theory that public policy must reconcile competing interests to allow consumers access to copyrighted works. Compulsory license schemes exist for the cable television and satellite industries, digital sound recordings, certain master recording uses, jukeboxes, public television, and public radio.

Conspiracy in restraint of trade The action of two or more independent entities to join together to restrict the free flow of commerce.

Contributory infringement A legally actionable copyright infringement that occurs by directly helping someone else infringe on a copyright, which also results in liability. This concept has been applied to hold online service providers liable for copyright infringement.

Copyright The exclusive rights granted by statute to authors to control and exploit their writings for limited times, to carry out the mandate of the U.S. Constitution to encourage creative expression.

Copyright Act of 1976 The major copyright legislation updating the 1909 Copyright Act to reflect technological and international developments.

Copyright Arbitration Royalty Panels (CARPs) Administrative bodies authorized by copyright law and empaneled by the Librarian of Congress to handle distribution of royalties and fixing rates under compulsory licensing systems. CARPs report findings to the Librarian of Congress, who issues final decisions.

Copyright Office The office within the Library of Congress charged with administering the federal copyright system and serving as a source of expertise to Congress and the public on intellectual property matters.

Copyright owner The individual or entity that holds the six rights comprising copyright. *See* Exclusive rights.

Copyright Royalty Tribunal (CRT) The federal agency created by the 1976 Act to manage compulsory licensing, dissolved in 1994 and replaced by the Librarian of Congress and the CARPs.

Corporation for National Research Initiatives (CNRI) A nonprofit organization created to promote the Internet, which brought a trademark cancellation action to recover public use of the word *Internet*.

Creativity A fundamental condition of copyright protection, requiring that a work have a modicum of thought.

CSS (Content Scramble System) A technical system that scrambles digital codes to hinder copying.

Cybersquatting Taking domain names in conscious derogation of the rights of trademark proprietors.

Database A collection of information. Whether protection should be afforded to the creators of databases has been a burning copyright issue and is not yet resolved. Proponents of such protection cite the considerable investment in constructing and maintaining databases, while opponents rely on the *Feist* decision and the public's right to access facts and government works.

DeCSS A computer program devised by a Norwegian teenager to defeat CSS. *See Universal City Studios, Inc.* v. *Reimerdes*.

Derivative work/derivative work right A work based on another copyrighted work. The right to control works derived from one's original work is an exclusive right of the copyright owner.

Descriptive marks Trademarks that specifically state the essential element of the product or nature of the service. Descriptive marks are at the weak end of the trademark protection spectrum and are not protected with evidence of secondary meaning.

Digital audiotape machine (DAT) A digital audio recording device, which, since 1992, has been subject to a compulsory royalty in the form of a tax on each machine transferred, to compensate those whose works are included in the digital recordings.

Digital distance education Distance education that uses digitally networked computers to reach students.

Digital Millennium Copyright Act (DMCA) The comprehensive copyright reform legislation enacted in 1998 to update U.S. copyright law to reflect technological developments since the Copyright Act of 1976.

Digital rights management (DRM) Systems for marking digital files to identify ownership and to control access and use.

Digital signature A method of controlling access to digital data by requiring a display before one can access it.

Digital sound recording compulsory license A license instituted in 1998 to compensate copyright owners for the use of musical CDs and sounds from digital media in Web pages.

Directors Guild of America (DGA) The association representing U.S. television and film directors.

Display/display right Traditionally, the act of placing works in public places for people to view; in the digital context, the word has been expanded to include viewing on computer screens. The display right is an exclusive right of copyright owners.

Distance education/distance learning Instruction that reaches students located outside a physical classroom.

Distribution/distribution right Dissemination of copyrighted work to the public, including electronic transmission. The right to distribute a work to the public is an exclusive right of copyright owners.

Domain name A unique combination of letters, numbers, and dashes that routes packets of information among computer users.

Droit de suite The concept that an author's interest in a work stays with it even after it has been sold. Under this principle, artists are entitled to share in the appreciated value of paintings and other art works as a result of sales long after the creator sold his original work.

Droit moral The Berne Convention principle that recognizes that, in addition to the economic interests an author has to exploit and benefit from a copyrighted work, certain noneconomic interests must also be protected. Under this concept, an author's honor and reputation are deemed part of his or her creative endeavors, and the artist and his or her heirs should be entitled to protect that honor from the degradation that occurs when an original work is altered.

Editing In the context of alteration of films, deleting content for a variety of reasons, including fitting films into time slots and removing offensive words or nudity.

Eldred **v.** *Ashcroft* A case before the U.S. Supreme Court in 2002. The key issue of the case is whether the 1998 law extending the term of copyright 20 years for new works and those already published violates the Constitution's "limited times" requirement.

Encryption The methods of coding content so that access to it will be denied unless the user's activity has been approved.

Ephemeral recording A temporary copy of copyrighted work that the copyright law permits to be made. In the case of music, a broadcast organization licensed to publicly perform a work may make an ephemeral copy, for example, to ease transitions between songs. The recordings may be used only by the organization that performed the recording, may be used only for local or archival purposes, and must be destroyed or archived 6 months after public use.

Exclusive rights Rights that the U.S. Constitution grants authors for limited times that, collectively, are referred to as copyright. These rights are defined by the Copyright Act as the rights to (1) reproduce the work, (2) prepare derivative works based on the original, (3) distribute copies to the public, (4) perform the work publicly, (5) display the work publicly, and (6) copy, publicly distribute, and prepare derivative works that are digital audio sound recordings.

Fair use A defensive claim alleging that use of a copyrighted work is not an infringement if the use meets certain purposes, criteria, and restrictions.

Fanciful marks Made-up terms that have no dictionary meaning but were created to signify a specific product. Their uniqueness grants them significant trademark protection.

Feist Publications, Inc. **v.** *Rural Telephone Service Co.,* 499 U.S. 340 (1991) The case in which the U.S. Supreme Court held that the names and phone numbers in telephone books are facts and hence not copyrightable. The process of collecting facts (so-called sweat of the brow) does not create a copyright interest in the facts.

Financial syndication (FinSyn) rules The rules of the Federal Communications Commission that prohibited the major broadcast networks from syndicating programming that originally aired on their facilities. The rules were eliminated in 1995.

First sale The copyright doctrine that gives the creator of a work the right to choose the forum of its first publication. It also allows the owner of a copy to loan, sell, or transfer that copy to someone else.

Fixation A fundamental condition of copyright, requiring that a work be embodied in a tangible medium of expression.

Formalities The rules (such as notice and registration) that were prerequisites to perfecting rights under the U.S. copyright system. Failure to comply with formalities resulted in loss of copyright protection. The 1976 Act eliminated them.

General Agreement on Tariffs and Trade (GATT) An international trade agreement that, among other things, is the basis on which Congress restored to foreign copyright owners the balance of their original terms if the loss of copyright protective status in the United States was due to failure to comply with formalities.

Generic marks Words referring to a category of goods or services and not one unique product or service. Generic marks cannot function as trademarks because they are inherently incapable of helping a consumer to distinguish one source from another.

Gilliam **v.** *American Broadcasting Companies,* 538 F. 2d 14 (2d Cir. 1976) The case in which the creators of the *Monty Python* television program sued ABC for severely editing their work for a network telecast. In a decision based on Section 43(a) of the Lanham Act, the producers prevailed in convincing the court that the altered show misrepresented their work.

***Goldstein* v. *California*,** 412 U.S. 546 (1973) The case in which the U.S. Supreme Court found that the duplication of audiotapes violated local laws of misappropriation, even though there was no copyright protection. The practice of selling the tapes on the street ultimately led to enactment of copyright protection for owners of sound recordings.

Harmonization The term used to characterize the efforts of nations to create international uniformity in copyright and trademark matters by establishing shared, common principles.

***Harper & Row Publishers, Inc.* v. *Nation Enterprises*,** 471 U.S. 539 (1985) A major decision on the subject of first sale and fair use. The U.S. Supreme Court held that *Nation*'s use of just 300 words out of a 200,000-word book constituted unfair use. *Nation*'s use scooped a publisher's planned book release and took President Ford's own words to describe his pardon of Richard Nixon (the "heart" of his book).

Idea/expression dichotomy The core principle of copyright law that ideas are not protectable but original and creative expressions of ideas are.

Incontestability The status of a mark 5 years after its registration by the Patent and Trademark Office (PTO) and the filing of a requisite notice and affidavit with the PTO. Incontestability does not mean there is no basis for challenging a mark, but in practicality, an incontestable mark is usually very secure.

Intellectual property (IP) The copyrights, trademarks, patents, trade secrets, and rights of publicity and privacy.

Intent to use (ITU) An application filed with the Patent and Trademark Office (PTO) stating the applicant's intention to use a mark in commerce. This filing allows for the reservation of a trademark, and the applicant has up to 3 years after the initial grant to actually start using the mark, provided the applicant files notice of *bona fide* intent to use every six months.

Internet The global electronic communications network that transformed the way works are published and forced updating and reevaluation of existing intellectual property rules.

Internet Corporation for Assigned Names and Numbers (ICANN) The organization that accredits the private registries that allocate domain names.

Internet Network Information Center (InterNIC) The U.S. organization funded by the National Science Foundation and managed by Network Solutions, Inc., of Herndon, Virginia (owned by VeriSign), that establishes and regulates domain names.

Internet service provider (ISP) Entity offering transmission, routing or providing of connections for digital online communications.

Lanham Act The U.S. law, originally enacted in 1946, that established the current system of trademark protection. The act was named for the congressional representative who then chaired the House Patent Committee.

Leapfrogging rules Geographical limits imposed by the Federal Communications Commission on which signals can be imported by cable operators.

Lexiconing An alteration to a movie in which pitch is altered while changing film speed to keep the sound level constant and mask the speed changes. *See Time compression/time expansion.*

Likelihood of confusion The test for infringement of a trademark; that is, whether the consumer is likely to be confused as to the source of two marks.

Limited publication A judicially created exception to the requirement that publication without complying with the formalities of copyright law prior to 1978 would divest the owner of copyright. This exception provided that a release of a very limited number of copies would not be considered a divestative publication.

Limited times The constitutional duration of time that an author has exclusive rights in a work. Copyright terms have been extended many times since the original act in 1790, most recently in 1976 and 1978.

Madrid Agreement Concerning International Registration of Trademarks An international treaty, to which the United States does not belong, that establishes a unitary international trademark system.

Market power The degree to which one entity controls a line of commerce.

Master use license The license to copy directly from a sound recording. Since 1972, sound recordings have been considered protected works under the Copyright Act. Therefore, taking music clips directly from a record or tape or CD without proper clearance is a copyright infringement.

Mechanical license A license that gives the holder the right to create his or her own version of published music for play on any mechanical device as long as a statutory fee is paid.

Mediated instructional activities Under the TEACH Act, activities supervised by an instructor and using works as an integral part of the educational experience.

Monopoly The situation that exists when one business can control prices to consumers or prevent entry by competitors.

Moral rights *See Droit moral.*

Morphing The technique of digitally altering video.

Motion Picture Association of America (MPAA) The association that acts as an advocate for U.S. motion picture and television production and distribution industries.

Musical Works Fund A statutorily created fund into which (along with the Sound Recordings Fund) compulsory royalties from the sale of digital audio recording devices are deposited. Monies from the Musical Works Fund are distributed to music publishers and writers.

Music rights The rights of creators and publishers that cover the public performance and licensing of the use of music.

Napster.com The website for the online music file-sharing technology that attracted millions of users in the late 1990s and 2000 and became embroiled in a conflict over whether facilitating such file sharing was a violation of the copyright rights of the owners of the music. Napster.com was sued by the recording companies and lost in *A&M Records* v. *Napster,* 239 F.3d 1004 (9th Cir. 2001).

National Association of Television Program Executives (NATPE) The leading association of program syndicators. The NATPE annual broadcast syndication trade show is where television executives look for programs for upcoming seasons.

The New York Times Company, Inc. **v.** *Tasini,* 429 U.S. 298 (2001) The case in which the U.S. Supreme Court ruled that reuse of articles by freelance contributors to newspapers and magazines in commercial electronic databases without additional permission from their authors constituted infringement of the authors' copyrights.

Nice Convention Regarding Classification of Trademarks The international treaty, agreed to by the United States in 1972, that organizes and categorizes trademarks into 42 classes of goods and services.

Nondisclosure agreement (NDA) An agreement that obligates the recipient of a trade secret to maintain responsible controls over the use of the secret.

North American Free Trade Agreement (NAFTA) An international trade agreement that, among other things, is the basis on which Congress restored to foreign copyright owners the balance of their original terms if the loss of copyright protective status in the United States was due to failure to comply with formalities.

Notice A formality required under copyright law prior to 1978 pursuant to which copyright owners were required to place the word "copyright" or the symbol "©" and information regarding name of author and year of publication on their works to claim copyright protection.

Notice and takedown Requirements imposed on online service providers as a condition of limitation on financial liability for infringement; that is, if an OSP becomes aware that infringing material is on its site, it must quickly and effectively remove the material or disable public access to the site or else face loss of the limitation.

Official Gazette **(OG)** The weekly publication of the Patent and Trademark Office that lists trademark applications that have been approved for registration or renewal.

Online service provider (OSP) Internet companies that provide software to link users to sites as well as store information on their servers, facilitating recordings and displays by users or subscribers. The DMCA provided a limitation on financial liability for infringement for OSPs that comply with certain conditions.

Originality A fundamental condition for copyright protection, requiring that a protectable work contain new expression.

Panning and scanning An alteration made to a movie by reducing the aspect ratio (height and width of screen image) from the rectangular, film format to the square, television format.

Paris Convention for the Protection of Industrial Property The 1883 international treaty that covers common standards for both trademark and patent laws.

Patent The right granted by the government to the creator of an invention to exclude others from making, using, offering, or selling the invention in the United States.

Patent and Trademark Office (PTO) The agency of the United States Department of Commerce charged with administering the federal system of patents and trademarks.

Performance license A license to perform music in public places, granted by composers and lyricists (authors) or their representatives, including ASCAP, BMI, and SESAC.

Performer's right The interest an actor has in his or her public or publicized performance. It should be distinguished from the right of the copyright owner to control public performance of a work. The person who delivers a work to the public via a performance does not, under current U.S. copyright law, hold a copyright in that performance.

Per-program license In music licensing, a license to perform a specific musical composition during a specific show, as opposed to a blanket license, which covers all programs broadcast every day and all songs in the licensing society's repertoire. The license fee is based on actual usage and calculated according to a complex formula.

Polaroid Corp. **v.** *Polarad Electronics Corp.*, 287 F.2d 492, (2d Cir. 1961), cert. denied 368 U.S. 820 (1961) The landmark case that establishes the principle of likelihood of confusion as the basis for evaluating a claim of ownership to a trademark. If there is a likelihood of confusion, usually the first to have used the mark prevails, and the second owner either loses the rights to the mark or finds its market severely restricted. If confusion is unlikely, the two marks can coexist.

Principal Register The main directory of federally registered trademarks.

Privacy right The right of the less-than-famous to anonymity; specifically, protection from intrusion into private affairs, public disclosure of embarrassing facts, publicly being placed in a false light, and misappropriation of name or likeness.

Publication The distribution of copies to the public or any other transfer of ownership by means of sale, lease, loan, or otherwise giving away copies of a work. Prior to the 1976 Copyright Act, publication was the event that triggered the need to comply with the formalities of federal law to preserve a copyright.

Public domain The status of works whose copyrights have expired, federal government works, and any other work not covered by copyright, which are free to be used and reused by the public without clearance or compensation.

Publicity right The right of famous people to control the use of their names and images.

Public performance/public performance right The rendition of a work before an audience in a public place or beyond a normal circle of family and friends. The right to control public performance of a work is an exclusive right of copyright owners.

Recording Industry Association of America (RIAA) The association of record publishers. RIAA has campaigned aggressively to expand rights of recording companies and shut down unauthorized copying of musical CDs.

Registration In the copyright context, a formality required under copyright law prior to 1978 pursuant to which copyright owners were required to register their works with the Copyright Office to claim copyright protection. In the trademark context, a process of filing a notice of use or intent to use with the appropriate authority (at the federal level, the Patent and Trademark Office; at the state level, usually the Secretary of State).

Retransmission consent The provision of the Cable Television Consumer Protection and Competition Act of 1992 that requires local cable systems to obtain permission from a local broadcasting station to carry its signal to cable subscribers.

Salinger v. Random House, Inc., 811 F. 2d 90 (2d Cir. 1987), cert. denied, 484 U.S. 890 (1988) The case in which an appellate court prevented Random House from including quotations from unpublished letters of J. D. Salinger in a biography of the author.

Satellite Home Viewer Act (SHVA) The law passed in 1988 to create a compulsory license system whereby satellite delivery companies pay a set fee per subscriber per month for the privilege of retransmitting off-the-air broadcast stations and their programming.

Secondary meaning The status achieved by certain trademarks that become well known to the public as originating from a sole source.

Service marks A word, phrase, design, image, or color associated with the provision of services that is a unique identifier as to the source of the service.

Society of European Songwriters, Authors and Composers (SESAC) One of the three major performing rights societies (along with ASCAP and BMI), which license the rights to perform songs on behalf of the songwriters and lyricists that they represent.

Sonny Bono Copyright Term Extension Act of 1998 (CTEA) The act that added 20 years to the term of copyright protection. The U.S. Supreme Court agreed in 2002 to hear a challenge to the constitutionality of this law. *See Eldred* v. *Ashcroft.*

Sony Corp. of America **v.** *Universal City Studios, Inc.*, 464 U.S. 417 (1984) The landmark case in which the Supreme Court held that sale of the Betamax machine to home viewers and its use for taping television programs was fair use.

Sound Recordings Fund A statutorily created fund into which (along with the Musical Works Fund) compulsory royalties from the sale of digital audio recording devices are deposited. Monies from the Sound Recordings Fund are distributed to musicians, vocalists, and the sound recording companies.

Spamming Sending unsolicited e-mail, often to millions of addresses, via the Internet.

Specimens Examples of materials that show a trademark in use for purposes of PTO applications.

Statutory damages The damages mandated by the Copyright Act ($750–30,000 per work infringed), which may be awarded in lieu of other damages to ensure that the copyright owner is properly compensated for infringement.

Suggestive marks Trademarks that seek to exploit words or phrases that already have an association in the consumer's mind and thus are suggestive of their content.

Supplemental Register The backup registry of trademarks that the PTO has concluded are descriptive (but not generic). If a mark is registered in the Supplemental Register for 5 years, its owner can petition to move it to the Principal

Register and claim full trademark rights. A Supplemental Register mark will also be used by a PTO examiner as a basis to reject someone else's application.

Synchronization (synch) license A license to copy music onto film or video and associate the words and songs with images.

Syndication exclusivity (syndex) rules The FCC standards that require a cable operator to delete a program from a distantly retransmitted station when it duplicates programs broadcast on a local station to which the local station had exclusive market rights.

TEACH Act The legislation introduced in Congress in 2001 that, when enacted, will update and expand the existing distance education limitation on the public performance and public display rights of copyright owners.

Technological protection measure (TPM) A method of or device for protecting digital copyrighted material.

Time compression/time expansion The practice of speeding up or slowing down frame speed of a film. *See Lexiconing.*

Trade dress The packaging of a product or overall image of a business.

Trademark A word, phrase, design, image, or color physically stamped on a good or a label attached to a good as a unique identifier as to the source of the product.

Trademark Trial and Appeals Board (TTAB) The body within the Patent and Trademark Office that conducts hearings on oppositions to trademark registrations.

Trade name The actual name of a business readily identified by additional words, such as *Company, Corporation, Ltd., LLC,* or *Inc.* A trade name often comes attached to a street address, a phone number, or an e-mail address. Unlike a trademark or service mark, which is linguistically an adjective that modifies a type of good or service, a trade name is grammatically a noun; it identifies a particular person or business.

Unfair competition Misrepresentation in commerce that harms a consumer or a competitor. Examples of unfair competition, in addition to direct misrepresentation, are false designations of origin, as well as misuse of names and trademarks.

Uniform Computer Information Transactions Act (UCITA) The uniform code promulgated by legal experts to address issues in the regulation of electronic commerce. One of the more controversial aspects of UCITA is the position that contractual arrangements set out in electronic licenses should be allowed to control all uses of content, potentially overriding copyright and consumer protection laws.

Uniform Domain Name Dispute Resolution Policy (UDRP) The policy imposed by ICANN in 1999 as a condition in its agreements with registries of domain names. Under the policy, parties seeking a domain name must agree to follow a prescribed process to resolve disputes regarding domain names.

Uniform Trade Secret Act (UTSA) The model code for states setting standards for protection of trade secrets.

***Universal City Studios, Inc.* v. *Reimerdes*,** 273 F. 3d 429 (2001), affirming 111 F. Supp. 2d 346 (S.D.N.Y. 2000) A leading case interpreting the DMCA, which held that decryption of a technological protection measure is not allowed.

Use in commerce The basis for common law trademark protection. Use in commerce is established by the sale or giveaway of goods or services.

Vicarious infringement A legally actionable copyright infringement that occurs when one indirectly supports or is responsible for the infringing activity of another. This concept has been applied to hold online service providers liable for copyright infringement. *See also* contributory infringement.

Visual Artists Rights Act (VARA) The law passed in 1990 to give visual artists a limited version of moral rights. It permits an artist whose outdoor sculpture or public mural falls out of contemporary favor to prevent the work from being removed or defaced and can ensure that a photographer's picture is properly credited.

Voluntary license A negotiated license between copyright owners and users, allowing performance, display, distribution, and production of works incorporating copyrighted material.

***Williams & Wilkins Co.* v. *United States*,** 487 F. 2d 1345 (Ct. Cl. 1973), affirmed by an equally divided court, 420 U.S. 376 (1975) The case in which Supreme Court affirmation left standing a Court of Claims decision that photocopying of an entire journal constituted fair use. The decision ultimately led to the enactment of Section 108 of the Copyright Act, which addresses photocopying in libraries.

Work for hire The copyright principle that allows an employer or person or entity paying for the work to own the work and to enjoy the economic benefits of the effort.

World Intellectual Property Organization (WIPO) The international organization that helps administer copyrights and trademarks. Most recently, WIPO established a mediation and arbitration center to address international domain name disputes.

World Wide Web (www) The section of the Internet capable of transmitting pictures as well as text.

Index

Page references followed by "f" denote figures.